ECONOMICS

ᵀᴴᴱ BASICS

Now in its third edition, *Economics: The Basics* continues to provide an engaging and topical introduction to the key issues in contemporary economics. Fully updated to take into account the global recession, ongoing problems in Eurozone economies, changing patterns in world trade, housing and currency markets, it covers fundamental issues, including:

- how different economic systems function;
- the boom and bust cycle of market economies;
- the impact of emerging markets;
- how price, supply and demand interact;
- the role of the banking and finance industry;
- whether we can emerge from recession and reduce poverty;
- the impact of economics on the environment.

With a glossary of terms, suggestions for further reading and new case studies covering subjects such as the choices facing developing economies, the impact of growth on the price of natural resources and the aftermath of the financial crash, this comprehensive and accessible guide is essential reading for anyone who wants to understand how economics works.

Tony Cleaver is a Visiting Lecturer at the Universidad de los Andes and at el Colegio de Estudios Superiores de Administración (CESA) in Bogota, Colombia. H⸱ ⸱⸱⸱⸱ ⸱⸱⸱⸱⸱⸱⸱⸱⸱ Senior Teaching Fellow in Economics at the University of

THE BASICS

ECONOMICS

THE BASICS

THIRD EDITION

Tony Cleaver

Routledge
Taylor & Francis Group

LONDON AND NEW YORK

Third edition published 2015
by Routledge
2 Park Square, Milton Park, Abingdon, Oxon OX14 4RN

and by Routledge
711 Third Avenue, New York, NY 10017

Routledge is an imprint of the Taylor & Francis Group, an informa business

First edition published by Routledge 2004
Second edition published by Routledge 2011

British Library Cataloguing in Publication Data
A catalogue record for this book is available from the British Library

Library of Congress Cataloging in Publication Data
Cleaver, Tony, 1947-
Economics : the basics / Tony Cleaver. -- Third edition.
pages cm
Includes bibliographical references and index.
1. Economics. I. Title.
HB171.C655 2015
330--dc23
2014004824

ISBN: 978-1-138-02353-6 (hbk)
ISBN: 978-1-138-02354-3 (pbk)
ISBN: 978-1-315-76200-5 (ebk)

Typeset in Bembo
by Taylor & Francis Books

MIX
Paper from
responsible sources
FSC
www.fsc.org   FSC® C013056

Printed and bound in Great Britain by
TJ International Ltd, Padstow, Cornwall

CONTENTS

A WORLD IN UPHEAVAL

You cannot make a lot sense of what goes on in the world without some knowledge of basic economics.

In my own lifetime, three major upheavals have shaken the world order to its very roots: the oil price shocks of the 1970s; the collapse of the centrally planned economies at the end of the 1980s, and now a widespread and long-lasting recession that is currently depressing the incomes of billions of people around the globe.

Quite apart from sudden cataclysmic shocks like these, there are also any number of other issues – some growing in importance with a slow burn, others just a dull persistent ache that never goes away – that demand our attention and understanding. All have important economic dimensions: climate change, bank panics, health care, world poverty, immigration, educational reform, even overseas military engagements ... the list is endless.

To fully understand the implications of these and many other issues requires serious, though not very difficult, economic analysis.

The aim of this text, dear reader, is thus to give you some insight into how some of these complex issues can be unravelled, how economics works and contributes to a balanced appraisal of controversial and contemporary affairs, and therefore how your own opinions can be better informed.

Let me say right here that economics is supposed to be value-free. Economists don't make the decisions, do not attempt to persuade; they are merely social scientists typically claiming to set out a dispassionate analysis of social phenomena, laying out the costs and benefits on either side, clarifying the assumptions and logic involved and thus allowing others to make their minds up. That is the intention, anyway! My apologies if you detect any undeclared biases.

ECONOMICS AND MONEY

You might be forgiven for thinking that economics is all about money. It is a popular misconception. Economics, in fact, is about analysing *choices*. What is the most economic course of action, given that resources are scarce and there are a number of possible options over how to employ them? Should governments provide better health care for their electorate, or invest more in the armed services and counter-terrorism? Should public money be used to bail out failing banks and what happens if not? Should drug companies pour more research into the causes of and remedies for flu pandemics or AIDS? Should you and I buy more food, clothes or electronic gadgetry?

Prior to making such choices we need to evaluate the alternatives. Economists use money as the measuring stick. Some people wrongly assume therefore that economics is only interested in what makes a profit ... but that is to confuse the aims of commercial business with the academic process of estimating economic costs and benefits. Should we build cheap, coal-fired power stations that pollute the planet, or less environmentally damaging but more expensive wind or thermal powered generators? A businessman with no restriction imposed by the state may choose the former option. *Should* the state intervene in this decision? An objective economist would want to calculate the costs to the planet of carbon emissions from low-tech, coal-fired power plants and then convert these environmental costs into monetary values on the way to measuring the *real* costs and benefits of the alternative strategies. Which power plant in which place is "best"? How do we define and measure that? Economics *is* about money – but as a means, not an end.

It is particularly when businesses lose money and people lose employment through no fault of their own that economists can be asked to explain what is going on. That was certainly the case in the Great Depression era of the 1930s when an unprecedented slump in trade destroyed the jobs, incomes and hopes of many innocent victims worldwide. At the time, in 1936, a brilliant economist and policy advisor – John Maynard Keynes – responded with a revolutionary analysis of the causes and possible remedies of the international crash that is in many important respects still relevant today. And sure enough, today, governments, businessmen, journalists and ordinary people affected by the current global economic downturn are again asking the same questions about what happened; why; who is to blame, and how do we get out of this mess?

We can use the example of the causes and ramifications of the present international slowdown as an introduction to basic economics. Critics might claim that this is a tough challenge. It is a bit like that old joke of the driver who gets hopelessly lost and pulls over to ask a local what is the best way to get to his destination. The reply comes: "Oh, aarh ... that's difficult. I wouldn't want to start from here..."

Nevertheless we are in the world where we are. Stuck in a complex mess that people generally want to understand. Just what are the precise reasons for the constrained economic circumstances we currently find ourselves in? How did we get in and how do we get out? It is a fascinating story that embraces both slow-moving, worldwide fundamental forces and more proximate, easily recognised foibles of specific time and place. Let us take up the challenge...

THE GREAT RECESSION

It is popularly held that it all started in the USA in 2007 with what is known as the "sub-prime mortgage crisis". This was the pricking of a bubble in house prices when a decade of steadily rising property prices was suddenly reversed.

The USA is a prime example of a market economy and as such – like all market systems – it is driven more by popular demand than by government diktat. Indeed, due to its unique history and traditions, there is probably a more active and pervasive distrust of centralised government in the USA than is the case in Europe and in most other developed nations. It was the increasing demand for home loans and the all-to-easy willingness of financiers to provide those loans, unrestricted by any central authority, which drove up house prices throughout the boom years of the 1990s. Both consumers and producers of this rapid expansion of US finance were too caught up in the enjoyment of inflated wealth to consider the longer-term picture.

Taking a longer view, however, we can see that all market systems are chronically unstable. For reasons that are still the cause of much argument, market economies are prone to cyclical booms and slumps and it was the false pride of many, outside as well as inside the USA, which led many to believe that in the 1990s we could escape this cycle.

The reality, as illustrated in Figure 1.1, is different. Considering only the period since the Second World War (that is, not even considering the enormous swings in economic fortunes caused by two world wars and an intervening Great Depression) the rate of economic growth of US gross domestic product (GDP) shows almost regular ups and downs.

A little explanation is called for: the 1950s was a decade of readjustment to life after one (world) war and during another (Korea) and thus accounts for a very variable growth record. The 1960s saw steady and positive growth as the US consolidated its position as the powerhouse of the Western world. The major oil shock of 1973–74 can be clearly identified with negative growth as large payments to the Organization of Petroleum Exporting

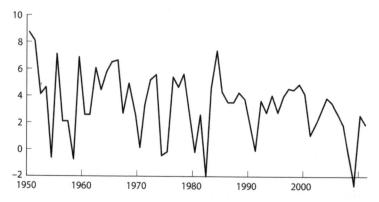

Figure 1.1 Percentage change in US GDP, 1950–2012. (Source: US Bureau of Economic Analysis.)

Nations (OPEC) were called for, repeated again at the beginning of the 1980s with the second oil price shock. After a brief hiccup in 1991, steady growth occurred (called "The Great Moderation") through the 1990s and into the new millennium (with a minor "dot-com" blip) leading to many observers thinking that cyclical ups and downs had been beaten ... until we run into the biggest downturn since the Great Depression from 2007 onwards. In memory of that major interwar slump, the developed world's current difficulty has been named the Great Recession.

Keynes called it "animal spirits"; Alan Greenspan, former chairman of the US Federal Reserve (the US central bank), called it "irrational exuberance". But whether it is the short time horizons of people who want to get rich quick; the infectiousness of group

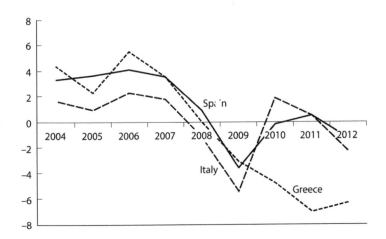

Figure 1.2 Percentage change in GDP, 2004–2012, Greece, Italy, Spain. The picture for Europe is not so very different from the USA until 2009 – and then the absence of European recovery is painfully obvious. This illustrates the Great Recession for three badly affected countries: A "double dip" for Italy and Spain who struggle to escape negative growth and prolonged, unrelenting misery for Greece. (The data for unemployment is an even more stark illustration of the Great Recession: steadily increasing from the onset of the crisis in 2007, unemployment at the end of 2013 was for Italy: 12.2%; Spain: 26.2%; Greece: 27.6%. These are figures comparable to the worst of the1930s.) (Source: World Bank.)

euphoria, or maybe that technological inventiveness itself follows the same cycle and blinds people who are caught up in it … whatever the reasons, market participants seem unable to avoid the herd-like behaviour that produces periods of over-indulgence and a rapid growth in asset prices, only to be followed some time later by a sudden collapse in confidence, prices and incomes.

The boom and bust in the US housing market, whilst undeniably a calamity for those involved, could not have been the tipping point for the international recession that followed, however, without a conjunction of a number of other factors operating over different periods in space and time. The most fundamental of these are the deep undercurrents that have been swirling away since the *other* two major upheavals in the world economy that occurred in the 1970s and late 1980s, mentioned earlier.

The first of these were the oil price shocks of 1973 and 1979. They emphasised how dependent the developed world is on imported petroleum, so causing a substantial redistribution of world incomes as consuming nations had to pay the higher prices that producers in the Middle East and elsewhere were demanding. Since the 1970s, the accumulation of REVENUES by the OPEC nations has varied over time in line with world oil prices and that in turn has given rise to the search for investment outlets – petrodollar recycling – as the capacity of those countries to spend such windfall riches has not always been able to keep pace.

The other world-changing event was the demise of the world's major command economies and their transformation into market systems. For China this was a gradual process of economic resurgence during the 1980s and thereafter, *not* accompanied (as yet!) by any radical change in political leadership. For the former Soviet Union and its Eastern European satellites it was a sudden, revolutionary change in capital ownership and control effected in and around 1989.

Add these two factors to too-clever financial wizardry that thought it had the world by the tail and we have a story of selfish greed, blindness, pride, bankruptcies, bail-outs, debt and depression.

GLOBAL IMBALANCES

We can track the path to the Great Recession directly from the late 1990s and a series of financial crises that hit East Asia in 1997 and then prompted the Russian rouble collapse in August 1998 (mainly due to investor doubts over the Yeltsin government's ability to manage a struggling transition economy). The clear message here was that the financial institutions of countries previously thought to be reliably based on either superstar growth (Korea, Thailand) or rich resources (Russia) were in fact dangerously vulnerable.

Add this notion to the economic realities of the new millennium: the economic growth of the most populous country on the planet was surging, creating an enormous demand for mineral resources to fuel its industry and, at the same time, much of the developed world was buying the cheap manufactured goods that China was exporting. Chinese trade surpluses were thus fast piling up, as were OPEC's again. Billions and billions of dollars were flowing into these countries' coffers, so where was the best place to put all these monies? Not in Russian nor East Asian banks, clearly, and the financial sector in China had not reached anywhere near the size and level of development as its manufacturing industry. The only place to pour them would be into the biggest possible pool of assets where those dollars would keep their value and hopefully cause the least disruptive splash, i.e. in the US money markets.

There are a number of ways of measuring the massive flows of wealth that were travelling around the world over this period and the impact these movements were having. Figure 1.3 first shows the

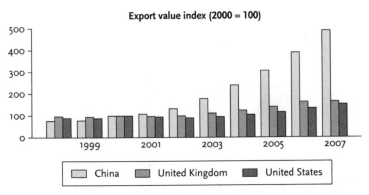

Export value index (2000 = 100)

Legend: China United Kingdom United States

Figure 1.3 Growth in value of exports, China, USA and UK, 1998–2007. (Source: World Bank.)

growth in Chinese exports compared to those of the USA and the UK. Using the year 2000 as the base year, it can be seen that Chinese exports increased by over 500 per cent in the period 1998–2007, whereas the UK and the USA barely saw a 50 per cent increase.

Figure 1.4 shows the trade balance for various countries in a single year: 2008. There are massive surpluses for the OPEC countries (Algeria, Angola, Iran, Iraq, Kuwait, Libya, Nigeria, Qatar, Saudi Arabia, United Arab Emirates and Venezuela) and China; with slightly less for Germany and Japan (two other export-based economies). These are contrasted with countries that have been importing far more than they have exported and thus have run up large deficits ... none larger than the unequalled negative balance of the USA.

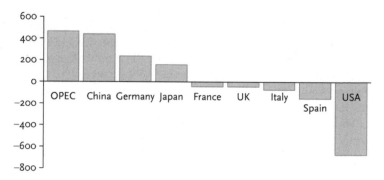

Figure 1.4 Current Account Balance, various countries, 2008 (US$ billions). (Source: IMF.)

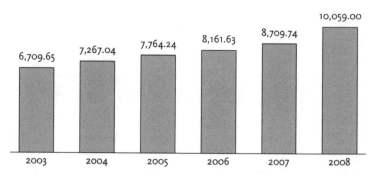

Figure 1.5 US Government Debt (US$ billions). (Source: IMF.)

These graphs give you some idea of the large amounts of money that were changing hands in exchange for exports of petroleum products and manufactures. Figure 1.5 shows where a lot of that money then ended up – recycled back into deposits in the USA! Because those countries with large trade surpluses were earning so much more than they were able to spend, they had to put the dollars they earned somewhere ... and that somewhere was in US government bonds and TREASURY BILLS. No other store of value was reliable and plentiful enough to soak up all that money. In 2008, therefore, over ten trillion dollars worth of assets were held by creditors inside and outside the USA.

Now this is where the story gets really interesting. All this cash pouring into the USA for over a decade was not just sitting there. US bonds and bills are like bread and butter to the money markets. They are in fact US government IOUs that are 100 per cent reliable and promise to pay you a steady stream of interest. As valuable assets, you can readily sell them on at any time to all manner of financial traders if you don't want to wait until the IOU eventually falls due. In this way, government securities become just the seed capital that forms the base for a huge expansion of subsequent money making.

All banks and finance houses are in the business of making money. In fact, as is explained in a later chapter, bankers can offer loans to as many people and businesses as they want to or consider safe – even though they may have very little cash at all in their own vaults. So, as customers deposit bills, bonds and other liquid assets into their bank accounts, it allows the managers of those accounts to create money, that is, *to loan out sums to a far greater multiple than they actually hold*. It is a numbers game. If you reckon that only one in ten customers will return to claim their deposits in any one period then you can create and loan out ten times more paper promises than you have assets to back them.

To whom do bankers want to lend money? Ideally, to those who are not only secure but who can also promise to pay back the most interest. Property is frequently the safest of bets. Bankers can see their money is being used for something that is (literally) concrete and not going to disappear overnight.

Who wants to borrow? With banks flush with funds and their managers looking for customers, it fuels the hopes and dreams of all those who want to own their own homes, or run their own businesses – especially if they have been frustrated in the past. Such people are frequently first in the queue to ask for loans.

I hope you can begin to see, therefore, that as billions of dollars are recycled back to the USA these monies can be multiplied many times over, by a series of transactions in very large and sophisticated money markets, into an even larger financial stimulus to property markets.

BANKS, BRAINS, TECHNOLOGY AND GREED

We enter now into the esoteric world of banking and a world of technological innovation, of mathematical whizz-kids, and of pure greed.

If you have a lot of money lying fairly idle on the one hand and, on the other, customers desperate for loans but with either inflated dreams or a history of bad debts behind them then this is a mismatch that calls for some innovative enterprise to bring the two sides together.

Bankers will normally want to charge a very high rate of interest in lending money to very risky (sub-prime) mortgage customers. But at such high rates, these customers will be too frightened to take out the loan. Frustration! The client doesn't get his mortgage; the banker doesn't get his sale. However, so long as there exists an unfulfilled demand, maybe some bright young financial dynamo can find a way to supply that need...

Here's what you do: add on some very risky customers to a line of other, more creditworthy clients that have come to you, involved with a host of other businesses, property deals and enterprising ventures of varying viability. Tot up all the money that the loans to all these outlets represent. Create a loan package that bundles all these clients together, thin slice this package to scores and scores of individual units and figure out the risk that any one component of the overall package will go bust. A lot of geeky mathematics will have to be calculated here in working out precise statistical probabilities of default on any one of these bits of paper. Give each of the financial securities that you have just created a fancy name, such as a "collateralised debt obligation" (CDO) and pay a credit-rating authority that you hire to give them an AAA stamp of approval. Now sell them on to whichever bank or finance house, home or abroad, wants what looks like a solid, triple A rated asset. (Don't worry about anyone unravelling the geeky maths and challenging the value of these bits of paper you have created. No one will understand it. Nor need they, so long as others stand in line, keen to buy and sell this paper at a speculative price.)

You now grant credit to all those customers who came to you for loans in the first place. If amongst them there is a dead-end client who buys a house, cannot afford it and fails to keep up with the repayments to you, then there is no problem. Simply kick the guy out, repossess the property (called "foreclosing the mortgage") and you can sell the place and recoup the money. Even better, if other financiers follow your lead with their customers – then loans will have multiplied, the demand for property will be booming and prices will soar. You cannot lose now: the house you sell nets more cash than you laid out in the first place.

Success in such a market place drives further growth. Risk of creditors defaulting on their loans can be insured against and, just as CDOs are invented to meet one need, so CREDIT DEFAULT SWAPS (CDSs) are invented to satisfy another. Banks, building societies, insurance companies, pension funds, credit rating agencies, hedge funds and every other related business all have the incentive to dream up other "needs" just so they can turn these into a profit-making opportunity. Massive bonuses are offered to those creating, innovating and engineering a regular alphabet soup of financial products since everyone is anxious not to miss out on the money to be made. And amongst such people there are always those who are prepared to dress up and sell snake oil to gullible, trusting folk who do not know the dangerous, unknown territory they are getting into.

AN INTERNATIONAL AFFAIR

Finance is a global industry that is highly competitive and very fast-moving. Money flows from one bank to another around the world at the touch of a button if the rate of return in, say, London or Tokyo, is higher than in New York.

If a bank takes a deposit anywhere in the world (which it will have to pay interest on) it will seek to lend out that money and more at a better rate of return, somewhere else. All finance houses everywhere therefore seek to balance liabilities with assets, gaining a profit on higher earnings than outgoings. As such, all round the globe there is always a high demand for AAA rated securities, especially for dollar–denominated paper originating not from questionable developing country markets but from the biggest and most secure financial source of all, the USA.

Big international banks that operate in countries far and wide, dealing with customers large and small, are not run by fools, you would have thought. (*Citigroup chairman, Charles Prince, explaining why his bank continued to trade evidently risky assets at a time when the sub-prime mortgage crisis was unfolding, said: "When the music stops, in terms of liquidity, things will be complicated. But, as long as the music is playing, you've got to get up and dance. We're still dancing."* (Financial Times, *9 July 2007.) He wasn't dancing in November of that year when he lost his job. Well maybe he was: he walked away with US\$ 38m...*) An ever-increasing supply of very complex, triple A securities, no matter what their source, you would expect to have been thoroughly investigated. The fact is, it didn't happen. Indeed, quite the opposite: the exuberance, optimism and sheer profitability of participating in the US financial markets caught on worldwide as financial assets here were eagerly purchased to bolster the balance sheets of institutions in a variety of financial centres around the globe. One can see in Figure 1.6 the rapid growth and phenomenal value of CDOs snapped up by financiers worldwide.

Banking is a very competitive business, as mentioned, and the pressure to perform is immense. The chief executive officers of

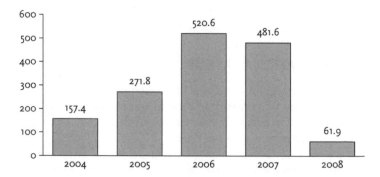

Figure 1.6 Combined value of CDOs issued around the world (US\$ billions). (Source: Securities Industry and Financial Markets Association.)

these prestigious institutions are rated according to their ability to generate earnings, compared to their peers in rival finance houses. Perhaps some of these officers, or their subordinates, did think these new-fangled CDOs were a bit dodgy. Perhaps they knew they were suckering others into buying financial products that would never live up to their promise but, hey, big profits were being made. *(In November 2013, JPMorgan Chase, the biggest bank in the USA, agreed to pay US$ 13bn in settlement of charges for knowingly selling "toxic" securities to homeowners, pension funds and others in the run-up to the 2007/2008 financial crisis. Although this is the biggest settlement in US corporate history, it represented only half the annual profits of the bank, and $7bn of that settlement is tax deductable. Some have said this is a sweetheart deal engineered between the bank and the US Justice Department and critics have demanded that criminal charges for massive fraud be brought against executives responsible.)* The incentive to pump up business earnings, share prices and personal reputations was too great. What started as a legitimate desire to help cash-strapped Americans to buy homes in the Mid-West ended up as a production line to equip banks all round the world with easy money. Except it turned out to be fool's gold...

THE CREDIT CRUNCH

Prices do not go up for ever. The US housing boom, driven by excess liquidity, began to go sour when an increasing number of mortgage holders – who should never have been given more money than they could afford – failed to keep up with their repayments. In 2001 just less than 5 per cent of all mortgage customers were 12 months behind with their payments but this percentage relentlessly increased, year-on-year, until in 2007 it was around 11 per cent who were a year behind. With evidence like this, the riskiness of this particular marketplace was hardly unannounced, therefore. Nonetheless, very few saw the bursting of the ballon that was to come. Forced sales of property as mortgages were being foreclosed eventually began to impact on the US market. In 2007, house prices began to fall. Seeing trouble looming, many holding property as a speculative asset also scrambled to sell – accentuating the problem. See Figure 1.7. The implications for

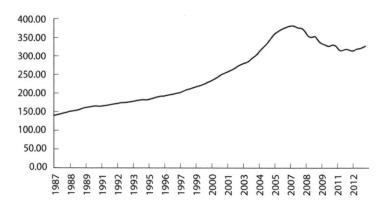

Figure 1.7 Quarterly Index of US house prices, 1987–2012 (1980 = 100). As can be seen, the rise in price of US real estate really began in the 1990s after the financial crises in Asia when international money turned to the USA to look for investment outlets. The speculative bubble caused by innovative ways to create greater and greater supplies of spending power eventually burst in 2007, the downturn accelerating in 2008. The upturn in 2012 indicates the USA is coming out of recession, or it is merely the result of increasing domestic money supplies, or both. (Source: US Federal Housing Finance Agency.)

the financial markets were now serious: as soon as house prices started falling, this implied that all those CDOs whose paper value was derived from the property they represented were worth less. How much less? It soon became obvious that *no one really knew!*

The extraordinary complexity of many of these financial products meant that it could take days for computers to perform the calculations needed to assess their true value … and in that time the base property prices assumed at the outset would have fallen even more. Worse, the lack of transparency as to who had sold what to whom, and which banks' balance sheets were loaded with these infamous bits of paper, meant that trust between financial traders evaporated. Which dealers were most in trouble? Impossible to calculate quickly and of course no one wanted to own up. So would you lend money to a business whose finances were opaque, and at a time when fears were rising? The answer was, obviously, no. This was the start of what was called "the CREDIT CRUNCH".

Finance houses "borrow short and lend long". That is, they borrow over the short term at low rates of interest and lend money out for long periods of time at high rates. Even though they have loaned out all their money for years at a time (20 years or more on home mortgages) they can repay their short-term debts by continually taking out other short-term loans. Rolling over credit like this allows you to make a profit on the differential interest rates … so long as you can continue to get the short-term funding. In the summer of 2007 this was no longer possible. Entire segments of the international banking industry dried up and provoked growing panic, with several US and European institutions facing collapse if others, and ultimately governments, didn't offer help. The US investment bank Bear Stearns was the first famous name to apply for a bailout in June 2007. Next was the UK mortgage house Northern Rock in September.

No one knew where the banking crisis would eventually spread to, and when it would end. For 12 months things got progressively worse, coming to a spectacular head on 15 September 2008 when – under a lot of popular criticism for bailing out and thus rewarding greedy bankers – the US Treasury refused to support the firm of Lehman Brothers.

Shock waves went around the globe. If such a large and prestigious investment bank was allowed to go bust, than *any* business, big or small, could go broke. No bank dared lend money to any private enterprise for fear they would go under, taking all their borrowed funds with them.

The rate of interest charged on overnight, interbank borrowing shot up; the flight of capital out of commercial paper and into government bills and bonds soared. (If you cannot trust your money with anyone else, you are safer holding on to government gilt-edged securities. Reputable governments, it was thought, will not default. US and European governments can always raise tax revenues if they have to pay debts.) There were even spikes in the prices of oil, gold and agricultural commodities as people rushed to take their money out of banks and property and put it anywhere else that they thought would hold its value.

GOVERNMENT DEBT

Assets such as people's homes, commercial property, paper promises, are only as valuable as the price people are willing to pay for them. The worldwide value of such assets collapsed in 2008 along with Lehman Brothers in the continuing credit crunch. This frightened everyone – including governments on both sides of the Atlantic. Other big banks, building societies, insurance companies and pension funds could not be allowed to go broke. Millions upon millions of innocent people would lose savings, houses, pensions, everything in a global banking pandemic. So governments had little choice – all these financial institutions had to be bailed out. American International Group (AIG), an insurance company, the Federal National Mortgage Association (FNMA or "Fannie Mae"), the Federal Home Loan Mortgage Corporation (FHLMC or "Freddie Mac"), General Motors, the Royal Bank of Scotland – these and many others were all saved by massive injections of government funds. On 8 October 2008 the UK government approved a £500bn bank rescue package; this was shortly followed by a $700bn Troubled Asset Relief Program in the USA. In consequence the government or sovereign debts of these nations soared. See Figure 1.8.

The situation in the 18 eurozone countries (Austria, Belgium, Cyprus, Estonia, Finland, France, Germany, Greece, Ireland, Italy, Luxembourg, Latvia, Malta, Netherlands, Portugal, Slovakia, Slovenia, Spain) on the mainland of Europe was and is a little more complex. On the adoption of the euro over the period 1999–2002, participating countries ceded control of their monetary policy to the European Central Bank (ECB) and the major influence upon that: Germany. The immediate advantage this brought at the turn of the millennium was cheaper borrowing since the euro was seen as a safer bet than previously inflation-prone currencies such as the Greek drachma, Italian lira and Spanish peseta. Households and governments thus went on a spending spree all over Europe as house prices and government deficits went up and, along with these, so did the debt ratios of households, businesses, banks and governments. Irresponsible borrowing cannot occur without irresponsible lending, however. Euro bonds issued by any government were assumed equally safe: that is, the rate of interest financial markets charged on Greek and Italian bonds were little different to

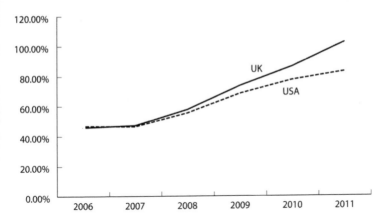

Figure 1.8 UK and USA central government debt as percentage of national income, 2006–2011. As illustrated, the sovereign debt of both countries has steadily increased over the period as their governments borrowed money and bailed out various commercial institutions in their respective fields. Getting hold of the money was no problem for the administrations concerned; the only difficulties were political – outraging various critics who said that broken businesses should not be bailed out and that governments should not incur excessive debts. Such critics, of course, did not need the support of millions of voters who would otherwise have been impoverished and/or unemployed. (Source: World Bank.)

those charged on those of Germany, despite the fact that the government debt/national income ratios differed markedly (prior to the crisis in 2006: Italy: 109.1 per cent; Greece: 128.5 per cent; Germany: 43.5 per cent).

When the credit crunch hit, bond markets belatedly woke up to the fact that not only were some government finances in a bad shape but the countries concerned had no independent monetary policy to address their problems and the ECB was constitutionally banned from bailing them out. *(The traditional remedy for a government heavily in debt with little chance to pay it off is to inflate the money supply and devalue its currency. Not particularly pleasant, but less painful than years and years of deflating incomes. This remedy is not available to countries who have joined a monetary union with others who refuse to take that option.)*

Market rates charged on loans to heavily indebted governments rapidly climbed – in effect shutting these countries off from borrowing any more. The major European power, Germany, would not countenance putting up its own taxpayers' money in euro-wide government transfers – so those countries with big debts were told to pay up. That meant enforced spending cuts: government austerity packages.

At the time of writing, the pain in the eurozone countries continues. Various combinations of government cutbacks have been tried in different countries: some public employees have been sacked, others had their wages frozen; pension ages have increased and payouts decreased; taxes have been raised; subsidies and loopholes closed, and numerous business contracts with the private sector have been cancelled. Alongside this, indebted households and businesses have been cutting consumption and with governments in the eurozone unable to offset this with their own spending the inevitable consequence has been a sustained fall in demand, an increase in unemployment, a fall in incomes and a deepening recession (see Figure 1.2). The problem of excessive sovereign debt, of course, has *not* been solved. If incomes are falling then even if you can manage to pay off some loans, the ratio of debt to income is not going to improve much. At the end of 2012 the government debt/income ratios for Italy, Spain, Greece, France, Portugal, Ireland were all close to or above 100 per cent. The misery will presumably continue for some time until people eventually realise that all debts cannot be repaid. A large number must just simply be forgiven; written off. Tough on a number of French, German and other banks that are holding these eurobonds but perhaps they should not have been so blind in lending in the first place.

WHAT HAVE WE LEARNED?

Looking back at recent economic history and setting the stage for the rest of this text, what lessons can we draw from the events listed above?

FREE MARKETS ARE UNSTABLE, AND CATCHING

First, markets fail. The dominant economic policy paradigm ever since it was first identified by Adam Smith in 1776 has been to allow the unfettered operation of private enterprise to generate business, wealth and economic growth. Smith wrote that each individual employs his own capital for his own gain with no necessary intent to promote social interest but in a free market he/she is led as if by "an invisible hand" to promote society's benefit "more effectually than when he really intends to promote it". From this early analysis has grown an enormous vested interest in obstructing government intervention in business. But whilst not denying the power of the free market economic engine, it cannot be allowed to operate without controls and regular servicing. Booms and slumps have proved to be inescapable and in a globalised world their effects are internationally communicable – like viruses – whatever their original causes and wherever they first impact.

INCENTIVES DETERMINE OUTCOMES

If financiers are given hefty bonuses for creating innovative forms of credit and suckering-in clients to taking it, and they are not penalised if these loans go bottom-up, then we can guess what will happen. They will generate more and more borrowing and increasing consumption until judgement day comes and the bubble goes pop! People respond positively to opportunities for personal enrichment, especially if the enrichment offered is substantial and any costs imposed on others are ignored.

BANKS ARE ESSENTIAL BUT NEED REGULATING

The role of banks and the international financial industry needs closer examination. The fact is that market economies need banks to collect funds from the billions of people who save and then recycle these savings to investment outlets that can use them productively. Without such recycling, spending power would not get spent, world AGGREGATE DEMAND would fall and production, incomes and employment will fall with it. That is what happened in the Great Depression and happened again with the Great Recession. But bankers cannot be trusted. Evidence has shown that they are prone to speculate with (not invest) other people's money; create more and more innovative loans with insufficient safeguards, and promote their own gain rather than the interests of society. Contrary to the argument of Adam Smith, above, US economist Joe Stiglitz has argued that, thanks to the deregulation of financial markets that has occurred since the 1980s, the free market hand is now not so much invisible; it is simply non-existent *(see* The London Review of Books, *Vol. 32, No. 8, 22 April 2010).* As a result, bankers accentuate booms with "innovative" (at times fraudulent) lending and deepen slumps when they catch fright and cut-back loans even to the most enterprising of small- and medium-sized businesses. More and better regulation is needed.

MORAL HAZARD

Bailing out banks prevented the 2008 worldwide financial crash from getting worse but it also highlighted MORAL HAZARD. If businesses are protected by governments from going bankrupt then what incentive do their leaders have in future to be more careful in the risks they undertake? We cannot be sure that businessmen and women will ever and always make wise investment decisions with the funds they are entrusted with, so they have to be punished if they are recklessly, or deliberately, irresponsible. How so, if their businesses are rescued? The answer surely is to safeguard insofar as possible the enterprise and employment of the innocent, but not those responsible for steering them into bankrupcy.

INEQUALITY OF DISTRIBUTION

The greatest injustice that has come to light over the Great Recession has been the inequity of sacrifice involved. This has a number of dimensions. It has been popularly argued that the incomes of the top 1 per cent of the developed world have risen over the last decades (particularly the incomes of those who engineered the boom in global finance); the real incomes of the other 99 per cent have not. Similarly, the incomes and welfare of northern European nations have increased, those of southern and "periphery" Europe have declined; finally the impact on the global environment of free market enterprise – both in boom and slump – has driven fears that the welfare of the planet has been ignored. Booming economic growth means more pollutants; whereas recession means environmental subsidies and safeguards are the first to be sacrificed in government cutbacks. All these inequities need addressing.

SURPLUSES MUST EQUAL DEFICITS

There is an urgent need to rebalance the world economy. So long as some countries succeed in running trade surpluses, even in the teeth of others' desires to cutback on their debts and rebuild household savings, then their deficits will not fall, income transfers must continue and, if they are not spent, it means aggregate demand for the world's goods and services must fall, and the Great Recession will go on and on.

Countries such as China, Germany, Japan, the OPEC nations have seen their trade surpluses shrink in aggregate as world demand has slowed. For example, 40 per cent of Germany's income comes from exports, much of those to the rest of Europe. As European spending has contracted so German growth has suffered. The solution is not to aggressively sell exports even harder because if this is successful, money will be siphoned out of circulation just more quickly, compounding the problem. In fact, of course, the whole point of earning money by selling your produce abroad is to enable you to go out and spend your increased income. Those countries with trade surpluses must learn to spend them! Not, you would have thought, a very difficult recommendation to put to the world's manufacturers and oil exporters. It does, however, require a rebalancing of the global economy – perhaps increasing trade in international services: Germans should buy more foreign holidays; the Chinese should invest in education, pensions and insurance.

A SUMMARY AND AN INTRODUCTION

If you have followed this tortuous story all the way so far, congratulations. This has not been the easiest introduction to economics. It has been a case study of how economic forces act and interact, for good or ill: how events on one side of the world have repercussions on the other; how actions can have unintended consequences; when what seems to be a good idea for one agent turns out to be a bad idea when all others get in on the act. There are many themes that have been interwoven in this narrative until now; hence, if you have found some issues insufficiently explained, then it is hoped that we can unpick and examine these in detail in the following chapters.

Economic affairs do tend to have implications spilling out in all directions in ways that are surprising and frequently not fully understood. How do you come to terms with a very complex world where all sorts of factors are operating all the time? The discipline of economics takes the approach of separating out key themes and influences and analysing them one at a time. That is the logic adopted hereafter.

To summarise, we have noted that the United States is a market economy and indeed the developed world as a whole tends to rely on market forces to organise its affairs, that is what ties the fortunes of people in one country to those of another. What a market system of organisation involves, its advantages and disadvantages and how it differs from command and traditional systems is explained in Chapter 2.

A fundamental, background force that is reshaping the way the world economy is evolving is the steady growth in incomes and, thus, demand for investment outlets from emerging markets, particularly China. Apart from snapping up US financial products, this has also driven up the price of oil and other raw materials. The flow of capital into US markets has facilitated a driving demand for mortgages in the United States that pushed up the prices of housing and, when that market could take no more, then the unsatisfied demand simply transferred to cause rising prices in government bonds, gold and even cereals. Analysing consumer demand in relation to supply; notions of substitutes and how a variety of factors can impact on prices is the theory studied in Chapter 3.

The particular industry that was at the heart of the credit crunch is banking and finance but the general analysis of costs and revenues, competition and the drive for profits that underpin all private enterprise is treated in Chapter 4.

It was earlier demonstrated that market societies have the characteristic of economic instability – of experiencing periodic booms and busts. The more penetrating macroeconomic analysis of how this happens, the theoretical controversies this awakes and how governments have attempted to smooth the cycle is further investigated in Chapter 5.

Technological innovation is an essential creative force in all business life, and it is the unique form that creativity has taken in primarily US financial markets that has been the more immediate cause of the speculative bubble that bloomed and burst. A further analysis of the nature of money, banks, bubbles and how this has impacted on the European sovereign debt crisis comes in Chapter 6.

The global transmission of bank failures and the credit crunch provoked the international recession as consumers and businesses worldwide struggled to cope with the loss of credit. Analysis of the circular flow of trade, money and incomes that takes place within a nation – dealt with in Chapter 5 – can also be applied to the circulation of world trade between nations. Analyses of a country's imports and exports, its balance of payments, of free trade or protectionism and how governments manage or mismanage global relations are explained in Chapter 7.

Finally, we finish in Chapter 8 with two major issues that are related but unmentioned in the story until now: is it possible that we can repair the state of affairs the world's developed, market economies have got themselves into and simultaneously reduce poverty and protect the environment?

What a challenge! Welcome to *Economics: The Basics*.

FURTHER READING

There is much published on the financial crisis of 2007/2008 and its aftermath as any cursory glance at the internet will show you. But a very readable text that looks deeper and analyses how modern economies function and why they malfunction is Akerlof, George and Shiller, Robert (2009) *Animal Spirits*, Princeton University Press.

QUESTIONS

1 How are OPEC and Chinese trade surpluses, Asian and Russian bank crises, Collateralised Debt Obligations and the free market paradigm all related to the housing bubble that built up in the USA in 1990–2007?

2 Explain how a collapse in the prices of housing in the USA could cause a worldwide recession.

3 Why do you think governments in the USA and the UK can borrow money cheaply from world financial markets but the government of Spain, with a lower debt/national income ratio than either of the other two, cannot?

A CHOICE OF ECONOMIC SYSTEMS

Planet Earth is a unique and immensely rich supporter of biological life forms. The most successful life form is, of course, humankind, and it has exploited the planet's richness to spread rapidly across the globe – and it has also, for some, developed lifestyles that are unprecedentedly sophisticated and luxurious. Dominant though the species has become, however, two important observations must be made as follows.

First, however richly endowed the Earth may be, its resources are not limitless. It is becoming increasingly apparent that the exponential growth in human activity is damaging to the planet's ecology. As more resources are commandeered for human consumption, not only do other life forms lose out in direct competition but also there is the danger that future generations of humankind itself will be deprived.

Second, just as other species have been unable to compete for the control of Earth's resources against the dominant life form, within humankind there are great differences in the ability of some to compete and succeed. A relatively small minority of the peoples on the globe enjoy great riches. The great majority of humankind survives with much less.

Unlike primitive plants and animals, however, what makes humankind different from all other species on the planet is our capacity for choice. We are not driven solely by instinct to the ends we find ourselves occupying. We can choose our own destiny. Acting on our own as individuals or acting together in society, we are blessed with the capacity to influence future outcomes.

Economics is the science of choice. In the face of limited resources, human society has evolved systems of decision-making that choose whose wants are to have priority, in what manner resources are to be exploited and whether – in the end – we make guns or bread and butter.

Whichever decision-making system society employs, however, it is in the nature of economics that the answers it comes up with cannot please all of the people, all of the time. Because fundamental issues and disagreements are at stake here, they have excited the passions of humankind throughout history. Revolutions have erupted, wars have been won and lost and demonstrations continue to this day in various cities and nations of the world about the proper distribution, use and abuse of the fruits of the planet.

Consider the criticism implied earlier. Some observers allege that we have squandered the riches of the Earth in creating inequitable opulence – catering for the greed of a few powerful parties while ignoring the needs of all other inhabitants of the planet. Is this true? If so, how has it come about, and what, if anything, should be done about it?

To address these questions, it is worth pointing out at the outset the difference between matters of fact and those of opinion, that is, between questions of POSITIVE ECONOMICS, which can be answered by resort to hard evidence and those of NORMATIVE ECONOMICS, which require the application of value judgement. Modern economists attempt to redefine most questions so that they may be couched in terms of the former, avoiding the latter (or at least identifying their own biases) so that the reader can make up his or her own mind.

That the Earth's riches are consumed more by some than by others can be quickly demonstrated. Consider an A to Z of the world's nations: one quick measure of relative wealth is the purchasing power of the average citizen in, say, Austria compared with Zambia and Bangladesh compared with the United States. The World Bank gives the data for the year 2012 (Figures 2.1 and 2.2).

Another yardstick would be to compare the consumption of primary energy sources of the average person in each country – because

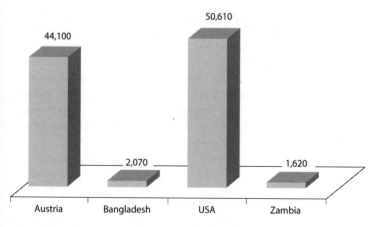

Figure 2.1 US$ average income per capita (purchasing power parity).

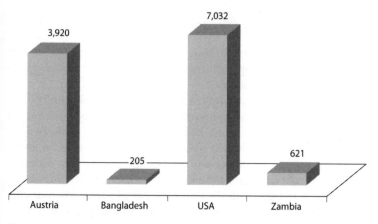

Figure 2.2 Primary energy consumed per person (kilogram of oil equivalent) (2012).

this is a direct measure of how much of a basic and essential resource (such as oil) is being used up by differing peoples.

These are crude measures. Many more sophisticated and more accurate surveys can be quoted but the basic point is made: there exist great extremes of wealth and poverty among the peoples of the planet. How such an unequal distribution has come about is a much more difficult question of positive economics. It is, in fact, an inquiry that runs through this book as an undercurrent beneath the various theories and analyses that form the backbone of this subject.

What, if anything, should be done about global inequality is, of course, not a question of positive economics at all. Like a scientist studying the workings of the solar system, or the internal organs of some animal, the economist is responsible for publishing the evidence and identifying what might happen if you make this change or that to economic systems, but he or she has no more right than anyone else to say what ought to happen in this world.

It is always easy to ask important questions in economics. It is easy also to make colourful and outrageous claims about the nature and conduct of economic affairs. (Have certain people really squandered the riches of Earth?) It is not always easy, however, to give balanced, objective and accurate responses to such questions and assertions. That is nonetheless the challenge of positive economics.

THREE DECISION-MAKING SYSTEMS

Let us return now to the study of decision-making systems that communities may adopt to organise their economic affairs. There are three examples as follows:

First, consider the economic activity within a small, student-run community – such as in a university college or hall of residence. In this example, we can imagine a fairly active social life exists, perhaps led and organised by a student committee: putting on discos, arranging a regular supply of drinks and snacks and maybe on occasions inviting outside agents and artistes to come and entertain the residents.

Now contrast this with the economic life of a large town or city: an enormous range of industrial, commercial and personal services are provided – too many to briefly enumerate.

Third, at the opposite extreme, we can consider the economic organisation of a small family home where housekeeping, maintenance and family care takes place.   ·

How is it decided in each of these communities what goods and services should be provided, how (where, when and by whom) these commodities should be produced and who should enjoy the benefits of their consumption?

Decisions as to what is produced, and how and for whom, may be taken in very different ways in these three examples.

Small college communities where everyone knows one another can often be run very democratically – people being elected for office and then asking around what goods should be ordered, what sorts of things people want to get done and so on. An efficient CENTRAL PLANNING mechanism may evolve – the community's wants are surveyed, passed up to the decision-making committee who then issue orders to outside suppliers or delegate production to internal groups (the bar committee, the dance organisers, etc.).

In a family home, there is unlikely to be any formal election of senior officers. Most economic decisions are taken by parents and family elders, and roles within the family evolve slowly according to TRADITION and the circumstances of individuals.

Most of the economic activity in a large city, however, is determined not by planning or by social custom but by the dictates of a free MARKET. If there is sufficient demand for a product or service, then, subject to its lawful production, it will be provided. (Governments can outlaw certain trades such that supplies are severely cut back – but as long as people are willing to pay high, BLACK MARKET prices, production will take place anyway. The free market can subvert government.)

These three decision-making systems introduced here can be found in operation all over the world. Their precise application in any one theatre of human activity will depend on the institutions and practices of the country concerned – some industries and some countries may demonstrate a distinct preference for one system above the rest; other economic organisation may rely on a combination of all three. Industry in almost any country will demonstrate some element of all three decision-making systems acting together, but let us look for examples where each regime can be studied more or less on its own.

TRADITIONAL AGRICULTURE

As an example of traditional practice, there is no better showcase to be found than to observe the work of the millions of people around the world tied to subsistence agriculture. They are bound to a system that – relative to other societies – has seen little change over centuries.

Evidence suggests that farm workers in poor countries are not themselves resistant to change – indeed they may respond rapidly to genuine opportunities to improve their welfare – but that given the circumstances in which they find themselves, their traditional agricultural practices are, in fact, rational and efficient outcomes that have evolved over generations of trial and error.

What goods does such a society choose to produce? Those that experience has shown to be the most reliable.

In farming some of the poorer lands on the planet, where climatic conditions may vary, where ownership of land and one's place in society is traditionally determined and where government is remote and as reliable as the wind, those who work the land tend not to take undue risks. They produce, therefore, what they know they can count on, using traditional technology that is home-grown and suited to the terrain.

Traditional agriculture tends to be self-sufficient because it has to be. To become dependent on a number of external suppliers in poor countries is to risk losses when they fail you. Furthermore, losses in this context mean not only losing crops or livestock but losing your life as well.

Social custom, therefore, determines much of the economic organisation that takes place in poor rural communities. What, how and for whom production takes place is decided by traditional practices that have evolved according to the particular institutions of the society in question. Within these given parameters, such economic organisation can often be highly efficient – much to the surprise of outsiders who expect to find backward or irrational production techniques.

The disadvantage of tradition, of course, is that no matter how appropriate established procedures are in their specific context, customary ways of life rarely prepare their followers to cope well with unprecedented changes (see Box 2.1).

BOX 2.1 EL SALVADOR: A CASE STUDY IN THE VULNERABILITY OF TRADITIONAL ECONOMIC PRACTICE

El Salvador became independent from Spain in 1839, and for some years thereafter, the country remained traditionally agricultural, with high birth and death rates, a small and stable population yet with sufficient fertile land to provide for all with no great extremes of poverty or wealth.

Standards of health and education were low in the mid-nineteenth century, but a British diplomat's wife commented that, in contrast with the major cities of England at that time, there was nonetheless a striking lack of poverty in this Central American republic. Land holdings were dispersed among the population with all families having access to their own property or to communal land, and a diverse range of agricultural goods was produced to support domestic consumption. The economy was basically one of self-sufficiency but with limited trade and economic growth.

The latter half of the nineteenth century, however, brought accelerating change. In a time of increasing world communications and trade, a growing El Salvador elite found in common with others around the globe that there was profit to be made in promoting exports. Most importantly, they found coffee. Suddenly, the ownership of coffee plantations became the key to wealth.

Families that started plantations found ways to increase the areas under cultivation. Indian village lands, worked communally for centuries, were said to be preserving a "backward" culture and came under threat. With no PROPERTY RIGHTS recognised in law, coffee planters bought them up, displaced the inhabitants but offered only limited plantation work at pitifully low wages.

El Salvador was eventually transformed – economically, politically and socially. Coffee dominated the economy and those who did not have coffee had little else. Land owning structures, land use patterns, labour relations and the distribution of economic and political power all changed. El Salvador is now a country where economic growth has occurred – though its benefits have been unequally distributed. Landless rural peoples have little control over their destinies, so the only remaining "tradition" that dictates what occupations poor people follow, what goods they produce and how they produce them is the continuing tradition of economic powerlessness. Their choices today are, in fact, more limited than in the past, thanks to the institutions that have overturned earlier social custom and have re-shaped their society.

Source: Burns, B. "The Modernization of Underdevelopment: El Salvador 1858–1931" reprinted as Chapter 10 in Wilber, C. K. and Jameson, K. P. (1996) *The Political Economy of Development and Underdevelopment*, McGraw-Hill.

MARKET AGRICULTURE

Contrast all of the above to agricultural organisation in modern market societies. Here, farms are typically located within a complex network of supporting suppliers and outlets in time and space, from which a wide range of inputs are purchased and to which outputs are sold. Crop farmers use formulaic combinations of fertilisers, pesticides and irrigation, employ agricultural machinery that is regularly serviced and use skilled, hired labour. In animal husbandry, there is similar dependence on bought-in feedstock and veterinary and transport services. Such farming practices are embedded in a modern, interdependent market society, and they could not survive without it.

What goods modern farmers produce depend on what prices and profits they can gain from the market. Whether it be organic foodstuffs or genetically modified crops, the market-driven producer will farm that which brings in the best returns.

The production methods employed are similarly dependent on market signals – where technical progress has brought down the price of machinery, seed varieties and/or breeding stock, the farm will be highly CAPITAL INTENSIVE. Alternatively, if the price of farm labour is cheaper, farming practices may be less capital intensive and more "hands on".

Finally, the rewards to farming will be divided between landowners, creditors, labourers and management according to the rates of RENT on land, INTEREST on capital and WAGES or PROFITS that rule in the market place. Certainly, if resources are not guaranteed the going market rate – whether it be a worker's wages or interest on a loan – then the resource involved, labour or capital, will seek better employment elsewhere.

Freedom to move is an essential pre-condition of any functioning market, and it is a key feature of this economic system that distinguishes it from traditional and planned systems. Consumers must be free to change their purchases, and resources their employment, if the market system is to work efficiently.

MOBILITY can only be meaningful, however, if people have effective choices. If there are no alternatives, then there is little freedom. Very poor people, in particular, may be unable to afford the glamorous variety of expensive products that are displayed on advertising hoardings and similarly unable to afford the upgrading of skills that might allow them to seek more rewarding employment.

For such reasons, certain governments in the past have attempted to introduce planned systems that guarantee all peoples in society access to basic essentials such as food, shelter, education and health.

PLANNED AGRICULTURE

A system of planning in agriculture was famously practised in Soviet collective farms and Chinese communes in the latter half of the twentieth century. Huge areas of land and millions of labourers were employed to produce targeted amounts of foods to be distributed to the nation's people at low, ADMINISTERED PRICES. Products that arrived on the shelves in the cities were those that the planners (not customers) ordered. Similarly, the type and quantity of resources employed on the farms were those that planners dictated. Private ownership of land, profit-maximising behaviour and the ability of entrepreneurs to employ the labour and determine the working lives of others were prohibited. The state directed the objectives of the collective farms/communes, gave the orders as to who was working where and with whom and restricted the freedom of individuals to do otherwise. Although this may seem completely alien to those raised in a world of democratic choice and economic plenty, a system that guaranteed food supplies and certain employment was extremely welcome to those who had suffered their absence.

What, how and for whom production takes place in planned systems is decided by a hierarchical organisation where last year's achievements are reviewed; tomorrow's requirements are identified and orders are given to all levels throughout the economy to co-ordinate production to meet the announced targets. Individual choice, thus, becomes subservient to the needs of the society as a whole.

The paradox, of course, is that society is made up of individuals. Thus, a key disadvantage with centrally planned systems is that beyond basic needs how can senior administrators know and make provision for what every individual wants? The Soviet and Chinese COMMAND ECONOMIES additionally suffered from politically determined payment systems that destroyed incentives and ultimately entailed that national outputs and incomes could not keep up with Western standards. No nationwide examples of centrally planned systems, thus, survive today, although within market economies some important and fascinating case studies are still to be found (see Box 2.2).

BOX 2.2 BRITAIN'S NATIONAL HEALTH SERVICE: PLANNING IN MEDICAL SERVICES

The largest employer in Western Europe is the UK's NATIONAL HEALTH SERVICE (NHS). It is a planned system of health provision that aims to provide free access to medical services to all Britons that require it. Set up originally in 1947, it is a huge organisation that provides nationwide coverage with relatively little competition from the private sector. The proportion of UK national income spent on the NHS is much lower than that spent on health by other developed countries, and it is, thus, a relatively efficient provider. There are a number of good reasons for this: first, it is a state MONOPSONY, that is, an immense, and only, purchaser of very large quantities of medical equipment, drugs, doctors and nurses, so it can, thus, drive prices (its costs) down. Second, it is a state MONOPOLY: a single, nationwide producer that is able to plan a network of hospitals and health care services that can avoid wasteful duplication and underemployment of resources. (Note finally, because it is a public monopoly and not a private one, the prices it charges are the very lowest it can get away with – not the very highest.)

In any planned system where consumers have little choice, there can be problems of indifferent service on the part of the providers. Insisting on professional standards and monitoring performance can go some way to alleviating this inherent disadvantage (applicable to state schools as well as hospitals), but there is increasing insistence on making hospitals compete and instituting patient choice in an attempt to improve efficiency and simulate a QUASI MARKET in UK health care.

Another problem when you have a valuable service made available to the public at next to zero price is excess demand. Anyone with any complaint goes to see the doctor. Because price cannot be used to ration out the scarce supplies, distribution is effected by executive decision, that is, some doctor, nurse or hospital administrator must decide who gets served when. For non-urgent medical treatment that tends to mean a long wait.

One other ongoing problem of the NHS is that it is dependent on state funding (i.e. government taxation) and raises relatively little revenue of its own. It is not free to sell its services at a profit nor can it divert resources to invest in those medical technologies that can guarantee the biggest financial returns. Some may well argue that this is just as well – wealthy millionaires who want cosmetic surgery cannot buy hospital time and resources that could otherwise be used to treat penniless car-crash victims. It does mean, however, that getting the money to pay for the latest in high-tech medical research means continually bargaining for government hand-outs.

Whatever the criticisms about the monolithic nature of the state-run NHS, however, the over-riding objective of this planned system has never been questioned – to provide an equitable health service for all at no up-front price to the patient. What, how and for whom medical services are provided is determined by medical administrators, not by the purchasing power of consumers.

EFFICIENCY AND EQUITY

In any context, whether it be how a whole economy functions, a particular industry or just the operations of an isolated farming community, judging the effectiveness of different systems of economic organisation means considering issues of EFFICIENCY and EQUITY.

Just how efficient is the organisation in generating outputs, creating wealth and improving welfare, and does its economic activity result in a social order and distribution of benefits that we can approve of and can defend on grounds of social justice/equity?

A beautiful and harmonious society may be perfectly equitable but extremely wasteful and hopelessly inefficient in providing for its needs – a community in peace but unable to fully feed its populace and lacking the means to defend itself against the ravages of disease or foreign invaders.

Alternatively, the society may be a ruthlessly efficient productive machine, its shops full of a wide range of foods and technologically advanced, sophisticated gadgetry – but based on exploitation of the powerless and blighted by sections of the public who are homeless, starving and capable only of thieving rather than productive employment.

Clearly, neither extreme is attractive. What is ideal is an economy that combines both productive efficiency and social equity.

The history of humankind is illustrated by the dramatic rise and fall of empires and civilisations and the success or otherwise of various experiments in social organisation – none more dramatic than the immense changes witnessed in the twentieth century. The past 100 years have seen wars, revolutions, economic depression, the division of the world into opposing camps of capitalism and communism, increasing wealth of a capitalist minority and the eventual collapse of the centrally planned, command economies behind the "iron curtain".

The process of evolution in the decision-making systems that society has invented must inevitably continue. Furthermore, as some systems become extinct, others replace them. In the new millennium, what has evolved as the most powerfully productive economic engine is a predominantly market-based dynamo capable of astonishing accomplishments but whose worse excesses – most would agree – have to be kept in check by the moderating influence of public authority.

The market model's efficiency has been severely questioned recently, but, relative to other forms of economic organisation, it has passed the ultimate test of outperforming the alternatives. It is on grounds of equity, however, that its performance is most vulnerable to criticism.

This chapter has already illustrated the great extremes of wealth and poverty that exist among the peoples of the world. The global picture is not easy to summarise but over the last half-century as market forms of economic organisation have increased their global reach, world trade and economic growth has increased, the number of people in the world living in abject poverty has fallen but inequalities have risen; this is particularly true of China but also true for Europe and North America (Figure 2.3). This might be expected. As mentioned in the last chapter, markets require resources to be

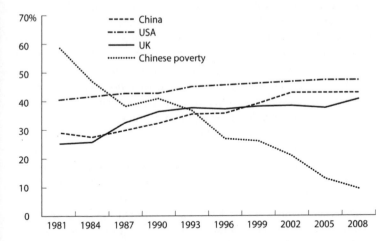

Figure 2.3 Inequalities rising as poverty decreases, 1981–2008. Data for USA, UK and China show inequality measured as a percentage where zero means perfect equality and 100% represents maximum inequality. The Chinese poverty gap is measured as the population percentage living on US$2 per day. Since the Chinese population is so large (19.1% of the world) the fall in poverty and rise in inequality in this country alone has biased world data in the same direction. (Sources: UK Institute of Fiscal Studies; US Census Bureau; The World Bank.)

mobile: to move their employment from sectors where demand is falling to those where demand is rising. Those most able and quickest to move will gain the highest rewards. Those less skilled, tied to traditional employments, geographically and occupationally immobile will lose out.

However, the inequities go further than this. Exponential growth in economic activity has visited increasing damage on the natural environment. Market systems that treat certain resources of the Earth as FREE GOODS (such as the oceans and atmosphere) have no incentive to conserve them. The monumentally productive market engine uses and abuses such free goods at will, dumps its waste products into the skies and seas and it is only relatively recently in our history that we have begun to understand the harm we have been doing to the biosphere. Priceless (literally) flora and fauna are rapidly diminishing in number, and we are, thus, reducing the planet's heritage that will eventually be passed on to our children.

If today's standard of living is only supportable by depleting the resources that are available for the future, then INTERGENERATIONAL EQUITY is being sacrificed.

Economist Kenneth Boulding characterised humankind's industrial activity as if it were operating within limitless frontiers – a "cowboy economy" played out under big skies and wide horizons where there is plenty of space and resources for all. Unfortunately, the growth of economic activity has now reached a point where the Earth is better appreciated as a crowded spaceship – where oxygen and other resources are scarce and some of the passengers are being more selfish than others. None of us should now go round like Buffalo Bill: burning the grass, shooting all the bison, using only a fraction of the carcass and leaving the rest to rot.

Evidence of how far the Earth's environment has been degraded is still contested – some claim that we are doing irreversible damage to the planet; others insist that such accusations are wildly exaggerated.

There will always be some people who have a vested interest in proclaiming one extreme or the other – all the more reason for economists to get their sums right. Measurement of many of the important variables is very often extremely difficult, but here are some data drawn from *The Economist* magazine and the environmental pressure group WWF (the World Wide Fund for Nature) (Figure 2.4 and Box 2.3).

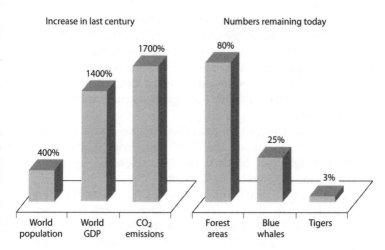

Figure 2.4 Changes in population, output, emissions and native species 1890–2013.

BOX 2.3 CASE STUDY: TIGERS AT RISK

Less than a century ago, it is estimated that 100,000 tigers ranged across all of Asia from Eastern Turkey to the Sea of Japan, from as far north as Siberia down over the equator to Indonesia. Now (2013) the World Wide Fund for Nature estimates that around 97 per cent of tigers are gone and fragile populations survive in small clusters in India, Indo-China and Siberia. Although poaching for illegal trade in tiger body parts is a continuing menace, the greater threat to the tiger's survival comes from loss of habitat and the consequent depletion of its natural prey.

Of eight tiger sub-species, three have become extinct in the past 50 years: The Bali tiger, Javan tiger and Caspian tiger. Of the others, the South China or Amoy tiger was estimated in 1998 to have a population of between 20 and 30 individuals only. Its future looks bleak.

As habitats fragment, the surviving tiger populations become separated from one another and a particular threat is then the loss of genetic diversity. Tiger fertility is reduced, litter sizes fall and cub survival rates decline.

The problem is that tigers compete with humankind in populating some of the most fertile, resource-rich places in East Asia. Look at Indonesia: having lost out in Bali and Java, the remaining battle for tiger survival is taking place in Sumatra.

A similar struggle continues in Bengal, whose famously beautiful tiger prowls the little remaining jungle in the India–Bangladesh borders not yet colonised by people hungry for economic development.

The painful reality of economics is illustrated here. Resources are scarce. Who should have first call upon them? This dilemma can be illustrated in two dimensions: first, should humankind continue its exploitation and depletion of the jungles that, unchecked, will lead to the extinction of tigers? How much is a tiger worth in terms of restricting the enterprise of local populations? If the cost of extinction is considered greater than the benefit of using jungle habitat for the use of local people, who decides that? How are such costs and benefits measured? It is easy for distant critics living in foreign cities to cry out in protest and insist that tigers are protected. Who is going to protect the livelihood of millions of poor children in Sumatra or Bangladesh? Only their parents who need the wood that protects the tigers' habitat.

Second, if the decision is taken to protect tigers in one specific location, as numbers diminish in this particular site, how should conservation agencies manage their manpower and resources to best effect? They have a choice of trying to safeguard the existing habitat in as wide a range as practicable ... but if tigers have not been seen in the district for some time (how long?) they might better use their resources to conduct surveys ... and if after surveying for some time (how long?) still none have been seen maybe they would be best giving up and moving their resources elsewhere? Just how should scarce resources be most efficiently employed? We return to issues like these in Chapter 8.

OPPORTUNITY COST

The most fundamental concept in economics is OPPORTUNITY COST. If you choose to use resources in one employment, then you must sacrifice the opportunity to use them in some other way. It is an old adage: you cannot have your cake and eat it. This sacrifice is frequently described as a TRADE-OFF. For example, if we use native forests to construct homes, build ships and fuel the fires of industry, then society must trade this gain off against retaining the natural habitat for wild animals to roam free.

North West Europe used to be carpeted from end to end in temperate rainforest. Very little remains today. There is no native, unspoilt natural vegetation left in Western Europe that has remained unexploited by man. Gone too are the bears, wild boar and a host of other species that used to run wild in the forests.

However, the trees felled in the past built the ships that first circumnavigated the globe, founded the trade and provided the energy that produced the modern industrial age. A much greater human population has now largely replaced the animal population that preceded it.

It is in the nature of economics that sacrifices must be made. The issue, therefore, becomes one of being as efficient and equitable as possible. Keep the opportunity cost of economic development to a minimum, so that we do not have to trade-off too much of one to gain more of the other.

The European lion may be extinct, although we might yet find ways to protect the Asian tiger. However, there are no guarantees. It takes time for society to learn to practise SUSTAINABLE DEVELOPMENT, and in the interim, more species may still die out. The long-term aim must not be to preserve all existing species, however, because this would inevitably preclude any further improvement of our own welfare. The opportunity cost in this case would be prohibitive. The appropriate aim is, thus, to match environmental costs with social benefits in such a way that the CAPITAL STOCK of our planet is not depleted. The garden I bequeath my children may, therefore, contain a different mix of flora and fauna to that which I inherited, but it should nonetheless retain all its phenomenal fertility and productivity. Future generations are, thus, not denied the opportunity to use the Earth in whatever ways their ingenuity allows.

THE MODERN, MIXED ECONOMY

We live in a world of constant change. What consumers demand today they discard tomorrow as tastes and preferences move on; what producers find technically impossible this year is revolutionised next year with the latest breakthrough. In such circumstances, achieving the twin goals of efficiency and equity in any economic system is a never-ending challenge.

Only the most flexible and fleet-footed economic organisations will survive to meet this challenge. This is evident at various levels: the success of some teams of more adaptable workers at the expense of others; the overtaking of old businesses and technologies by new ones; by the demise of inefficient centrally planned Eastern European economies that could not match the growing wealth of their western neighbours. It is also evident in the economic stagnation of nations with inequitable regimes in sub-Saharan Africa and elsewhere that confine riches to a few and, thus, fail to harness the productive capacity of most of their peoples.

Getting the perfect mix of market systems, government controls and national traditions just right in any one country is frustratingly difficult because there is an infinite variety of combinations, and the global economy is moving all the time. However, of course, it is just this endless diversity that makes the world what it is and the study of economics so fascinating.

There is a continual debate, in particular, over the extent to which governments should intervene in markets. It must be emphasised that markets need government and could not survive without them – the art is in knowing just how far to exert the guiding (corrupting?) influence of central authority and examples are given throughout the following pages to illustrate this point.

That markets cannot develop without government protection is easily demonstrated. Contrast the experience of a consumer trying to purchase something as basic as a shirt in different cultures. In a modern city store, the buyer would choose the selected item from a range of alternatives on display – all carrying designated price tags on cards that additionally provide information about the shirt size, quality of cloth and design type employed. The customer next takes the shirt across to the sales assistant and quite possibly hands over a plastic card to effect a transfer of money from the consumer's bank account to that of the store. The buyer taps in his card number or signs the till receipt, picks up the packaged item and leaves the store. Sale concluded.

In another culture, the process may be very different. The consumer enters the bazaar and is confronted with a wealth of colourful alternatives, none of which appear standard. After a period of indecision, one particular shirt perhaps seems attractive. An eager stallholder – if not already present – soon arrives and, recognising a potential sale, engages in conversation with the customer pointing out how wonderful this particular product is and how astute his client is in picking out this item so soon. When it comes to price, there is quite a debate. One party starts high and the other much lower. In the process of HAGGLING, the eventual EQUILIBRIUM PRICE emerges according to the bargaining strength and verbal acuity of the participants. Payment is accompanied by minute examination of the means of exchange proffered. If all goes well, the stallholder accepts the cash and the customer moves away with his purchase, wondering if what he has bought is as good as he hopes it to be and whether the price will subsequently turn out to be exorbitant...

The physical characteristics of the shirt in both examples might be exactly the same, although a case can be made for saying that in the latter market place, the customer has paid for the social interaction as well as the product.

The economic reason for the differences described above relates to the nature of institutional support for the markets in question. In the second case, much time and effort are devoted to CLIENTISATION: the process by which the two parties become known to one another and their credibility established. Without the back up of a reliable system of contracts and law enforcement, one party can always cheat on a deal and get away with it. To overcome this, personal credibility has to be established with a certain extravagant interaction (hidden agenda: is the other worthy of entering into business with?) otherwise the "price" agreed on will be all the higher to compensate for the increased risk involved.

If the buyer distrusts the seller, then the latter will have to pay the "price" of no deal or gaining less cash than he bargained for. If the seller distrusts the buyer or his currency, then he will charge all the more. Better for both parties if they deal with each other frequently and have already established a respectful relationship or, failing that, one comes with the personal recommendation of a third party who is known and respected by both (hence the importance of extended family, or a patron, in such societies).

Without the support of contract law, reliable currency and trust that each is indeed the rightful owner of the property that is to be exchanged, the market society in the second example – however colourful and attractive to the tourist – cannot extend very far. The TRANSACTION COSTS and INFORMATION COSTS involved limit its scope to personal trade only between recognised dealers. It is too costly, too risky to engage in transactions with total strangers. Therefore, this simple market economy will never grow. It is, indeed, characteristic of what goes on in villages and towns that are found throughout the poorer countries of the world.

How much easier it is to buy products in a modern (albeit impersonal) market economy. Both parties are assured that if they are cheated, they have recompense in law. With central authorities providing the essential institutions to protect property and facilitate trade, risk is reduced and market dealers can get on with their business. Today, people can purchase goods and services on the internet, which minimises transaction costs and allows greater expansion of commerce. Dealing with strangers is quite normal; one-off trades where you are unlikely ever to see the other party again do not mean you are going to be exploited. Revealing details of your bank account over the phone or on-line is so safe that it has become common practice. It might be impersonal, but it works.

In fact, because it works, it has become more impersonal. Where trust can be taken for granted, the market economy grows. Furthermore, as it grows it facilitates greater and greater economic specialisation, interdependency and thereby wealth. You can book a foreign holiday, buy the flight tickets, reserve hotel rooms, hire a car and pay for it all without leaving your computer – safe in the knowledge that the tickets will arrive on-line or in the post, the car will be waiting at the foreign airport and the hotel room will be ready for you whenever you say. A range of specialised contracts have all been fulfilled across different frontiers, not one party having personal knowledge of the ultimate customer: you. However, insofar as these trades are successfully concluded, all dealers profit from the arrangement and are encouraged to expand their businesses, offer more services, employ more resources and spread the benefits ever wider.

There is a powerful clue here to explain why some communities grow rich and others do not. Where society has evolved institutions to underpin markets and facilitate trade, wealth can be created. Where trust breaks down, where people cheat and get away with it, trade and economic growth fails too. Wherever the institutions that form the foundation for economic exchange are undermined, markets cannot develop any further; wealth cannot grow. This is an important conclusion in basic economics and one to which we will return.

SUMMARY

- Economics analyses how societies choose what, how and for whom goods and services are produced.
- Tradition, central planning or free markets can be employed as mechanisms to organise production and distribution.
- The choices made and end results achieved by different economies can be judged according to the efficiency and equity of the processes involved.
- The real or opportunity cost of achieving any goal is measured in terms of what has been sacrificed in achieving it.
- Wealth is created and economies develop insofar as market trade is facilitated and enhanced by institutions that protect property, enforce contracts and minimise risk.

FURTHER READING

North, D. (June 1994) "Economic Performance Through Time", *American Economic Review*, Vol. 84, pp. 359–68. This is a very accessible article by a Nobel Prize winner of how institutions underpin trade and how this accounts for the economic progress of North America in contrast to the relative stagnation of South America.

Schultz, T. (1964) *Transforming Traditional Agriculture*, Yale University Press. A classic text on its subject.

Wilber, C. K. and Jameson, K. P. (1996) *The Political Economy of Development and Underdevelopment*, McGraw-Hill. Not positive economics but a provocative set of readings that emphasise the exploitation of poorer by richer nations. Note the chapter on El Salvador.

World Wide Fund for Nature, wwf.panda.org. Again, not positive economics but a source of selective information on environmental matters.

World Bank, *World Development Report 2002: Building Institutions for Markets*. The World Bank publishes an authoritative report each year on a topic of economic importance, reflecting the trends in current academic interest. This issue is recommended if you want to read a more balanced reference on how markets develop.

World Bank, *World Development Report 2010: Development and Climate Change*. The dangers of climate change affect all countries, but low income countries are the most vulnerable. The benefits of high income are enjoyed by the rich; the costs incurred by their high carbon emissions are borne by the planet – and especially the poor.

Lastly, I have to recommend: Friedman, M. (1953) *Essays in Positive Economics*, University of Chicago Press. Also, Friedman, M. and Friedman, R. (1980) *Free to Choose*, Harcourt. These are very readable classics on the philosophy of economics by the late, most famous, provocative and distinguished economist since Keynes. His emphasis on the importance of free markets will never fade.

QUESTIONS

1 Each year the demand for places to study medicine at university tends to exceed their supply. How would a free market PRICE MECHANISM solve the problem of the allocation of university students to these places, compared to a system of central planning? Examine the advantages and disadvantages of either system.

2 In many countries, the supply of cars to the domestic marketplace is determined by the price mechanism and consumers' ability to pay. The supply of roads in these countries is, however, determined

by command and will only increase subject to government planning. Particularly for countries where average incomes are rapidly increasing, examine the issues that arise in such mixed economies and how might any problems be resolved – by market or command remedies.

3

PRICES, MARKETS, COFFEE AND REAL ESTATE

Durham Cathedral soars above the centre of the old British market town as it has done for almost a thousand years. But just down the road from the Norman cathedral and the castle that defends it, a new coffee shop has recently opened. Amongst the cluster of shops and stalls which crowd Durham's market place, this newcomer has now opened its doors to tempt the passer-by with the pungent aroma of fresh-roasted coffee. (At least it has at the time of writing. By the time you read this yet another entrepreneur may well have taken over the business and be displaying fashion wear or computer games or some other such service which attracts the buying public!)

There are few places on Earth that are not touched by the continual changes of market organisation. Humankind is a restless species and is always seeking out new and better ways to produce things, more and different goods and services to acquire. But by what mechanism is it decided what is produced where, and by whom? How is the organisation of society's economic affairs carried out?

A hot cup of coffee is a perishable commodity: how come coffee, milk, sugar, skilled labour, specific equipment and every other resource necessary all arrive from their separate origins to deliver a satisfying product to your hand just at the very moment you want it? We take it for granted but a simple cup of coffee represents in fact a complex coming-together of a unique set of ingredients that makes up a distinctive and time-sensitive product. Any breakdown in the multiple chains of organisation that are involved in bringing you this good will result in the costly failure to produce anything palatable that anyone would want to buy.

Coffee from Colombia, sugar from the West Indies, milk or cream from a British farm, a china cup and saucer from somewhere local or distant (China?), water from the regional utility, an espresso machine from Italy, local labour and enterprise, plus a variety of other resources that go to make up the total experience of visiting this coffee shop: who organises all these resource flows to bring you a cup of coffee?

THE PRICE MECHANISM

Adam Smith called it the Invisible Hand. He wrote in 1776 that each individual's pursuit of personal gain ensured that, in aggregate, society's wants are better met this way than if some philanthropic enterprise had indeed set out consciously to organise the same.

Many economists have since shared this view. They argue that the automatic functioning of unrestricted trade and free market pricing will ensure efficient economic organisation that cannot be bettered by the combined actions of any number of well-meaning planners, administrators and public servants.

Prices make up the key signalling mechanism in a market economy that indicates which needs are most urgent, which production strategy should be utilised, who is to be employed and how much they should be paid.

Suppose the tastes of the public change such that they are increasingly interested in buying coffee and health-food sandwiches and are tired of consuming additive-packed hamburgers and technicolour pizzas? Who is best placed to signal this to restauranteurs and fast food producers – government planners or individual consumers?

In a free market, by the pattern of consumer spending, hamburger bars and pizza parlours will lose sales and the owners of coffee shops will be earning extra. Prices of those products out of favour may well fall at first to try and tempt back more custom; prices of those commodities in hot demand may well rise at first as competitive bidding forces them up. But if consumer trends continue there will be an irrevocable change in suppliers' profits – out of the pockets of loss-making hamburger sellers and into those of coffee shop keepers. If they cannot continue to pay their costs (typically high rents in city centre locations) then owners of the former enterprises will want to sell up; owners of the latter may well negotiate to buy them instead.

The range of commodities on offer in Durham market place, like any other, thus automatically adjusts to meet consumer DEMAND. A new coffee shop is just one small piece of evidence of how markets evolve – the prices of products and profits of entrepreneurs signalling the way that changes must go.

THE ALLOCATION OF RESOURCES

In this particular example, as a result of changing consumer demand, the employment of a number of specific resources was affected. Consider, first, the small corner of land occupied by a hamburger bar that converts to a coffee shop.

LAND AND TRANSFER EARNINGS

Land in the centre of any market place is usually in much demand. A fixed SUPPLY of land in a restricted area where many traders compete to gain control of a given site means the price of this resource is forced up and up. Though fixed in space, this land thus becomes extremely OCCUPATIONALLY MOBILE – it can be bought up and employed in the service of a cafe, a retail store, a solicitor's office, an estate agent's or a bank – according to whichever business is prepared to pay the highest price. (Ever wondered why the centres of the largest business districts are dominated by banks?)

Geographers can map the employment of land in cities going out in concentric circles from the highest earning inner ring to progressively less and less economically productive sites. A coffee shop with a rapid turnover selling an attractive product to equally high-income-earning inner city employees may well earn just enough to cover its costly OVERHEADS. Typically, however, with high rents to pay, such enterprises are run on a financial knife-edge such that any slight change in the quality of its product or in consumer preferences will have an immediate knock-on effect on profits and thus the business's long-term survival as indicated earlier.

Land in city centres can therefore transfer its employment relatively rapidly if it does not earn enough – which explains why so many stores do indeed close down and reopen transformed in a new guise and under new management. The same fate may also apply to people but since individuals, unlike land, have feelings about the work they do and can express their opinions vociferously then the allocation and reallocation of their labour supply embraces many issues that are not solely economic.

LABOUR AND WAGES

Nonetheless, precisely because the price and employment of labour is such an emotive issue, we can take time here to briefly analyse and understand the economic forces that determine outcomes in this particular market.

Economics is a seemingly cold and cruel science that, like it or not, treats labour just as any other resource. People will be employed only in so far as they are productive. Generally speaking, coffee shop assistants will be taken on if they possess the necessary skills, attitudes and enthusiasms at a competitive price. Employment is not a right. In a market society, any resource will only find it is in demand if it can help produce something that consumers are willing to buy. If this is the case, then as above, the scarcer the resource, the more it will command a high price.

Scarcity is a relative concept. There are millions of footballers all over the world but the supply of footballers of the specific talents of individuals such as Lionel Messi are very few, relative to the demand for their services. Hence such talent can command an exceptional price.

MISMATCH UNEMPLOYMENT

People can become amazingly specialised in the occupations they perform. The degree of talent and training required to become a professional in one employment or another varies enormously and this in part determines the speed at which newcomers can enter any particular labour market. Labour as an economic resource, therefore, is divided and sub-divided into many non-competing groups. Someone whose abilities do not match those skills in demand will thus be unemployed – unless and until either the individual retrains or the jobs on offer change. For example, there may be a shortage in the supply of accountants to balance the books of our coffee shop and employing someone to do so may be very difficult (and therefore expensive) if access to this profession is restricted. There may be a large pool of willing and able workers who can be taken on as shop assistants but even extensive unemployment of such relatively cheap labour will not necessarily increase the supply, and bid down the price, of those accountants who possess differently honed skills and attributes. Increased specialisation reduces the occupational mobility of labour.

DEMAND-DEFICIENT UNEMPLOYMENT

As mentioned earlier, the demand for a particular specialist service is DERIVED from the DEMAND for its product. In the extreme, in a severe recession, a slump in consumer spending throughout the nation means businesses in all sectors may lay off their employees – white-collar workers of rare skill as well as some horny-handed manual labourers – if there is no demand for their products. This is large-scale, DEMAND-DEFICIENT UNEMPLOYMENT that is associated with the cyclical slumps, referred to in the first chapter. In such a downturn, governments may be petitioned to provide support for those the market cannot employ. This means pumping state money into the economy to bolster consumer demand, though this sort of support is dependent on for how long, and to what extent, the central authorities can sustain large debts, and really the only long-term solution is for an autonomous recovery in the business cycle.

DEMAND, SUPPLY AND THE THEORY OF PRICE

Whether it be the price of coffee, the rent on land, a worker's wages or the profits of an enterprise, all are a measure of the demand and supply of goods and services in a market society and these prices signal to all and sundry the relative shortages and surpluses that exist. Not only this, they also provide incentives for market operators to respond and remedy any imbalances. Coffee in demand? Its price will go up to ration out existing supplies and meanwhile tempt new producers to enter the market. Falling profits for hamburger bars? The least efficient will close down. Accountants are earning high wages? More will take up the training. The price mechanism is a ruthlessly efficient organiser.

Since prices are demonstrably at the heart of all economic organisation it should be clear by now why economists focus so repeatedly and relentlessly on the theory of price. If we can theorise about what exactly determines price movements it enables us not only to explain what has happened in the past, and why, but it also gives us a basis for predicting what will happen in the future.

One comment on theorising before we begin: Milton Friedman, the most famous economist of the late twentieth century, said that no matter how abstract and seemingly unreal are the assumptions on which a theory is based, "the only relevant test of the validity of a hypothesis is comparison of its predictions with experience". As you will see, though many assumptions in economics make perfect sense (for example, we assume consumers and producers behave rationally) they are not necessarily true for all time. These assumptions do not matter so much, however. In positive economics we are most of all concerned about whether or not a theory's predictions are confirmed by hard evidence. So long as it produces workable results, even the most unrealistic hypothesis must be taken seriously. With that in mind, let us begin with analysing demand.

CONSUMER EQUILIBRIUM

Assume that all consumers wish to maximise their UTILITY: their "level of satisfaction". They are thus motivated to consume that combination of goods and services which, given their income, yields the most utility. Individual tastes differ such that your pre-ferred shopping list features items totally different from mine – you may prefer coffee and ice cream and I access to public parks and footpaths – but in both cases we opt for combinations that best satisfy our particular wants. A change in relative prices between some goods and others or a change in our levels of income will affect our chosen purchases but factoring in these changes we will always adjust our consumption to maximise our total utility or satisfaction.

Considering the demand for coffee, we can assume for the purposes of illustration, that an individual divides his purchases between coffee and all other goods (Figure 3.1).

Given constant prices and incomes we can represent the choices available to this consumer in the above OPPORTUNITY SET.

Figure 3.1 shows that if a consumer spent all his fixed income on coffee he could afford to buy amount A. Alternatively, if he spent it entirely on other goods he could afford amount B. He thus has the

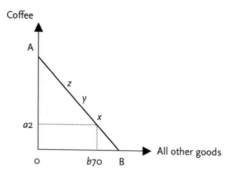

Figure 3.1 Consumption alternatives: coffee and other goods.

opportunity to buy any combination of coffee and all other goods bound by the BUDGET CONSTRAINT triangle 0*AB*. Given this opportunity set, the individual thus chooses that combination of goods which best maximises his utility. Let that be at point *x* where he would consume *a2* of coffee and *b70* of all other goods. He could have chosen any other point along his budget constraint *AB*, such as *y* or *z*, but we have said that combination *x* represents the highest level of satisfaction for this individual. At this point, the consumer is at equilibrium in the sense that he cannot rearrange his purchases to reach a higher level of utility (Box 3.1).

BOX 3.1 MAPPING INDIVIDUAL PREFERENCES: INDIFFERENCE CURVES

Economists have invented a unique way to map an individual's tastes and preferences on a two-dimensional diagram. It is called an indifference map and it shows lines (similar to contour lines on a topographical map) which illustrate higher and lower levels of satisfaction and when taken together map out the shape of a consumer's preferences just as contour lines map out the shape of the land.

Consider Figure 3.2. The map of INDIFFERENCE CURVES or preference lines shows increasing levels of utility as consumption of both goods increases from zero. The closer together or further apart are the lines, the faster or slower an increase in consumption leads to increasing utility. Any

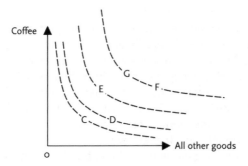

Figure 3.2 An indifference map.

one line, however, joins places of equal satisfaction. That is, the consumer is indifferent between all combinations of purchases along the same line. (Just as going up or downhill is represented by crossing contours on a geography map, so maintaining the same level means moving *along* a contour.) Thus the combination of coffee and all other goods represented by consumption point *G* is preferred to combinations *E*, *D* and *C* (and all are clearly preferred to zero). But the consumer rates the combination of goods at point *F* at the same level of utility as point *G*. He is indifferent between these two combinations of purchases.

Note that another individual might have a completely different map of preferences between the two dimensions shown. It all depends on individual tastes (Figure 3.3):

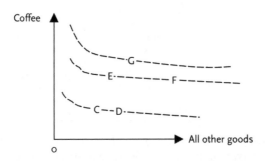

Figure 3.3 A coffee lover's indifference map.

The combination points of goods *C* to *G* remain unchanged here. However we are now illustrating the preference map of a coffee lover who is indifferent between points *C* and *D*. The indifference curves are relatively flat, showing that a great deal of other goods must be substituted for a small reduction in coffee if this consumer is to retain the same level of satisfaction. A small movement vertically in the direction of consuming more coffee, however, rapidly takes this individual onto higher levels of utility, for example to points *E* or *F* (again he is indifferent as to which). *G* in this case represents the highest level of satisfaction illustrated.

Returning to the original case discussed above, where the consumer has an opportunity set constrained by his budget to o*AB*, of all the possible combinations of goods that the consumer can choose between, which one will the individual choose?

Given his fixed income, he will choose that combination which maximises his utility – that which allows him to reach the highest level of satisfaction. That is, the combination of *a2* and *b70* represented by point *x*, which we can now see, courtesy of this individual's map of preferences, is clearly higher than the levels of satisfaction represented by points *y* and *z* (Figure 3.4):

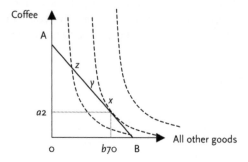

Figure 3.4 Consumer equilibrium.

What happens now to this individual's demand for coffee if its price falls? Given his income, if he chose to spend it all on coffee he could clearly buy more (represented by a move from *A* to *C* in

Figure 3.5), though if he chose to buy no coffee at all then since the price of no other good has changed he is still constrained to point B. This consumer's new set of choices made possible by the price change is thus illustrated by the budget line CB:

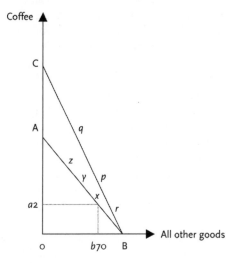

Figure 3.5 A price change.

Which consumption point will the consumer move to? It will be that point which maximises his utility somewhere along the line CB. Let that new equilibrium be point *p*. Note that although this consumer's NOMINAL INCOME has not changed, since the price of coffee has fallen his REAL INCOME has risen such that he now has the opportunity to increase his purchases of all goods as illustrated by the additional sector *ABC*. According to this consumer's preferences he could equally choose point *q* or even *r*.

Different people have different preferences. A real coffee lover, given the fall in price of coffee represented above, may choose to move from consumption point *x* to point *q*. That is, he or she may choose to consume much more coffee and actually buy less of all other goods. Alternatively at point *r* there is illustrated the option of buying the same amount or even less coffee and buying more of other things. Point *p* represents the choice to buy more coffee as its price falls, all other purchases remaining the same.

BOX 3.2 DIMINISHING MARGINAL UTILITY

If the price of coffee falls, exactly how much more would you buy? Think about it. Doesn't it depend on how much you have already, and how much you value a bit more coffee compared to the cash you would sacrifice in buying that bit extra? Generally speaking, if you have already bought a lot of something, the increase in total utility you would gain by buying more of it would be relatively little. That is, your *marginal* utility has diminished. The more you have something, the less you want more of it.

This important principle is true for all goods and services consumed. Some people's marginal utility diminishes more slowly than others, however. A chocoholic, for example, will no doubt be keener to consume more and more chocolate bars than I will, but even an addict will find that the first item consumed increases his total utility by more than that gained from the last of, say, ten items consumed.

Given a price fall for a given product, an individual will increase consumption until his marginal utility diminishes to just equal its price – that is, the value of the cash that could be spent on all other goods. Suppose this week, King Size Deep Pan-fried Pizzas are on special offer: each one for £1. Assuming you like these things, wouldn't you buy more ... up until the point where the sacrifice of £1 (which you could spend an all other things) is not worth it? The extra or marginal utility to be gained from one more pizza purchase is now adjudged to be less than the value of its price. Whether you knew it or not, you have just reached "consumer equilibrium" – where the marginal utility per pound or dollar (or MU/£ or $) on one item in your shopping list is equal to that for all other items.

The analysis in Box 3.2 illustrates all the options open to one consumer. Summarising, we can say that a price fall of any one good that features in an individual's regular shopping list represents not only the opportunity to increase purchases of that good itself but also, since it represents a marginal change in real income, it opens the opportunity to alter purchases of other goods as well. The more a certain good takes up an important slice of a person's budget, however, the more its price change will affect that individual's overall pattern of purchases.

MARKET DEMAND

We can now move from the analysis of one individual's consumption decisions to consider the demand for one product from all consumers added together.

Following a price change, if the decisions of all consumers in a specific market for, say, cups of coffee are aggregated together we can thus construct a market demand curve. There may be some individuals whose decisions run contrary to all others (for example, an individual who chooses point *r*, in the analysis described above) but their influence on the overall market will be negligible. The normal demand relationship is illustrated above – as the price of coffee increases, demand for it will fall, and vice versa, assuming all other factors influencing the market remain unchanged.

The *slope* of the demand curve illustrated here is important. It shows just exactly how much demand will contract as price increases a little or, conversely, how much demand extends as price falls. This slope, of course, relates the change in quantity consumed to the relative change in price. The responsiveness of demand for a good consequent to a change in its price is known as ELASTICITY (Box 3.3).

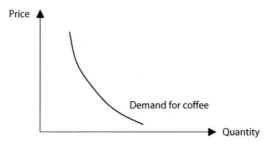

Figure 3.6 Coffee demand curve.

BOX 3.3 ILLUSTRATING PRICE-ELASTICITY

Price-elasticity is mathematically expressed as the percentage change in quantity demand divided by the percentage change in price. Thus if a 5 per cent increase in price of a good causes a 10 per cent fall in demand then price-elasticity equals −2. Equi-proportionate changes in demand and price will give unitary elasticity, equal to −1. Demand is said to be price-elastic for any ratio above −1. If, however, a 5 per cent change in price causes a 2.5 per cent change in consumer demand then demand is price-*in*elastic – equal to −0.5. Where demand is price-inelastic – where price changes are greater than demand changes – then the ratio will be less than 1.

Price-elasticity is often illustrated in a graphical form. All things being equal, the flatter the demand curve the more responsive or price-elastic is demand. That is, it shows a situation where a small change in price is met by a large change in the quantity demanded – but take care with the horizontal and vertical axes: in Figure 3.7, the illustrated price-elasticity is in both cases the same.

The flatness or steepness of any curve illustrated depends entirely on how scale is represented on the respective axes, so it is best to refer to the elasticity of demand mathematically. Nonetheless, graphical illustrations

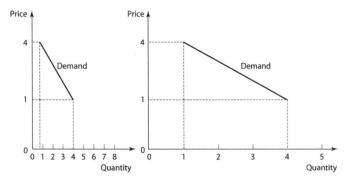

Figure 3.7 Different scales, different slopes, same price–elasticity!

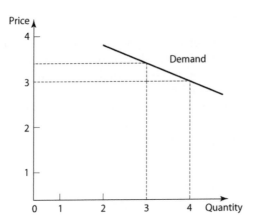

Figure 3.8 Price–elastic demand. A relatively small change in price induces a larger change in demand for this good.

of demand and supply are common and so Figure 3.8 illustrates relatively price-elastic demand on the assumption that the axes are equally scaled. Conversely, a steep demand curve illustrates *ceteris paribus* a less responsive or inelastic relationship to a price change.

Generally speaking, the more one good can be substituted for another in a person's pattern of spending, the more price–elastic it is likely to be in demand. Where a specific good or service has a number of competing substitutes (for example a particular brand of cereals) then demand will be very price-sensitive (with elasticity much greater than 1). In contrast, a commodity for which there are no or few substitutes will have low elasticity (a price-elasticity of less than 1). For example a 400 per cent increase in the world price of oil in January 1974 led to a minimal reduction (say 6 per cent) in demand. That gives a ratio of 6/400 or 0.015! Note that although the demand for all oil is price-inelastic in the short term, the demand for any one *brand* (say, Shell oil) will be price-elastic since if one petrol station puts its price up, drivers will simply fill up somewhere cheaper. The competition between rival oil companies is fierce (see Chapter 4).

SHIFTS IN DEMAND

Analysis above has referred to price movements, "all other factors remaining unchanged". But what factors other than price have an important influence on market demand and how do they affect the theory being developed here?

For any one commodity, a whole range of other factors can be listed. World demand for coffee, for example, is affected by changes in consumers' incomes, by industry advertising, by collective fashions, tastes and preferences, by competition from alternatives or complementary goods, perhaps even by global changes in the climate. Whatever the price of coffee, if any of these other factors changes it will cause − to a great or lesser extent − a *shift* in demand.

Suppose, for example, the International Coffee Organisation sponsored a successful world-wide advertising campaign to promote the consumption of coffee. Then, whatever the going market price, we can expect that many more consumers would enter the market and buy coffee. In Figure 3.9, at price *P1*, for example, demand shifts from quantity *Q1* to *Q2*.

Demand for coffee can change for any number of reasons, therefore. A contraction (or extension) in demand caused by an increase (or decrease) in price is illustrated by a movement *along* the demand curve. A fall (or rise) in demand caused by any other EXOGENOUS CHANGE is illustrated by a *shift* in the whole curve (Boxes 3.4 and 3.5).

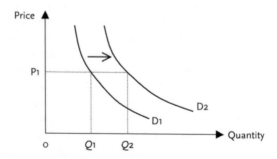

Figure 3.9 A demand shift.

BOX 3.4 ENDOGENOUS AND EXOGENOUS CHANGES

A two-dimensional diagram can only illustrate the interactions between two variables – in this case, the effect of price on demand. In this example, an increase in price is an endogenous change, that is to say within the dimensions of the model, and its effect can be studied on the dependent variable: causing a fall in demand illustrated by a contraction along the demand curve. A change in some other factor outside the model, in this example advertising, is an exogenous change and this causes the relationships between the two original variables to shift. The distinction between endogenous (internal) and exogenous (external) changes is important and will be referred to continually through this text.

BOX 3.5 COFFEE PRICES

All this analysis may seem a bit pedantic but, as you will see later on, it is actually important in separating out causes and effects of major crises in world markets. A quick example should help explain. Coffee is (after oil) the world's second most important traded commodity. The livelihood of 25 million small producer families and more than half a billion other people linked to the coffee trade in poor countries is directly influenced by the price of coffee. In October 2001 the world price of coffee bottomed-out at 42 US cents per lb., a 100-year low, depressing the incomes, and lives, of millions, but it has since bounced up and down again, falling 37 per cent from February 2012 to February 2013. Prices continue to be very volatile – hurting particularly the smaller farmer who cannot insure against risk. Did the 2013 price fall because world demand was low or did some other factor cause the slump in prices? And what causes these sudden and great reversals in prices and fortunes? This is not an insignificant matter. Careful analysis is called for...

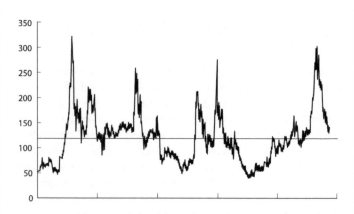

Figure 3.10 Coffee prices, 1980–2013 (US cents per lb). This graph
        illustrates the changing price of coffee future contracts, that
        is the price agreed before harvest for future delivery – which
        will be less volatile than "spot" or day to day prices. None-
        theless the variation shown is the result of great movement
        in supply and demand conditions. (Source: Trader2Trader.)

MARKET SUPPLY

The incentive for any business to supply goods to market is to make
profits – to sell his/her product at a higher price than the COSTS
OF PRODUCTION involved in offering it for sale. Whether it be
a personal service, such as providing haircuts, the assembly of a
luxury motor car with inputs from all over the world, or selling
advertising space on-line to invisible consumers, these goods and
services will only be supplied if the market price agreed on with the
buyer sufficiently rewards the entrepreneur for his/her efforts.

Assume that all suppliers wish to maximise profits. Given that
production costs and all other factors affecting the supply of a certain
good remain constant, then producers will increase supplies to the
market if prices rise. Conversely, supply will contract if price falls.

There are many costs involved in offering coffee for sale in a
given market place. At low prices per cup, only the most efficient,
low-cost suppliers can afford to produce this beverage and the
quantities offered for sale will be limited. If consumers are willing

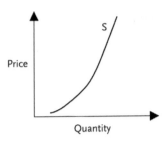

Figure 3.11 A supply curve.

to pay higher prices, however, then other suppliers will be tempted to enter the market and existing producers will also increase their provision. At very high prices, businesses which had never previously thought of making this product may well switch production plans and become coffee suppliers.

We can illustrate the relationship between the price of a product and the quantity supplied by the supply curve S in Figure 3.11.

Note that, as before, the slope of the supply curve indicates the responsiveness of producers to alter supplies as price changes. If, for example, a small increase in price calls forth a proportionally large increase in quantity then supply is said to be price-elastic. The rather steep curve shown here illustrates the opposite: relatively low price-elasticity of supply (though the same qualification about horizontal and vertical scales mentioned in Box 3.3 should be emphasised).

Price-elasticity of supply is affected by time – the longer businesses have to adjust production plans, the more responsive they can be to any market changes. A sudden increase in demand for almost any product cannot be accommodated instantly, no matter how high a price a customer is prepared to pay. Supplies of oil, cars or coffee for example are fixed by current stockpiles. If someone is desperate to buy something then a high price may persuade another con-sumer to leave the market (as in an auction) but supply itself cannot be increased.

Over time, depending on the technology involved in production, high prices call forth greater supplies. For oil, more may be pumped out of the existing wells and refineries. More cars can roll off the assembly line. In the case of coffee, if all existing stocks are already committed, consumers will have to wait until the next harvest.

Typically, economists can identify three trading periods: the instantaneous or SPOT MARKET, when supplies are fixed to existing, identifiable stocks; the SHORT TERM when supplies are price-inelastic and the LONG TERM when supplies are price-elastic (Figure 3.12):

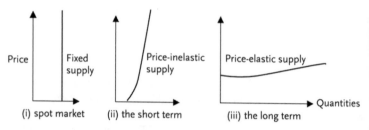

Figure 3.12 Price-elasticity of supply and time (i) spot market; (ii) the short run; (iii) the long run.

The dividing line between the short term and long term is a matter of judgement. The short term usually refers to the increase in supplies that can be gained by relying on existing resources and working them harder; the longer term tends to imply employing more factors of production.

SHIFTS IN SUPPLY

What other factors than price affect supplies? A supply curve for any good or service shows the distinctive relationship between just one variable, price and the quantity of supplies that each price will call forth to the market. As before, if any exogenous variable outside of this relationship changes then the original supply curve will shift in its entirety – showing that at whatever price that existed before, now at that same price a new supply relationship exists.

Any sudden change in production costs, say due to a technological breakthrough or breakdown, an increase in wages, any transport and distribution hold-up, will all effect a shift in supply. Government tax and regulation can also affect supplies of certain goods and services (Figure 3.13).

If a local brewery was prepared to supply quantity *Q1* of beer to town at a price of *P1* and then the government raises the beer tax

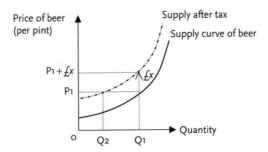

Figure 3.13 A shift in supply. In this example of a government tax on quantity supplied, the supply curve shifts up vertically at all prices by the amount of the tax.

by £x per pint sold then this will shift the supply curve as shown. That is, the brewery will only be prepared to sell the same quantity as before at a price of *P1* + £x. Equally, if they had to pay the tax at the old price *P1* then the brewery would only be prepared to supply the much-reduced quantity *Q2*.

PRICE DETERMINATION: CASE STUDIES

We now have all the analytical components in place to complete our theory of price. To recap, price changes signal how resources in the economy must automatically re-allocate so as to match consumer demand to potential supplies. How does this work? How are sudden changes in market preferences or in production conditions accommodated in an economy and what are the implications for the people involved? Let us look at a case study.

REAL ESTATE

The abstract analysis of how the price mechanism works as described earlier can be applied to how demand and supply changes affect prices in real estate markets – for example in residential housing. We can, thus, illustrate and explain the speculative bubble that has led to booming house prices in a number of countries up until 2007 and their sudden and precipitous fall from grace thereafter (see the graph of US house prices in Figure 1.7).

Although it is true that the supply of any one property in a specific location is absolutely fixed, the supply of housing in general is not. As mentioned earlier in this chapter, land is *occupationally* mobile, so that if the return on building residential homes rises, then the land designated for offices, factories, farm buildings or any other use will transfer its employment as builders construct more houses, apartment blocks and so on. Indeed, old buildings will be demolished to rebuild whatever is demanded to give the construction industry greater profit.

We can, therefore, say that the supply of existing housing stock increases in direct relation to prices, although it will be very inelastic in the short term – depending on how quickly other buildings can be converted and how much time it takes for the construction of new homes.

Meanwhile, the demand for homes depends on a number of factors – some more volatile than others. Clearly, demand falls as prices rise and force buyers out of the market, as noted earlier, but the level of incomes and the price and availability of mortgages also are key influential factors (see Box 3.6). Added to this, as we shall see, are notions of confidence and future expectations.

Assume for the time being that a normal demand curve *D1* meets a price-inelastic supply curve for housing in a specific market location. Suppose this is a given town where there are a range of consumers with different incomes and abilities to purchase a three-bedroomed property and there is a somewhat more restricted range of such houses on offer.

If the local estate agent marketing these properties asks for too high a price, say *h3* in Figure 3.14, then he or she may find more willing sellers (*q3*) than buyers (*q1*). Conversely, we can imagine that if the agent asks for a house price that is too low, then there would be too few willing to sell their properties compared with the many more willing to buy.

Ask for too much and excess supply forces sellers to bring the price down. Too low and competitive bidding forces prices up. This particular market would eventually reach an equilibrium where demand meets supply at price *h*★ and with a quantity traded at *q2*. (This is one unique market outcome. Note that regional differences in house prices are accounted for by differences in the position of demand relative to supply. Wealthier, more populous regions will

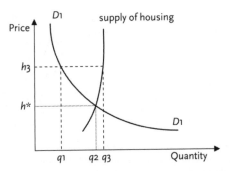

Figure 3.14 The price of housing. At high price (*h3*) supply exceeds demand so sellers will likely reduce what they are asking for until demand equals supply at equilibrium price (*h**). In this case, the number of houses offered for sale will contract a little *q3* to *q2*; the number of interested buyers increases greatly from *q1* to *q2*.

have the demand curve further to the right relative to their supply, thereby determining higher equilibrium prices.)

So far, to consider the interaction of demand, supply and price in a simplified form, we have considered all other factors affecting the real estate market as unchanged. Let us now take this analysis forward and study the impact of other exogenous influences.

BOX 3.6 INTERDEPENDENT MARKETS

The demand, supply and price of mortgages (long-term loans to house buyers) are closely linked to the market for housing. If the supply of mortgage finance increases, this is an important factor increasing the demand for housing (see Figure 3.15).

The supply of mortgages depends on the willingness of finance companies to lend out money. Generally speaking, they will lend out more if customers are willing to pay more. The supply curve is positively sloped *Sm1*. If these companies either find that the cost of getting hold of more money is falling, or they can come up with innovative ways to invent more mortgages, then they in turn will be willing to increase supplies. *Sm1* shifts right to *Sm2* and the price of mortgages falls from *r1* to *r2*.

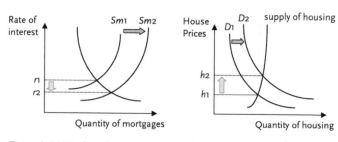

Figure 3.15 Markets for mortgages and housing: as rates of interest fall, house prices rise. In the left-hand diagram of the market for mortgages, the price of mortgages is the rate of interest. As the supply of mortgages increases, the rate goes down, *r1* to *r2*; the demand for houses in the right-hand diagram thus goes up, pushing house prices up with it.

Cheaper loans therefore lead to an increase in the demand for housing. As *Sm1* shifts to *Sm2* this means the demand for housing *D1* shifts to *D2* and house prices rise *h1* to *h2*. The two market places are interdependent.

For reasons already described in Chapter 1, the availability of money in the USA rose steadily from the late 1990s, reducing interest rates and making it easier for people to secure mortgages. Granting cheap loans particularly to low-income families to enable them to buy their own homes was becoming financially possible, commercially profitable and both socially and politically desirable. The demand curve for housing above shifted to the right, *D1* to *D2* (see Figure 3.15), driving the average price higher.

Now, as property prices rose, it generated along with it feelings of confidence, consumer wealth and well-being, and also financial innovation. As the price of assets rises on the one hand, people feel naturally wealthier and there inevitably comes the temptation to go out and spend that wealth. Bankers catering for this demand will therefore create means whereby house owners can cash in on that wealth – taking out second mortgages, for example. The increase in demand for property begins to gather pace (Figure 3.16).

A shift right in demand *D1* to *D2* causes a rise in price which causes an increase in confidence, money supplies and thus further

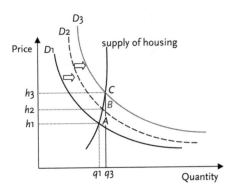

Figure 3.16 The effects of a spending boom.

demand. *D2* moves to *D3*. A virtuous feedback loop, or price–confidence–price spiral, exists: *h1* moving to *h2* and then *h3*. Notice how, because the supply is very price-inelastic in the short term, relatively small shifts in quantities demanded cause greater than proportional rises in price.

However, people who were slower off the mark, and typically those who are poorer, see house prices beginning to rise out of their reach – and these are the ones that society was hoping to support. They clamour for help, hence providing the opportunity for smart bankers to invent ways of lending them what seemed to be extremely cheap mortgages.

There is yet another feedback loop to send this booming scenario skyward: finance houses can create money according to how much capital they hold. Suppose they can create loans to the value of ten times their assets listed in reserve. *If banks themselves* have a lot of assets in the form of properties which are increasing in price in this buying boom, then as the value of these assets appreciates so they can loan out even more mortgages. The demand curve for housing shifts right even further as more and more money becomes available with financiers casting around the markets looking for profitable ways to loan this out.

Rising prices induce existing suppliers to put more houses up for sale in this market – represented by an extension along the supply curve from points *A* to *B* to *C* in Figure 3.16. Will the supply curve of housing also shift right as more builders move into the

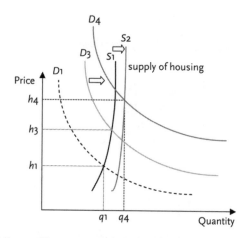

Figure 3.17 Favourable expectations and financial innovation drive prices
higher. The supply of mortgage finance driving the increase in
demand for houses *D1* to *D4* will always outpace supply *S1–S2*.
Hence prices rapidly increase *h1* to *h4*.

market chasing the increasing profits to be made in a construction
boom? Yes … but the speed at which housing can expand *S1* to *S2*
will never catch up the speed at which banks can create and lend
money *D3* to *D4*. Prices soar to *h4* and quantity traded to *q4*,
where *D4* intersects with *S2* (Figure 3.17).

We have seen that widely available credit has fuelled a rapid
increase in property prices, free from any central authority restraint.
That credit, although easily won, requires new householders to
keep up with their mortgage repayments … and those who were
worried about the security of lending to people with little or no
regular income were hardly surprised when payments fell short,
houses were repossessed and forced sales began to increase.

The market now saw a shift right in the supply curve as mortgage
companies moved to sell off housing stock they had acquired. A small
number of sales would hardly cause a dent in prices but large numbers
of sub-prime customers who were hoodwinked into taking loans that
they could not afford must inevitably increase the downward pressure.
S2 shifts forward to *S3* just as demand is moving in the opposite
direction as consumers cannot pay and mortgage companies cut
back credit. Prices slump to *h5* where *S3* cuts *D5* (Figure 3.18).

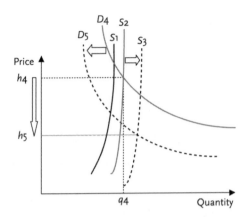

Figure 3.18 Housing foreclosures prompt falling prices.

As was explained in the first chapter, the sub-prime mortgage crisis led to a credit crunch. Innovative mortgage-backed securities that were behind the great expansion of credit were now seen to be of uncertain value. Uncertainty frightens financial markets. Availability of credit therefore virtually dried up. The demand curves that were shifting right just a little while ago were now rapidly shifting left. House prices slumped … and this, by the opposite sequence of events to those described above, meant that the assets and lending power of finance houses was falling by a multiplied extent. The cumulative spiral was now impacting in an opposite direction to the earlier boom and demand curves were backing off just as fast as was possible.

In such circumstances, much housing stock would be taken off the market – better to hold the property empty than attempt to sell it when prices are at rock bottom. The final scenario illustrated is where both *D6* and *S4* are further to the left than their original starting positions, the quantity traded is halved at *q0.5* and price is lower at *h6* (Figure 3.19).

The price system here links an implosion in the financial sector to a collapse in the real estate market. In market economies, the destinies of consumers and producers in one sector of an economy are entwined with others elsewhere. Shocks that impact in the system in one place are rapidly communicated via trade links to others. That is all fine and good when the impulses are positive and bring

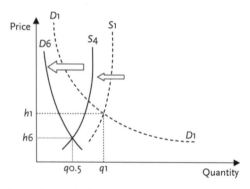

Figure 3.19 The credit crunch forces a further collapse in the real estate market. Some housing stock is taken off the market rather than sold for a low price *S1* to *S4* but the credit crunch and flight from property invokes a far greater shift back in demand *D1* to *D6*. House prices collapse.

rising incomes and other benefits to participants (the original housing boom generated increased wealth for many involved in the production of consumer durables, travel and tourism, as well as financial services) but the downside is just as communicable – bringing falling trade and incomes to all just as quickly when things go awry. This worrying instability of market systems is analysed further in Chapters 5 and 6.

SUMMARY

Resources transfer their employment in response to price/income signals, subject to their occupational mobility.

Consumers buy those goods and services that maximise their utility, subject to income constraints. A change in price of any one good that a consumer purchases represents a marginal change in real income such that it may effect a change in consumption patterns of this good and/or others.

Demand or supply for any good is said to be price-elastic if it is very responsive to a change in price; price-inelastic if not.

Other factors which affect demand for goods can be consumers' incomes, tastes, advertising, etc. Other factors affecting the supply of goods and services can be sudden changes in costs or technology or exogenous shocks and disasters.

Any change in the factors affecting market demand or supply will trigger price changes and thus a reappraisal of consumer and producer decisions.

A market society thus automatically responds to consumers' wishes and to exogenous shocks, and although rapid increases in trade, production and incomes are thus possible, and broadly welcomed, free markets are also vulnerable to opposite and painful slumps in demand and supply.

FURTHER READING

The theory of supply, demand and price determination is at the very heart of economics and any elementary text will give an explanation and illustration of this analysis. For further exposition of indifference curves, turn to a first-year university text such as Begg, D., Fischer, S. and Dornbusch, R. (2008) *Economics*, McGraw Hill.

For the economics of coffee, have a look at one formal, mainstream source and one fascinating, critical and rather different point of view:

International Coffee Organization, Coffee Market Reports, www. ico.org

http://blackgoldmovie.com/economics-of-coffee

Two websites that carry lots of information on housing and real estate are www.housingmarket.org.uk and www.globalproperty guide.com

QUESTIONS

1 The International Coffee Agreements were an attempt (relatively successful until 1989) to establish quotas, or fixed limits, on the export of coffee to world markets, thus restricting supplies and keeping prices up.

Illustrate by means of supply and demand curves how such agreements operated.

Who would you predict would be the winners and losers when these agreements successfully held?

What are the difficulties in maintaining such agreements?

2 Producers of primary commodities, like oil, coffee, copper, etc., stand to gain higher revenues if they sell their product at a high price. In contrast, sellers of many manufactures and services, from motorbikes to fast foods, will likely gain more revenue if they keep their prices down. Can you illustrate and explain this seeming paradox? (It's related to differing price-elasticities of demand...)

4

THE BUSINESS OF SUPPLY

It is time now to analyse in detail the factors that influence the supply of goods and services to market. How are resources organised in production, and what are the economic constraints involved? How do costs and revenues impact on prices and outputs, and how does the state of business competition affect a firm's decision-making? First of all however, consider the very foundation stone of a market society.

PRIVATE PROPERTY

Private property rights represent a fundamental building block of modern, developed economies. Being able to define what is mine and what is yours enables us to trade, agree prices and thereby organise the allocation of society's resources. Property rights are, thus, an essential starting point – if we cannot agree ownership today, we cannot bring together diverse resources, invest in production and distribute future rewards according to some arranged formula.

Peruvian economist Hernando de Soto has argued that what holds back people in poor countries is lack of legal title to the assets – land they live on and buildings they have constructed – they informally possess. Because their possessions are not legally recognised, banks are unwilling to lend them capital to start a business. With no collateral to offer, poor people are trapped in a low-income equilibrium, and even if they are enterprising and inventive, they cannot raise funds beyond the meagre sums their families can provide.

In modern capitalist states, however, one of the most important socio-economic inventions that underpinned the Industrial Revolution and drove subsequent economic growth was the creation of the JOINT STOCK COMPANY. A large number of owners of relatively small amounts of capital could together pool their assets, pledge this stockpile as security to raise even more in the form of bank loans and thereby equip a large factory, a ship or some other productive enterprise capable of securing future profits.

Not that production always needs to be on a large scale. However, whether large or small, business cannot be conducted without rules and without contracts enforceable in law. A promise to deliver a given supply at some time in the future must be kept if economic organisation is to be successful. If people do not trust one another to complete a deal, then no progress can be made. Everyone would have to provide everything for him or herself because no one else would be relied upon to fulfil their part of the bargain. What standard of living could you then aspire to if you had to provide for all your own shelter, clothing, food and transport – let alone other, less urgent needs? However, this is precisely the reality faced by many in societies that fail to codify private capital.

Property rights protect owners and facilitate trade. Specialisation becomes possible. Market values can be estimated, and this allows for subdivision and exchange through time. You can buy or sell a share of some existing or future asset and can have the confidence that you can retain this for the long term, so that when you die this property will be passed on to your heirs. Such confidence in the future promotes investment and, thus, growth.

Poor peasants, meanwhile, who may have farmed communal lands for ages may have no recognised assets, no means to raise capital and no pathway to increase incomes. Quite the opposite, they risk eviction if they have no formal title to the lands they work, and they may lose any crops or livestock that they may possess if they cannot physically defend them.

CAPITAL, INVESTMENT AND GROWTH

CAPITAL is a stock of assets that is capable of producing consumer goods and services. It will include a business's plant and machinery, its resources in the process of production and even abstract concepts such as its logo, certain business ideas and customer "goodwill" – provided they can be defined in law and ascribed a value.

INVESTMENT is a flow of funds that is devoted in creating more capital. It may be from funds retained out of past profits, or from private savings or it may be loans gained from a bank, but the action of allocating finances to build capital stock defines investment. For existing production to be maintained in any business, it requires that old capital stock is replaced as it wears out (DEPRECIATION); plus to secure growth, capital stock must be increased. Investment must respond to both business needs.

In addition as capital stock increases, requirements for other resources (land and labour) will change, and it is most likely, for example, that a business will also need to invest in its labour force or its HUMAN CAPITAL with improved training programmes.

The relationship between land, labour and capital and the effects of increased investment lie at the heart of analysis of production and market supply. We resort to economic theory to clarify the issues involved.

PRODUCTION THEORY

Increasing the supplies of any consumer good or service requires the relevant producers to employ more resources and/or to increase the PRODUCTIVITY of each resource. Leaving aside productivity for the moment, consider the issue of how many and what sort of factors of production to employ. What is the ideal mix of resources to secure the most efficient level of output for any one consumer good, and given this factor combination, is there some ideal size or scale of enterprise to produce the good or service in question?

The first question relates to the optimum employment ratio of land/labour/capital; the second refers to the optimum size of the firm.

THE LAW OF DIMINISHING RETURNS

If an entrepreneur experiments with employment ratios to find the ideal blend of, say, labour to capital in production, he or she will run up against one of the oldest laws in economics. Consider the employment of labour and capital in, for example, running a coffee shop in the centre of town.

What would be your choices if you were the entrepreneur making the business decisions? Suppose first of all that the service you provide is winning you lots of custom – people are queuing up to come into your premises. Clearly, you want to expand the service – sell more coffee and make more profits – but if there are so many customers that you cannot maintain the same high standards, you will lose the opportunity to make money as potential sales are lost to rival suppliers. Therefore, the solution is to employ more waiters and bar staff.

Taking on one more worker may boost sales and profits significantly. If customers keep on coming, you may need to employ more and more labour.

However, what about capital equipment, additional seating, the crockery and cutlery, the espresso machine and so on? If there is no corresponding increase in these inputs to match the increase in labour to your business, then you cannot expect your profits to keep growing.

Therefore, if all other factors remain fixed, each additional input of labour soon results in the erosion of increasing gains. What at first may have led to a 25 per cent increase in outputs may soon lead to an increase of, say, 10 per cent then 5 per cent then 2 per cent then less and less. Each additional worker hired brings falling benefits. It is THE LAW OF DIMINISHING RETURNS: a principle as old as economics itself. Output grows with additional inputs – but in steadily decreasing amounts. There is clearly a limit to how much growth can be stimulated if you continuously increase employment of only one factor when others are fixed. (This law was famously outlined by Thomas Malthus in 1798 who argued that there was a tendency of the population, if unchecked, to increase faster than the food supply until poverty for all resulted. More and more people trying to farm the Earth would lead to smaller and smaller increases in outputs: a pessimistic scenario shared by many environmentalists today.)

This having been said, there are still great differences between businesses as to what is the optimum combination of capital to labour and, therefore, when the point of diminishing returns sets in. Generally speaking, service industries tend to have a higher proportion of labour to capital compared with manufacturing – but even that is changing. Improvements in technology embodied in the latest capital equipment can, for example, greatly increase productivity, increase the most efficient capital to labour ratio and thereby postpone the onset of diminishing returns to the employment of capital. (This may change the demand for labour – creating jobs for some, creating unemployment for others. For example, information technology has completely transformed employment in banks and financial services. Far fewer office clerks and secretaries are now employed per unit of capital in such workplaces whereas higher skilled job opportunities have mushroomed.)

THE OPTIMUM SIZE OF FIRM

Whatever the eventual decision on which mix of land, labour and capital to employ in production, assuming a given state of technology, what happens if all inputs are, say, doubled? The same mix of resources is maintained but now at a much larger scale of enterprise – does efficiency increase or decrease?

The results can be measured by considering the AVERAGE COSTS of production. Does the unit cost of producing, say, a cup of coffee, or a haircut, or public transport or a barrel of oil increase or decrease as the scale of production increases?

Answers differ according to the product in question. In general, the more that consumers want a standard, homogenous product, the more this will lend itself to large-scale production. In contrast, the more individualised the good or service in demand, the smaller will be the most efficient size of firm. Oil refineries, therefore, can be huge, capital-intensive complexes that churn out millions of litres of petrol per day – each one identical in its composition (car engines would not work if the chemical content was variable). Meanwhile, a giant, centralised hairdressers supplying identikit haircuts is unlikely to efficiently meet consumer demand!

As demonstrated, the OPTIMUM SIZE OF FIRM will differ between industries according to the nature of the product in demand

and the technical possibilities in production but, in addition to this, most if not all businesses will experience a similar cost–efficiency relationship as they vary their own scale of production.

ECONOMIES AND DISECONOMIES OF SCALE

Starting at low production levels, average costs of production will be initially high and, as scale increases, efficiency is likely to increase – and unit costs fall – until the optimum size is reached. Beyond this point, inefficiencies begin to appear in the production process and unit costs begin to rise again (Figure 4.1).

What are the reasons for this pattern of costs? They relate to the balance of advantages and disadvantages of bigness in business.

As a firm grows in size it benefits from certain cost advantages or ECONOMIES OF SCALE. For example, storing or processing goods in a large container is cheaper per unit volume than producing them in small packages. This is relevant to processes that involve constructing buildings, transporting oil, selling boxes of soap powder and indeed in making almost anything. Second, a large firm buying inputs in bulk can negotiate better discounts than those gained by small firms. Lastly, the capital threshold for technologically sophisticated products may be very high such that large

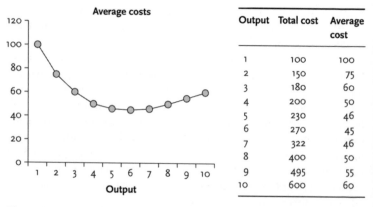

Output	Total cost	Average cost
1	100	100
2	150	75
3	180	60
4	200	50
5	230	46
6	270	45
7	322	46
8	400	50
9	495	55
10	600	60

Figure 4.1 A typical profile of average production costs. (Note that the optimum scale of output in this example is at 6 units.)

sums have to be invested even before production can begin. Thus the research costs and start-up costs of implementing new ideas may well be prohibitively costly for small enterprises.

Over certain production ranges, depending on the nature of business in question, size may not confer significant benefits such that total costs rise almost exactly in proportion to output and there are thus CONSTANT RETURNS TO SCALE. There may nonetheless come a point where the complications involved in producing more and more leads to greater inefficiency and rising average costs. These DISECONOMIES OF SCALE are most often related to the difficulties of management in complex organisations. Any bureaucracy where decisions are made at some distance from the scene of operations is likely to make mistakes but delegating management to the lowest effective level becomes more difficult the larger the firm. Discriminating between which issues should be centralised and which delegated cannot be practicably determined for every single business decision.

A SHIFT IN AVERAGE COSTS

Derivation of the standard, U-shaped, average cost (AC) curve is explained above but this does not allow for the impact of sudden changes in production circumstances. Growth of the firm so far analysed has considered steady increases in the employment of all factors of production (internal growth) but we can hypothesise two causes of sudden exogenous transformation. The firm in question may take over or merge with another enterprise (external growth) or it may experience a technological revolution that transforms its business practice.

Whatever the cause, such indivisibilities in the growth process are illustrated by a *shift* in the AC function. The AC curve may shift a number of times, trending upwards or downwards, according to the number of exogenous shocks experienced and their overall impact on long-run costs.

The long-run AC curve is illustrated by the darker "envelope" curve in Figure 4.2. (Note this example shows almost constant long-run returns to scale over the middle range of outputs between Q1 and Q2 where there is no unique optimum size of firm which enjoys a distinct cost advantage.)

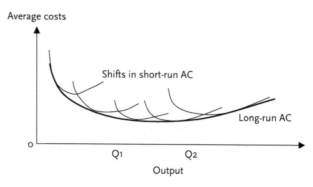

Figure 4.2 Long-run average costs with exogenous shocks.

COMPETITION, PRICES AND PROFITS

Costs of production are one element in the analysis of supply but we now need to contrast this with an understanding of prices and profits. However cost-efficient an enterprise may or may not be, whether it can stay in business, or fail, depends on its ability to make long-term profits.

A company can weather a short-lived downturn in trade only so long as it can cover all its costs and return a reasonable profit over the longer run. This depends on the success of each individual firm in the market place: can it deliver what consumers want to buy at the right price? If not, if the price at which a firm sells its goods cannot be maintained above its average production costs, then losses will be made. If these continue, the firm will close down.

This raises the interesting notion of how market prices are influenced by the setting up or closing down of firms. Assume for the time being there is a stable, unchanging industry demand for a given good – if the number of firms producing this good decreases, and industry supply therefore decreases, a shortfall in market supply will push up prices (see Chapter 3). Conversely, an increase in the number of producers may lead to falling prices over time. The state of competition in industry, therefore, affects prices and thereby profits of all involved.

In some industries there may be thousands, if not millions of suppliers. In the market for coffee or tea, for example, if one more producer enters or exits the industry it will have a negligible effect on overall supply and therefore price of the product. The entry of a new airline company in long haul, transatlantic flights, however, may well have a significant impact on ticket prices.

PROFIT MAXIMISATION UNDER PERFECT COMPETITION

Consider, first, the market structure where there are many competing suppliers but no one in particular is big enough to exercise a commanding lead. In such a scenario, typical of agricultural commodity markets such as coffee, tea or wheat, the product of one supplier is a close if not identical substitute to that of another and the price of this product is set in the market place by the competing forces of demand and supply. An individual producer, therefore, has no effective power over the important decision as to what price to charge for his/her product (the enterprise is a price taker, not a price maker) and can only decide how much to produce, given that price.

If we assume that the supplier aims to maximise profits in this competitive situation, we can deduce that output will expand so long as each additional unit produced adds more to revenue earned than it does to costs. That is, production can continue so long as selling prices are maintained above costs – but, as we have seen, costs eventually begin to rise. Profits will thus be maximised where the cost of the very next bag of coffee/tea rises to just equal its price. To produce beyond this point incurs a loss on each additional unit sold.

Economists define this point of profit maximisation in terms of MARGINAL REVENUE being equal to MARGINAL COSTS. That is, the point where the revenue earned from the sale of one extra unit equals the costs incurred in the production of that unit (Box 4.1).

BOX 4.1 TOTAL, AVERAGE AND MARGINAL COSTS AND REVENUES

To clarify the issues involved here requires us to discriminate carefully between total costs and revenues; average costs and revenues; and marginal costs and revenues.

Note our earlier outline of total and average costs given in Figure 4.1. We can add an extra column illustrating the increase in total costs as output increases: from 1 to 2 units the increased total cost is 50; from 2 to 3 the increase is 30; and so on. This is the column of Marginal Cost seen below in Table 4.1.

What would be the profit maximising output if the price of the product, determined in world markets, was stable and given as 60 per unit? That would give a table of total, average and marginal revenue as shown in Table 4.2.

Table 4.1 Total, Average and Marginal Costs

Output	Total Cost	Average Cost	Marginal Cost
1	100	100	–
2	150	75	50
3	180	60	30
4	200	50	20
5	230	46	30
6	270	45	40
7	322	46	52
8	400	50	78
9	495	55	95
10	600	60	105

Table 4.2 Total, Average and Marginal Revenue

	Price, or		
Output	Total Revenue	Average Revenue	Marginal Revenue
1	60	60	–
2	120	60	60
3	180	60	60
4	240	60	60
5	300	60	60
6	360	60	60
7	420	60	60
8	480	60	60
9	540	60	60
10	600	60	60

In this example, profits are maximised at where output equals 7 units. Check, if you wish, the total revenue and total costs at each output level and you will find the greatest difference between the two occurs at 7 units. The quickest way to find this profit maximising output, however, is simply to compare marginal costs (MC) and marginal revenues (MR). At output 7, MC equals 52, just short of MR at 60. That is, the cost of the seventh unit is less than the revenue it earns and so it is worthwhile producing it. The eighth unit, however, has MC of 78 – much higher than the MR of 60. The enterprise loses by pushing production this far.

Note that the ruling price is determined in world markets (at 60) and the individual producer compares this to his/her costs of production. With average and marginal costs as illustrated, the profit maximising output is shown at 7 units. At this level of output, the marginal cost rises to equal the marginal revenue (equal to price).

Total revenue (TR), total costs (TC) and total profits (TP) can all be derived from Figure 4.3:

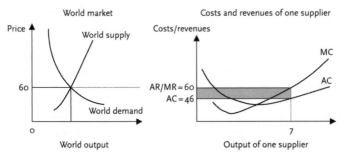

Figure 4.3 Short-run profit maximisation for a competitive producer.

TR equals the price (AR) times output: 60 X 7 = 420
TC equals the average costs times output: 46 X 7 = 322
TP equals TR – TC, or AR – AC times output: 14 X 7 = 98

> Thus total profits, which are maximised at 7 units of output, are illustrated by the shaded area in the diagram. It shows the difference between the price (AR) and unit costs (AC) at that level of output (7) where marginal revenue (MR) is closest to marginal costs (MC).

If there are large profits being made in a competitive market place there is bound to be an incentive for outsiders to enter and seek to do the same. This raises the theoretical notion of NORMAL, as opposed to ABNORMAL profits. Normal profits can be defined as a just and sufficient reward for an entrepreneur to conduct his/her business. Any less than this and the entrepreneur would not be getting enough compensation for the hard work and risks undertaken; any more than this and the business would be earning an excess above what is considered necessary. An enterprise earning less than normal profits would thus leave the market it is operating in and go look elsewhere to conduct its business; conversely a market place where existing businesses are earning above-normal (or abnormal) profits would act as a magnet for other firms to enter. (Note: since entrepreneurs would not set up a business without the promise of normal profits, economists would define this level of reward as an essential cost of enterprise. It may at first acquaintance seem confusing to call "normal profits" a sort of cost but that is indeed what they are in the view of economic theory!)

In a competitive market place, if outsiders are not restricted from entry, abnormal profits would lead to more businesses setting up, thereby increasing industry supply. The higher the original abnormal profits, the stronger the signal would be to attract outside interest and the more new entrants would flood in. The longer-term outcome is not difficult to see (Figure 4.4). As industry supply grows (illustrated by a supply curve that shifts further and further to the right, see Chapter 3) the more market prices will fall, squeezing down the profits earned by everyone until only normal profits remain for the latest newcomer.

> Note the difference from Figure 4.3. Abnormal profits (the shaded area in Figure 4.3) have all been eroded as market prices have fallen. The long-run equilibrium for producers in a competitive market is thus where prices and marginal

revenues equal marginal costs just where average costs are at their lowest and no abnormal profits remain to tempt the entry of further competition. Two conditions of equilibrium now exist – for the individual firm and for the industry as a whole. The firm or enterprise is at its profit maximising equilibrium where its marginal costs equal its (lower) marginal revenue, and the industry is in equilibrium with only normal profits being available and thus where no further movements of suppliers in or out of the market place will take place.

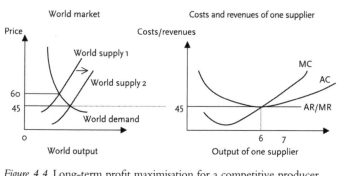

Figure 4.4 Long-term profit maximisation for a competitive producer.

High short-term prices and profits for internet companies – the so-called dot.com boom – led precisely to this outcome in world markets at the turn of the millennium. First there was a rush to create all sorts of dot.com businesses – which attracted much media interest, promised great future profits and thus prompted soaring share prices for start-up outfits that seemed to have nothing but young entrepreneurs with big ideas. Then a bust followed the boom when an oversupply of such enterprise could not return anything like the profits that were originally hoped for.

Note that a highly competitive market environment is generally considered to be the most efficient and equitable form of economic organisation. Profits are earned by catering for public demand and the more successful the producer is in this respect, the more other competitors will follow. Increasing rivalry drives each business to look for ways to reduce costs and economise on society's resources and, simultaneously, so long as competition prevails it prevents any one producer from accumulating excessive profits and abusing its market power.

MONOPOLY AND OLIGOPOLY

The reality in many business contexts, however, is that a small minority of giant firms dominate the market place such that small producers feel relatively powerless. For almost any industry you can think of you can probably also think of the handful of famous names that bestride it – from sophisticated, high tech products like passenger aircraft (Boeing, Airbus) to mundane household items like washing powder (Proctor and Gamble, Unilever); from things you can hold in your hand (Nestlé, Coca-Cola) to abstract ideas and entertainment (AOL TimeWarner, Sony).

A monopoly is a single large firm that sells its product in a market place with no effective rival. If such a development were allowed in the supply of an essential good or service, the monopolist would exercise great economic power – customers would have to pay the price the monopolist wanted or go without, since there would be no alternative supplier. Most countries therefore have legislation to prevent the growth of private monopolies to anything greater than 25 per cent of market share, with the result – as mentioned above – that industrial concentration stops short of single-firm dominance and thus competition occurs between a small number of very large firms. This is a market structure known as OLIGOPOLY.

Industries dominated by a few big rivals still means that each business wields an impressive economic influence, however. The European Commission calculates that 0.2 per cent of the total number of businesses on the continent control over 37 per cent of market sales and these large firms, on average, employ over a thousand people each. When it comes to multinational corporations – businesses that own and control assets in more than one country – the top 200 multinationals across the globe jointly produce about one-third of the world's total output. Not much evidence here of the forces of competition preventing the accumulation of market power.

What accounts for the prevalence of such large corporate enterprises and why has their growth to such dominance not been constrained by follow-my-leader-competition as theorised above?

In some cases it can actually be the forces of competition, over time, leading to the survival of the fittest. The more efficient firms in an industry may be able to reduce costs and prices below those of their rivals, drive them out of business or take them over and thus convert what was a competitive market place into one dominated by a few large corporations.

Modern banking has sometimes been described in these terms. The nature of banking as a business lends itself to over-optimistic expansion on the one hand, followed by financial crashes where the weakest go to the wall. Where this process has worked its longest – in Europe and the USA – a few very large enterprises have emerged, each with considerable financial muscle that supposedly(!) acts as a safeguard against crises that would destroy smaller brethren and also provides a key competitive advantage. (Bigger, safer banks are more likely to attract more custom.)

Note, however, that this process of industrial or commercial evolution could not succeed in producing a dominant few – in banking or anywhere else – if the businesses that remain could not somehow retain a competitive edge: some advantage that inhibits the entry of new, lean and hungry enterprises looking to capitalise on the profits that the lead oligopolists feed off.

BARRIERS TO ENTRY

Economies of scale provide one explanation for oligopolies being able to resist dilution of their market power by the entry of new businesses. Financial and risk-bearing economies are relevant in the case of banking referred to above (large financial enterprises can buy and sell money in bulk and thus can offer lower price deals to customers) but other economies of scale include technical factors. For example, in aerospace, the oil industry and also in pharmaceuticals, the capital threshold that new firms have to cross before they can bring their costs down to a level commensurate with existing suppliers is simply immense. Where technically complex production processes are involved in bringing goods to markets, then the set up costs for new entrants are a natural barrier to the forces of competition. In some sectors, only very big businesses can be efficient and the market place – even worldwide – may not be large enough to support more than two or three firms. (For example, just two enterprises dominate the world market for long range, wide-bodied jets: Boeing and Airbus.)

We can discriminate, however, between barriers of entry like those above which are structural or due to real economic forces and those which are behavioural, or due to the manipulation of power by existing oligopolists. Massive advertising campaigns, for example, may be resorted to by existing firms which inflate production costs on the one hand and create a brand image on the other, which new producers find hard to overcome. The technology involved in producing carbonated soft drinks, for example, is hardly rocket science (quite the opposite, it is one of the first industries that low-income countries can invest in to develop their own emerging industrial sector and serve their own peoples). Nonetheless, the powerful presence enjoyed by the duopoly of Coca-Cola and PepsiCo greatly reduces the room for poor countries to promote industrial expansion in this particular market place.

Product differentiation is a strategy pursued by large firms to increase the range of items they sell. Varying superficial qualities of the product – colour, packaging, logos, special offers and other marketing gimmicks - helps create a different BRAND in the mind of the consumer. Thus the many supermarket offerings of breakfast cereals seem to the untutored eye to illustrate very active competition between a large number of rival producers but, on closer inspection, the scores of different brands on display are all produced by two or three large oligopolists. (Even supermarket "own brand" items are simply purchased from these same producers and retailed in cheaper packaging.) Product differentiation is a ruse employed by such enterprises to block out the market. Any genuine new entrant to this industry therefore faces having to establish its identity against a wealth of dazzling alternatives.

Vertical and horizontal INTEGRATION refer to directions of industrial growth that large firms may indulge in to exercise greater market control. In the late part of the nineteenth century, Rockefeller's original Standard Oil company (SO) accumulated vast profits by buying up or building all the pipelines serving North Eastern US markets with oil from the Southern producer states. This was HORIZONTAL integration – monopolising all business at one stage of the production process, in this case the transporting of oil. (In 1911, Standard Oil was broken up by US anti-trust legislation as a result of this abuse of its power. It was such a huge business, however, that the several parts into which SO was cut up all evolved to become international oil majors in their own right!) As a result of this experience, many oil producers have since resorted to VERTICAL integration to ensure they always have some degree of control over supplies and markets – buying up, building or signing exclusive long-term contracts with upstream suppliers or downstream distributors in the production chain. Modern day Exxon (which Esso became) therefore owns and controls a stake in all the processes involved in the international oil industry – from oilfields, to pipelines and oil tankers, to refineries and gas stations that operate all around the world.

Finally, an important reason for industrial concentration, if not actual monopoly, is government legislation or patronage. An innovating firm may apply for a PATENT or sole licence to supply a unique product or process. Drug companies, for example, may spend fortunes developing a new medicine but such innovations, though costly to develop, may be very cheap to imitate. Without patent protection, therefore, such firms would be unlikely to invest in new ideas. Monopoly status is thus conferred with an official patent that sets a time limit to the innovation – guaranteeing the firm sufficient time and thus reward to recoup the investment before other imitators can enter the market.

State monopolies or nationalised industries are those enterprises owned and controlled by public authority where the law actually forbids competition. There has been a worldwide trend to privatise much state enterprise so fewer examples now remain today but nonetheless in many countries the post office remains a monopoly, as are certain public utilities (the distribution of gas, electricity and water). In defence industries and in the provision of nuclear energy the state may or may not own the production process but via exclusive government contracts it will determine outputs and restrict competition in this area for security reasons.

In all these cases, where monopolists or oligopolists dominate a market place they are able to exert greater control over prices and thus their sales and profits. Industry supply in these circumstances will differ from the perfectly competitive model described earlier in a number of vital ways.

MONOPOLY DEMAND

There is an important distinction between the demand conditions for monopoly and for oligopoly and this is examined here and in detail in the boxes that follow.

First, the more a large firm monopolises a market place the more the demand for its particular product will come close to that for the industry's output as a whole. Oligopolists attempt to mimic this situation which is why corporations invest large sums in product differentiation. The objective is to create customer loyalty – that is, the monopoly of a brand. ("The one and only – accept no substitute!")

The ideal situation for the firm is that demand for its product thus becomes price-inelastic: consumers are so accustomed to buying their favourite brand that sales do not fall appreciably even if its relative price rises.

Profit-maximising enterprises operating in conditions of monopoly will deliberately restrict production if this forces prices up more than unit costs. We can predict that if margins between average prices and costs can thus be widened, and BARRIERS TO ENTRY to the industry can be maintained to frustrate new competition, then abnormal profits can be realised even in the long run (Box 4.2).

BOX 4.2 PROFIT-MAXIMISING MONOPOLY

In the case of a pure monopoly where there is only one producer and no competition whatsoever, the demand curve for the firm must be identical to that for the industry. Unlike a competitive firm that must accept whatever price the free market dictates – see diagrams in Figures 4.3 and 4.4 above – the monopolist in contrast is a price *maker*. The firm dictates what price will rule simply by deciding what level of supply to produce. Restricting production will push prices up since consumers are forced to outbid each other to secure their purchases; increasing supplies will cause prices to fall.

Note the effect this has on marginal revenues. For a normal, downward-sloping demand curve, since the monopolist must reduce prices if sales are to be increased, marginal revenue (earnings gained on the last item sold) must always be less than the average.

Check the derivation of average and marginal revenues in Table 4.3 and in Figure 4.5.

Total revenue (TR) is derived from multiplying the price (P) of the good, times the quantity (Q) sold. Note, in reverse, that dividing TR by Q gives you P which is the same as Average Revenue (AR). This relationship shown between price and quantity is actually the demand curve of the firm – which in the case of a pure monopoly is the same as the demand curve for the industry.

The marginal revenue curve (MR) shows the increase in total revenue brought about by the sale of one extra unit and it falls faster than average revenue.

Remember that no profit-seeking enterprise will expand production to the point where the last good sold nets less revenue than it costs to produce. That is, the firm – whether it be operating in conditions of competition or monopoly – will produce only up to the point where marginal costs equal marginal revenue. In Table 4.3, check that the monopolist will produce 4 units of output but not 5. In Figure 4.5, the firm is at equilibrium at 4 units of output

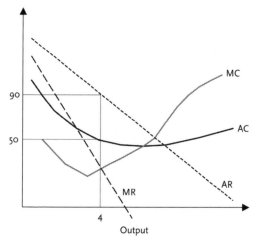

Figure 4.5 The profit–maximising monopolist.

Table 4.3 Monopoly Costs and Revenues. (Note: Marginal costs and revenues are calculated on the difference between one level of output and the next which is why they are recorded between the lines.)

Q	TC	AC	MC	P/AR	TR	MR	TP = TR − TC
1	100	100		135	135		35
			50			105	
2	150	75		120	240		90
			30			75	
3	180	60		105	315		135
			20			45	
4	200	50		90	360		160
			30			15	
5	230	46		75	375		145
			40			−15	
6	270	45		60	360		90
			52			−45	
7	322	46		45	315		−7
			78			−75	
8	400	50		30	240		−160
			95			−105	
9	495	55		15	135		−360
			105			−135	
10	600	60		0	0		−600

where Price/AR is 90 and AC is 50. Total (abnormal) profits (TP) thus will be maximised at 90 − 50 X 4 = 160, confirmed by reference to the table of data.

Note: The profit maximising equilibrium as illustrated is stable only so long as new competitors are barred from entry to the industry. If, in time, new suppliers gain access to the market then the demand/AR curve for the existing monopolist will shift back as sales are lost. This squeezes out some of the abnormal profits as the distance between price (AR) and unit costs (AC) closes.

OLIGOPOLISTIC RIVALRY

Oligopoly, remember, is a market structure where there are a few, very large corporations sharing power in an industry with substantial barriers to entry restricting access to any other firms. In such a situation rivalry is intense: every firm has to keep a close eye on the actions of its competitors.

Driving prices down to the limit where average revenues equal average costs and only normal profits remain is the inevitable outcome of competitive industry where new entrants cannot be excluded. But where barriers to competition limit production to a few, very large businesses, each one warily watching the other, it is extremely unlikely that the rivals would want to engage in price wars. More likely they would want to collude and push prices up to all firms' mutual advantage. The oligopolists thus act as one – joint profit maximisation – which is the typical outcome of a CARTEL (Box 4.3).

Fixing prices is against the law, however. Active collusion must be avoided since it can be severely punished – though this still does not remove the incentive, under oligopoly, for competition to be constrained. What results, therefore, is TACIT COLLUSION: a passive, unspoken (and thus unpunishable) understanding not to excessively stir up deep waters.

BOX 4.3 CARTELS

It is precisely the tendency to COLLUSION that governments need to monitor and legislate against in order to prevent the public from being exploited. Setting up a cartel – a formal agreement between rivals to rig the market – is illegal in most countries, though cartels between international operators are more difficult to outlaw since there is no one world body that can be relied upon to stop them (especially if it is national governments that actively collude!).

The Organization of Petroleum Exporting Countries, OPEC, is frequently cited as a cartel but in fact it has been far less exploitative than the cartel of major oil companies that preceded it and formerly controlled international oil supplies. The national governments represented by OPEC now regularly meet to arrange production quotas between them but disagreement is common.

> What conditions are likely to be conducive to the successful operation of a cartel? Under what circumstances, that is, must governments be most vigilant to protect the interests of consumers?
> Collusion is most likely to succeed:
>
> 1. the smaller the number of rival producers and the higher the barriers to entry;
> 2. where the interests and objectives of each producer are similar;
> 3. where the product is homogenous, difficult to differentiate and thus highly substitutable;
> 4. where the actions of each producer are highly visible to all;
> 5. where market demand is stable;
> 6. where legal restrictions can be easily bypassed or bought off.

There is an inevitable reluctance to engage in extremely rivalrous and damaging "cut-throat" price wars and instead a preference to move competition into the realms of advertising, marketing, "special offers" and other sales promotions. Investing in large marketing divisions and resorting to creative ways to practice NON-PRICE COMPETITION can also be costly but it is a safer, less unpredictable business practice and mutually beneficial to the existing rivals in that it builds up even higher barriers to potential new competition.

OLIGOPOLY DEMAND

The demand curve for the firm – which shows the relationships between the price of the product and its quantity sold – given the oligopoly conditions just described can be quite unique. Consider what would happen if one of, say, five rival corporations was determined to change its selling price: as Firm A cuts its price, so too would Firms B, C, D and E. The sales of all products in the market place may grow a little overall but the individual demand for each firm would not change by much. If, in contrast, Firm A puts its price *up* then it is unlikely that any of its rivals would follow suit. Firms B, C, D and E would benefit from extra sales if they kept their prices low, picking up consumers of product A who would now switch to the rivals' lower price alternatives (Box 4.4).

BOX 4.4 PRICE STICKINESS

With asymmetric demand in the market for the products of oligopoly, the shape of each firm's average revenue/demand curve would be kinked at the point of the current ruling price, P^* as illustrated in Figure 4.6:

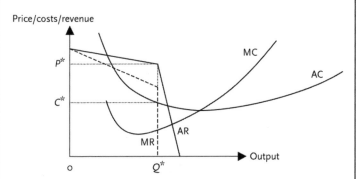

Figure 4.6 Profit-maximising oligopoly.

Adding the oligopolist's cost structure to the pattern of demand identifies the firm's equilibrium price P^* and output Q^*. Abnormal profits are given by the box $(P^* - C^*)$ Q^*. Note that the effect on this equilibrium of any increase or decrease of MC and AC here would be minimal, whereas a shift back in demand (AR) caused by any increase in competition from rivals would have, in contrast, a serious impact on price, output and profits.

Prices under oligopoly tend to be stable, therefore. At least they will be so for relatively long periods until something occurs to upset the equilibrium. The sudden appearance of a new competitor, a technological breakthrough or a revolutionary new product or process may then turn the relative stability of the status quo into turmoil. For a brief period, an intense battle over market shares will take place as the original "pecking order" or hierarchy between rivals is challenged. Cut-throat price competition may be resorted to in order to eject an upstart interloper from the market place or to re-examine the economic efficiency and thus supremacy of the remaining firms. After a period of aggressive activity where short-term profits are sacrificed in the quest for a new order, eventual calm will be restored as all survivors realise that mutual interests are best served again by tacit collusion. Interdependence in oligopoly – the reality that one business's action has a direct and observable impact on another's – makes this form of market structure unique. At one extreme, monopolists can ignore competition. At the other extreme, perfectly competitive businesses operate with so many others that the effect of any one's actions on the industry is negligible. Oligopolists, however, know only too well what will happen if they cannot match innovative actions on the part of a business rival. They thus try to anticipate their competitor's moves in advance in order to determine their own best action. Such strategic behaviour can best be understood and simulated in GAME THEORY.

BOX 4.5 THE PRISONERS' DILEMMA

Game theory is best introduced by this classic, involving two players. Two suspects of a crime are caught by police and interviewed in separate rooms. They are each told that if you confess you will get off more lightly than if you stay silent. If both confess they each get two years in prison. If both stay silent they take the chance of only getting one year. The worst case scenario for both is if one stays silent and the other confesses. Then the silent one gets five years and the one who talks gets off free.

The specific PAYOFF MATRIX of this game is given below. The rewards or payoffs for each decision are crucial in setting up this game and thus determining its outcome:

		Alf	
		Confess	Silent
Bob	Confess	A: 2 years B: 2 years	A: 5 years B: free
	Silent	A: free B: 5 years	A: 1 year B: 1 year

What is the outcome?

Note that if prisoner Alf stays silent then the other, Bob's best strategy is to confess. Alternatively, if A talks, then B's best strategy is to confess as well. In this game, therefore, the DOMINANT STRATEGY for both players, independently, is to talk. The outcome therefore is the NASH EQUILIBRIUM where both get two years.

(This type of game is famously associated with John Forbes Nash, the Nobel Prize winner in economics and schizophrenic portrayed by Russell Crowe, in the 2001 film *A Beautiful Mind*.)

The sort of game oligopolists might play is over a decision whether or not to decrease output, and thus hopefully drive up prices and profits. Clearly if all decide to do so, all profit. If one oligopolist cheats however, and increases output at the same time as all others *reduce* production then the higher prices will bring the highest rewards to the cheating one who sells most! Note the similarities here to the game known as "The Prisoners' Dilemma" (see Box 4.5): when rivals decrease output, the firm benefits most by expanding production; yet if others expand then the firm would be foolish not to do so as well. The dominant strategy for the individual firm in such a scenario is always to produce more and so the Nash equilibrium in the industry is for increased output and for market prices to fall.

Strategic business decisions in the real world will typically involve more moves than the one-shot game of The Prisoners' Dilemma, however, and so collusion becomes more likely in repeated games. Predictability is another matter. As players learn more about their rivals' behaviour, so game theory must embrace more and more complex interactions. Note also that payoffs might not be so easily calculated. The information set available to players might be incomplete or asymmetric and when we add in random, exogenous shocks – government intervention, banking crises, new entrants to the industry – then outcomes become very difficult indeed to foresee (Box 4.6).

BOX 4.6 THE WIDE-BODIED JET GAME

In many games, unlike in The Prisoners' Dilemma, the player who commits first may enjoy first mover advantage. That means taking the initial risks, of course, and to pour billions into research that may or may not pay back sufficient returns is certainly a brave move. In the 1960s, Boeing Company failed to win the US airforce contract for a large military transport, and their design might have been written off as yet another dead investment ... but it was subsequently converted into a passenger aircraft that changed the face of aviation: the 747 or jumbo jet.

The world's first wide-bodied, long-haul passenger jet entered service with (the now defunct) Pan American Airlines in January 1970, and over 1,500 jumbo jets have been produced in varying formats, bought by 80 different airlines carrying more than 3.5 billion passengers over 35 billion miles. The 747 has been the immensely profitable cash cow that has enabled Boeing to see off all competitors (outselling the DC-10 and taking over its producer, McDonnell Douglas, in 1997) until the arrival of its European rival, the even bigger Airbus A380, or superjumbo, which made its first commercial flight in 2007 with Singapore Airlines.

Can the A380 see off the competitive advantage forged by the 747? The Airbus superjumbo benefits from all the most modern technology with development costs rising well above US$ 12 billion; however, it is very late into the market, and it is doubtful whether it will ever be as profitable as its famous American predecessor. The increasing success of Airbus has nonetheless prompted a move by

Boeing to the WORLD TRADE ORGANIZATION (WTO) to investigate allegedly unfair European government subsidies.

In a repeat game, as rivals learn more about each other's strategies, it can pay to collude and avoid a low-profit equilibrium. It has always been known that Boeing benefits from large federal handouts for its defence contracts, and in response, Airbus has approached European governments (principally Germany, France, Spain and the United Kingdom) and won launch aid to assist with technological developments. The two companies signed a deal in 1992 to agree limits on the amounts each received in state aid. Such deals reduce costs, limit costly tit-for-tat competition and help to protect the large commercial aircraft market from any potential newcomer (maybe Russia or China?).

However, as the superjumbo became a reality and, particularly, the mid-sized A350 appeared with its threat to the Boeing 777, in 2004 Boeing boss Harry Stonecipher took the decision that these were strategic moves that could not go unanswered. On 31 May 2005 he complained to the WTO that the increasing size of the European subsidies was a barrier to free trade.

This was a bet that Airbus subsidies were more vulnerable to investigation than Boeing's. Another risky first move! The two companies have ever since been locked in a litigious battle – one side complaining it is getting more state support than the other.

The WTO investigation reported in May 2011 that (according to trade agreements both have signed) illegal subsidies have been received by both companies and should be paid back. The specific sums were disputed (somewhere between US$ 5 and 18 billion!), as were the pay periods demanded but Airbus reported on 1 December 2011 that it had fulfilled its obligations under the WTO findings and called upon Boeing to do likewise in the coming year. The USA promptly denied the claim that Airbus had complied with the ruling and that Boeing had not. Accusations have since been batted to and fro, both sides claiming (mid-2013) that its position has been vindicated. Will hostilities escalate or will there be a return to negotiation, collusion and deal-making?

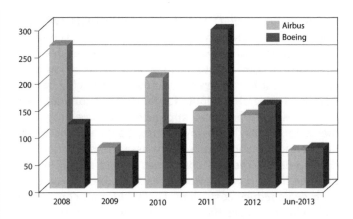

Figure 4.7 Wide-body aircraft sales. Boeing had been losing sales to Airbus from the mid-1990s to 2010 until the strength of the competition made them raise their game. *Gulf Business* reported in November 2013 that, according to Shep Hill the president of Boeing International: "The emergence of Airbus has made us tougher, better, more customer-focused and a more innovative company. I like competition, I think it is good for you." (The Dubai Air Show, the world's biggest aviation showcase, in November saw Boeing gain more orders than their rival.) *The Economist* noted (January 2014) that Airbus regained the lead in overall aircraft sales (wide- and narrow-bodied) in 2013, totting up 1,503 net orders compared with Boeing's 1,355, though Boeing actually delivered more planes to airlines: 648 to Airbus's 626. (Sources: Reuters; ft.com; Gulf Business, *The Economist*.)

Repeat games tend to be characterised by the latter outcome, especially if the market becomes contestable by an outsider. (At the time of writing, Boeing and Airbus have 50 per cent each of the wide-body aircraft market but Canada, Brazil, China and Russia are possible future rivals). In the mean-time, Boeing and Airbus have been straining every muscle to sell their aircraft all round the world (Figure 4.7).

Many examples of oligopolistic rivalry can be quoted where, in between the extremes of intense competition or secretive collusion, the pre-occupation of business leaders in protecting market share and pursuing profits seems to be at the direct expense of the public's interest. Big tobacco companies have deliberately suppressed information of the harmful effects of their products; international banks have promoted cheap loans and increased the indebtedness of poorer peoples before hoisting up interest rates; pharmaceutical giants charge exploitative prices for AIDS vaccines and other life-saving medicines that consumers must purchase, or perish.

Large, oligopolistic corporations that have built up business empires that span the globe wield an enormous amount of economic power, therefore. The challenge to governments is how to channel all this corporate muscle so that the ends it pursues suit public, as well as business, interests.

Many who have a direct, vested interest in free markets and in restricting the intervention of governments like to quote Adam Smith (1776) who wrote that the individual in a market economy "is led by an invisible hand to promote an end which was no part of his intention. By pursuing his own interest he frequently promotes that of society more effectually than when he really intends to promote it." That sentiment still exerts a persuasive influence on Western economic policy-making: the claim that all will be for the best if only private enterprise is left alone. Oligopoly theory predicts otherwise.

CONCLUSION

The dominant concern of any oligopoly is to preserve or increase its economic power in the market place. In an ever-changing world where markets are subject to sudden fluctuation and where business rivalry is intense, an individual firm may at turns appear very aggressive, or defensive, or very passive in its operations. But, subject to short-term expediency, the analysis so far leads to the following conclusions:

Oligopolists will

- attempt to increase their share of whichever market they operate in;
- sacrifice short-term profits in order to secure long-term, competitive advantage;
- generally prefer to collude rather than compete on prices;
- keep prices high and stable for as long as conditions allow;

- exploit economies of scale to widen the difference between prices and unit costs;
- pay handsomely for any innovation that gives them a lead on their rivals;
- drive out or vigorously resist entry of new competitors;
- manage the media, public opinion and government contacts to resist any restriction on their operations;
- not initiate any increase in supplies that weakens prices and profits;
- exploit any consumer dependency on their products.

It is not intended to portray all executives of big business as heartless, greedy capitalists intent on grinding the fate of others under the wheels of the corporate machine! Most business people are hard-working family types intent on doing a professional job and keeping their budgets in balance and their heads above water. It is just that the structure of modern, competitive oligopoly rewards ruthlessness, not compassion.

Where the temptation exists to make a fortune by bending the law, oligopolists may frequently go too far. Large business empires can then go bust frighteningly quickly – especially where rivals are only too happy to exploit any weakness amongst their number. This merely increases the penalty of failure and yet, by the same token, rewards are always greatest where others fear to tread. Thus the incentive still remains to choose investments that are morally questionable but highly profitable. It is in such circumstances that ordinary members of the public must hope that elected governments can set the rules of the game to prohibit corporate abuses – and that they get to their political leaders before big business does.

The father of economics knew. In his famous book *The Wealth of Nations* from which the quote earlier was taken, Smith also wrote: "People of the same trade seldom meet together, even for merriment and diversion, but the conversation ends in a conspiracy against the public, or in some contrivance to raise prices". Also: "To widen the market and to narrow the competition, is always the interest of the dealers ... It comes from an order of men, whose interest is never exactly the same with that of the public, who have generally an interest to deceive and even oppress the public, and who accordingly have, upon many occasions, both deceived and oppressed it."

It is a warning to public authorities everywhere that oligopoly needs policing.

SUMMARY

Market economies are built upon recognised private property. Only if ownership is defined and protected in law can contracts be entered into, trade expanded and economic growth secured.

If an enterprise increases *either* its labour force *or* its capital stock alone it will find that output grows but in steadily diminishing amounts.

A business experiences economies of scale if, by increasing *all* inputs in proportion to one another, it becomes more efficient and reduces average production costs. In contrast, diseconomies of scale will lead to an increase in average costs as the size of the business expands.

Any profit-maximising business will expand production up to the point where the cost of the next product just rises to equal the revenue earned – that is, up until marginal costs equal marginal revenue.

In a perfectly competitive business environment, the nature of competition keeps prices down level with average costs so that only normal profits are earned.

Monopoly results from erecting barriers to the entry of new firms. One producer can then dominate a market, keep prices high and enjoy abnormal profits in the long run.

Oligopoly is a market structure where there is an inevitable temptation for a few, very large enterprises to collude to make profits at the public's expense. In the last resort it is incumbent on government watchdogs to safeguard the public interest.

FURTHER READING

Any book on microeconomic theory will devote a number of chapters to competition, monopoly and oligopoly. For example: Krugman, P. and Wells, R. (2013) *Microeconomics*, Worth.

To keep up with the rivalry between Boeing and Airbus you will have to track the news reports on the internet. For a popular book, see Newhouse, J. (2008) *Boeing Versus Airbus: The Inside Story of the Greatest International Competition in Business*, Random House.

An insider's story of how big oligopolists can abuse their economic power is Cruver, B. (2003) *Enron: Anatomy of Greed*, Arrow Books.

QUESTIONS

1 Explain the difference between diminishing returns and diseconomies of scale.
2 Illustrate what happens to a monopolist's equilibrium price, output and profit when a new and innovative competitor successfully enters the market.
3 List the main oligopolistic rivals in an industry of your choice. Give examples of forms of non-price competition that are employed in this industry. Is there any one example that you think is particularly effective? Why?
4 You start up a profitable educational business, providing on-line answers (at a price) to homework questions submitted to you by troubled and time-constrained student customers. (a) A rival enterprise enters the market providing the same service at a lower price. What strategies would you employ to fight off this competition? (b) Are there any criticisms, disadvantages or social costs, to the successful growth of such an educational business? How would you answer these criticisms?

5

INFLATION AND UNEMPLOYMENT
BOOM AND BUST

The wonderful, automatic mechanism of market forces has a powerful hold over the mindset of most economists. Unrestricted competition between buyers and sellers leads to the evolution of a market price that equates scarce supplies to effective demand. Market equilibrium results with costs close to revenues, normal profits rewarding enterprise and prices signalling what, how and for whom goods should be produced. The role of government in such an ideal world is to establish market institutions and enforce the rules of trade – especially outlawing monopolistic practices that threatened the public interest.

There are many critics of such a system of economic organisation, however. Many ordinary people complain about its inequity: incomes are determined by the fickle nature of consumer demand; essential goods may be priced out of reach of those in need; precious environmental assets may be degraded. This is an argument of normative economics: one that accepts that the market mechanism works – but it produces outcomes which some people consider socially unacceptable.

The argument that will concern us first, however, is one of *positive* economics – one which expresses doubt about the market mechanism's efficiency. Will it actually work to equate demand and supply of all resources as its advocates say it will? Economists have argued between themselves for decades about whether or not the unregulated market is capable of reaching and sustaining general equilibrium for a country as a whole. This is the ongoing debate over MACROECONOMICS.

There is no doubt that markets work very efficiently in the production and distribution of fresh food. They have for centuries – from medieval market places to sophisticated modern supermarkets. As mentioned in Chapter 3: we take such complex organisation for granted, but producing and distributing such perishable produce as coffee, milk, oranges, etc. is generally amazingly successful. We neither trip over rotting fruit and vegetables in city centres nor are we starved of choice – markets clear with no waste. Vast populations are catered for around the world in a mind-boggling maze of trading relations that ensures demand meets supply.

If the market for perishable fruit achieves balance then surely all markets together will similarly secure GENERAL EQUILIBRIUM of an economy as a whole?

THE FALLACY OF COMPOSITION

Not necessarily! Because one action on its own is efficient, it does not mean that all similar actions added together will bring about the most efficient, economical ALLOCATION OF RESOURCES as a whole. That is the FALLACY OF COMPOSITION.

Suppose you leave work early to avoid the rush hour and miss all the traffic. That is a perfectly reasonable and rational action that succeeds on its own. But if everyone chose to do likewise then, in aggregate, this action fails. Everyone gets stuck in the traffic.

John Maynard Keynes, the brilliant twentieth-century economist who revolutionised the subject, applied the same logic to money, incomes and employment. Let us look at three examples:

First, consider the role of savings. If you and I save a larger pro-portion of our income this year then next year we will be that much richer. Put, say, 10 per cent of our income away then next year not only will we have 10 per cent more but we might get added interest too. Save more this year and we earn more next year.

Now think through the consequences if the whole country did the same. If everyone stopped spending 10 per cent this year and saved more, then national consumption will drop. All businesses would sell less, earn less and thus would have to reduce costs and outputs – lay off workers and/or cut wages. National income would fall by 10 per cent. So: if everyone saves more, everyone loses.

Next look at the case of wages. Market economics asserts that if, in your job, you ask for wages that are too high you won't get taken on by employers. Conversely, if wages are too low there may be plenty of businesses willing to employ such cheap labour but there will be too few workers willing to sell their skills for so little. Wages will adjust over time, therefore to a level that just equates the amount of work offered to the supply of the labour willing to take it on. The equilibrium wage equates demand (from employers) to the supply of labour.

This is the key function of the price mechanism – to clear markets. By this argument, there can be no unemployment. If there was, the excess supply of labour would bid wages down and employers' demand for labour would increase such that the unemployment would gradually disappear.

You should be able to see that this self-adjusting mechanism, even if it does work in one labour market, cannot work in all markets added together. A fall in wages in one sector, say the restaurant trade, might well attract employers to employ more waiters, kitchen staff, etc. But if wages fell across the whole economy, then assuming no immediate and corresponding fall in prices, national income would again fall, aggregate consumption must fall, there would be less business for everyone, and so employment in all sectors would fall in the short run, not rise.

For the third example, reconsider the issue of world trade, discussed in the opening chapter.

If one country successfully exports more than it imports then it makes a trade SURPLUS … which appears on the face of it all well and good for the country concerned. An excess of sales over purchases means an increase in revenues over outgoings.

The world as a whole, however, is a closed economic system so gains in one place must be matched by losses elsewhere. What happens to those gains, to that trade surplus made by a successful exporter? If they are *not* spent by the country concerned or loaned to another to spend, then the world as a whole must experience a net fall in aggregate consumption. And that must therefore mean a net fall in world earnings…

We thus enter the world of *macro*economics – the economics of all markets in a system aggregated together. We need different theories, analyses, models to understand the workings of entire nations since, as has been demonstrated, what works efficiently at the level of individual consumers and producers need not work in aggregate for society as a whole.

THE CIRCULAR FLOW MODEL

For the analysis that follows, we use the nation state as the model for macroeconomics – subdividing one economy into a society of households and firms; where we assume households save and firms invest. Exactly the same model could be used to simulate a circular flow of spending and saving on a global scale but for the sake of simplicity and consistency, we will use the nation state as the model.

Assume households on one hand act as *consumers* of all final goods and services; they also act as *owners* and providers of land, labour, capital and enterprise: an economy's productive resources. Firms, in contrast, act as the *suppliers* of consumer goods and also as the *employers* of all resources. Households and firms, employment of resources and the demand and supply of all consumer goods and services are all linked together in one system-wide circular flow as illustrated in Figure 5.1.

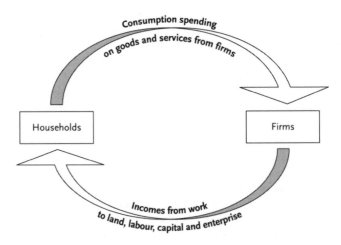

Figure 5.1 The circular flow of incomes and consumption.

Note that the top half of this diagram illustrates a market for all consumer goods and services: money and goods are exchanged between buyers and sellers; and the bottom half represents the market place for factors of production: where employers pay for the productive resources they wish to hire.

Money flows around the economy therefore in the direction of the arrows – in the form of spending on consumer goods and services in the top loop, and in the form of incomes exchanging for the hire of resources in the bottom loop.

There is a qualification we need to make to this national circular flow, however. Not all household income is immediately spent on CONSUMPTION. Some fraction may be saved and, of course, some percentage of income is always taxed away by governments.

For the time being we can ignore the influence of government taxes and concentrate on what happens to SAVINGS – all money not spent. Where does income saved actually go?

In modern, financially sophisticated economies, much of those savings will go into banks. Nowadays a variety of commercial financial institutions have evolved to hold your savings in one form or another – private banks, building societies, savings-and-loans institutions, unit trusts and pension funds. The more trustworthy the financial infrastructure in an economy, the higher a fraction of a nation's savings will find its way into these accounts.

In the circular flow diagram illustrated in Figure 5.1, all savings represent a leakage from the system – a decision to postpone current consumption. Insofar as these savings are placed in financial institutions there is the possibility, however, that these funds can be recycled back into the national economy: banks make loans to firms in order to fund INVESTMENT.

For the sake of simplicity, we need to consider only bank loans which finance industrial investment (in reality, many savings go to finance consumption but we can ignore these and assume these funds never left the circular flow in the first place). The issue that is important for macroeconomic purposes is what happens if the flow of savings which leak out of the system on the one hand does *not* equal investment which is injected back into the economy on the other. There is, after all, no reason why these two flows should be equal since they represent decisions by very different people and institutions in the community (Figure 5.2).

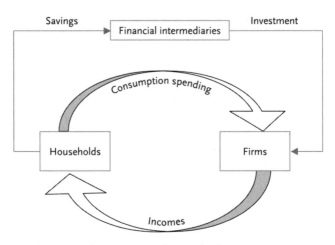

Figure 5.2 Savings and investment in the circular flow.

It should be seen that, as in any fluid system, if the LEAKAGES from the flow are just a little more than INJECTIONS then the aggregate level of money and incomes circulating the economy must slowly decline. Conversely, if injections into the flow are larger than leakages, aggregate incomes must rise over time.

We can begin to see here the illustration of what Keynes called the PARADOX OF THRIFT: that, although saving seems to be a virtue for the individual, if a whole community saves then aggregate incomes fall. There is no guarantee that national income will remain stable therefore, so long as savings and investment are out of line.

Free market economics is not so easily confounded, though. It is asserted that a country's banks act as FINANCIAL INTERMEDIARIES – dedicated to matching up savings on the one hand with loans (for investment) on the other. What happens if these two flows do not equal each other? Banks in a free market will set into operation the price mechanism to ensure financial, and thereby national, equilibrium. We return to the operation of demand and supply that was analysed before:

Consider that savings represent the supply of funds into financial markets; loans that go to facilitate business investment represent the demand for funds. If supply exceeds demand the price of funds will fall. Conversely, if demand exceeds supply the price of funds will

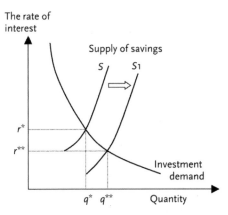

Figure 5.3 The financial marketplace. The supply of savings increases, *S* to *S1*, and so the rate of interest falls, r^* to r^{**} ensuring that investment increases and so savings therefore equals investment again. The circular flow of income remains in equilibrium, thanks to the automatic workings of the price mechanism applied to the financial industry.

rise. Changes in the price of money – known as the market RATE OF INTEREST – act like prices in the market for oranges, or coffee, to ensure that there is always equilibrium (Figure 5.3).

According to mainstream, or NEOCLASSICAL ECONOMICS, the supply of savings in a country rises as the rate of interest (the reward for saving) increases. Conversely, the demand for funds for investment will fall if borrowers have to pay too high a price. The two conflicting objectives meet at the market equilibrium rate r^* where the aggregate total of savings just equals the aggregate total of investment at q^*.

What happens if there is an exogenous rise in the country's savings *S* to *S1*? The equilibrium rate of interest will fall to r^{**} and investment will extend to q^{**} so that there is no occasion when leakages and injections to the national income are not matched up.

In this case, therefore, financial markets play an enormously important role in the national economy – adjusting interest rates in order to secure balance between leakages and injections into the flow of incomes, between savings and investment, so that the economy as a whole experiences neither INFLATION nor RECESSION; neither boom nor bust. With flexible markets, therefore, the economy as a whole attains general equilibrium at full employment where the AGGREGATE SUPPLY of goods and services creates just sufficient income to generate an equal and opposite aggregate demand.

BOOMS AND SLUMPS

If only it was always like that! The fact is that there are times when economic events do not work out as market theorists maintain and, in such times, it is very difficult to give an explanation as to what is going on and what is the best that should be done.

The 1930s Great Depression was just such a time – when millions were thrown out of work in all developed countries around the world – and similar fears are being expressed today in the current international slowdown, as explained in the first chapter. Depression, or recession, is a time of rising unemployment and – in the extreme – DEFLATION (falling prices). When prices are falling, though it seems welcome, it means people tend to stop spending. This is yet another example of the fallacy of composition. For you and I, if we can buy certain goods later at lower prices than today then it makes sense: we make money by delaying purchases. But if *everyone* stops spending, waiting for prices to fall further, then the circular flow of money, consumption and incomes in the country decreases. The national income goes down and unemployment will certainly rise. The policy of stopping and waiting means that some will never get the chance of buying later!

In the global circulation of incomes and spending today, leakages and injections to the circular flow have *not* been balanced by movements in world rates of interest, as market economics dictates. In deflationary circumstances, net leakages from the economy are still positive even though rates of interest are at rock bottom. (See Chapter 1, particularly the unspent trade surpluses exceeding the deficits, in Figure 1.4. See also the build-up of savings in the form of US Treasury Bills, Figure 1.5, despite the very low returns they offer.)

As was said at the opening of this chapter, free market theory has a powerful hold over the mindset of many economists. The dominant PARADIGM, or worldview, so influences thinking that it is a struggle to see phenomena in any other terms. It takes genius, plus the accumulation of lots of other evidence, to shift received perceptions. In 1936, the Great Depression provided the evidence; Keynes provided the genius.

Re-read some of the circular flow analysis above – and now consider how savings differ for low, as opposed to high, income countries. This implies a different way to model savings and investment in an economy than neoclassical market economics.

Keynes argued that the main determinant of the volume of savings in an economy is *not* the market price of money (the rate of interest) but *the level of income*. That is, if rates of interest increase by a relatively large amount, people will still not save more in their bank accounts. But if people's incomes rise substantially then they *will* put money aside. (It can thus be argued that savings are price-inelastic but INCOME-ELASTIC in supply.)

Keynesian macroeconomics holds that savings are a leakage from the circular flow and that they are primarily a function of income, rising from some negative amount at very low income levels but then increasing more steeply as incomes rise.

In contrast, the demand for funds for investment – the key stimulus to the economy – is neither primarily determined by rates of interest nor levels of national income. The most potent influence on investment is business EXPECTATIONS of future profits. If the outlook is profitable then even high rates of interest on borrowing will not dissuade the eager investor, and equally if future expectations are gloomy then it is likely that even very cheap loanable funds will not change the entrepreneur's pessimistic mood. Investment is thus exogenously given by a factor other than income. It is assumed fixed at Q, by forces (expectations) outside this simple model.

Simple though it is, Figure 5.4 carries a very powerful message. Look what happens at low income levels, that is below the level Y^* illustrated. Over this range of incomes – from 0 to Y^* – the level of savings or leakages in the national economy is less than Q, less than the level of exogenous investment. So long as more money is being injected into the system than is being taken out, the circular flow of incomes and spending must therefore grow.

Conversely, at levels of national income greater than Y^* the amount of savings leaking out of the circular flow is greater than the level of injections. National income must decline. Either way,

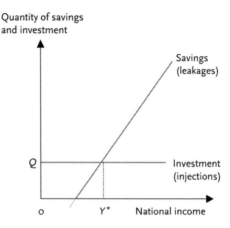

Figure 5.4 Savings and investment functions. Savings rise with income; investment responds to expectations and is assumed exogenous (at level Q)
with regard to income. (The rate of interest is a minor, somewhat
irrelevant, influence, according to KEYNESIAN ECONOMICS.)
There is thus a unique level of equilibrium income (Y*) where savings
equals investment. Now consider the consequences of a decline in
expectations such that investment shifts down below the level Q.
What happens to equilibrium National Income?

the economy moves to a unique equilibrium at Y* – *through a
movement of income levels.*

This needs emphasising. According to the Keynesian macroeconomic model any imbalance of savings and investment, leakages
and injections, in the economy is not matched up by a mere
movement of interest rates in financial markets but by a relentless
movement up or grinding down of all income levels in an economy.

What are the implications of this? It means that if, for some
reason, business confidence in aggregate is low and there is thus a
fall in the general level of investment in the country then, despite
financiers' temptations to lower interest rates and practically give
money away, there will be a net flow of un-recycled money piling
up in banks and finance houses. Aggregate spending will fall, profits
will fall, industrial production will either fall or result in increasing
stocks of unsold inventory, unemployment will eventually rise and
the country's level of income will slowly, relentlessly fall. The
economy will enter a slump, which will be prolonged until

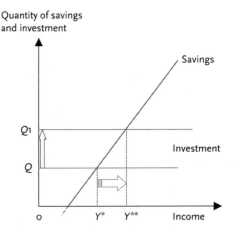

Figure 5.5 An increase in investment. Investment rises from Q to Q1. At original income level $Y^\star$, the amount of investment or injections (the distance 0 to Q1) is now much higher than savings/leakages (0 to Q). National income grows therefore from $Y^\star$ to $Y^{\star\star}$ where the two flows are again equal.

incomes fall low enough for the level of aggregate savings to decline to the already low level of autonomous investment. We can call this the LOW LEVEL EQUILIBRIUM TRAP.

The opposite scenario is now easy to predict: if business confidence and investment rises then, at the existing level of national income, injections will exceed withdrawals from the system and so the circular flow will increase. Income levels will continue to rise until the new equilibrium is reached, as illustrated at $Y^{\star\star}$ in Figure 5.5.

Note that how far income grows, given an increase in investment, depends on the slope of the savings function. The steeper this line, the less income will grow; conversely the more slowly savings rises with income, the more any given stimulus to the economy will cause greater growth of income (see Box 5.1, Figure 5.6).

BOX 5.1 THE INVESTMENT MULTIPLIER

Any autonomous increase in investment in an economy may have a multiplied impact on incomes. Suppose, for example, it was decided to build £10 million worth of more houses in a given region. First of all there would be purchases of land, increased employment of labour, more spending on construction materials, etc. This represents an injection of £10m to the incomes of resources immediately employed. The households receiving those increased incomes would, subject to a certain propensity to save, then increase their spending on a whole host of consumer goods. This flow of spending promotes a second round of income increases as the providers of these consumer goods benefit from the surge in spending. Then, in turn, the recipients of second round incomes increase *their* spending and so we can begin to see that what started as an increase in construction spending in one part of the economy slowly spreads and multiplies around the entire economy. What began as an injection of £10 million could result in an increase in aggregate incomes of very much more than this as the impulse of spending goes round and around the circular flow.

The extent to which incomes multiply in the economy is determined by how much of the injection in spending is passed on as extra consumption, as opposed to saved (or leaked) out of the system. If the MARGINAL PROPENSITY TO SAVE (that is, that fraction of an increase in income that is saved) is high then clearly not much will be passed on to local traders in the form of extra spending. Incomes will not multiply very much. If this propensity to save is low, however, then spending rapidly passes on to others who pass it on to yet more others, and still others, and national income as a whole will keep rising until, eventually, total savings just rises enough to equal total investment again – but now at a much higher income level.

This principle is illustrated in Figures 5.5 and 5.6. The marginal propensity to save (*mps*) is illustrated by the slope of the savings function – it shows how fast savings rise as incomes rise. A high slope, or high *mps*, as shown in Figure 5.5 means that less income is re-cycled and thus a given injection of investment leads to a small MULTIPLIER. Income grows from Y^* to Y^{**}. In Figure 5.6, however, the *mps* is much lower and so with the same injection it

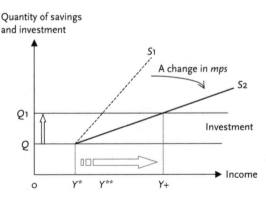

Figure 5.6 A larger multiplier. A fall in *mps* leads to a higher impulse on national income, consequent upon any increase (*Q* to *Q1*) in injections. *Y** thus grows to *Y*+.

produces a greater increase in income, *Y** to *Y*+. (Exogenous changes in a country's *mps*, though uncommon, can arise due to momentous national events, such as the recent major financial crisis, or may slowly build up over time as a result of social or cultural pressures – an ageing population and more media emphasis on consumerist lifestyles have both led to falling savings propensities.)

An important implication of this Keynesian model is that a country's income level need not be stable over time. Contrary to the market paradigm, it suggests that there are no guarantees that the movement of prices will always keep the economy in some happy balance. The variable flows of savings and investment may bring the economy to rest at some level of aggregate spending too low to secure employment for everyone or, conversely, spending may be greater than domestic production can satisfy – in which case a surge in inflation (continually rising prices) may be the result. Neither outcome is particularly pleasant.

In the short run, a country's stock of productive resources is given. The maximum level of potential national output – which corresponds to the maximum level of national income – that can be produced in any one year is thus relatively fixed. Whether this level – which is consistent with full employment of all resources – is actually produced or not depends on the aggregate level of demand in the country.

Consider Figure 5.6. Suppose that savings rises with income as illustrated by *S1*, investment varies between *Q* and *Q1* yet full employment of the economy is only reached at income level *Y***. The problem is that investment is a volatile variable, dependent on (fragile) business confidence. Clearly there is no *a priori* reason why exogenously determined investment should equal savings, and the economy thus be in balance, at the precise income level *Y***. Investment and thus equilibrium income might just as well be below this (at *Y**) in which case some resources in the economy will suffer unemployment; or equilibrium might be above this level (at *Y+*) in which case, if production cannot rise above *Y***, then inflation will persist. (Aggregate spending will exceed the economy's capacity to produce.)

Result? The Keynesian model predicts that national income is inherently unstable – that is, booms and slumps in fortunes are to be expected – all depending on the size of injections to and leakages from the circular flow of aggregate demand.

THE CONTINUING DEBATE

So, is the market economy a fully automatic, self-regulating system capable of securing general equilibrium for a country as a whole? The Keynesian critique, above, says no. Unemployment at one extreme or inflation at the other are the inescapable consequences of an economy where aggregate demand adds up to either insufficient, or too much, spending to balance aggregate supply. Any self-righting market forces within the economy (in this case, the movement of interest rates) working to restore balance between injections and leakages will be too weak to be effective.

This is a major, positive-economic criticism of the market system and, since its first articulation way back in 1936 (in Keynes' *The General Theory of Employment, Interest and Money*) it has provoked an ongoing controversy.

That all economies experience periods of inflation and unemployment is self-evident. What accounts for these unwelcome phenomena is something much more contestable.

The Keynesian argument is clear – that variations in unregulated aggregate demand (particularly caused by the instability of private investment) are the prime culprit. Note that the important twentieth-century policy recommendation derived from this thinking was that if private markets were too volatile to keep injections equal to leakages at the full-employment level of national income required, then governments had to intervene. Governments should increase their own spending when aggregate demand was otherwise too low and decrease their spending when aggregate demand was so high as to be inflationary. Such a policy recommendation was known as DEMAND MANAGEMENT (see Box 5.2).

In his time, Keynes' writings were so revolutionary that he became the world's most famous economist and his legacy on the subject as we know it today is immense. His theories and the policy implications that flowed from them changed the accepted paradigm such that the post-Second World War international economy was dominated by governments, think tanks and policy makers of all stripes all advocating demand management policies.

BOX 5.2 DEMAND MANAGEMENT AND GOVERNMENT BUDGETS

Governments spend money on education, health, transport, defence and a whole range of services to the nation which must be paid for – if not by direct pricing – by levying taxes. The balance of public sector spending on one side, against tax revenues on the other, is recorded in the government's BUDGET. Note that government expenditure acts as an exogenous injection into the domestic economy, whereas taxes act as a leakage to reduce people's incomes and spending. This fact enables governments to use their budgets in an active FISCAL POLICY to directly influence the circular flow of national income.

Suppose business expectations are pessimistic, investment is less than aggregate savings and financial markets cannot induce further investment, even though interest rates are rock bottom. National income will fall as recession grips the economy. In such circumstances, Keynesian economic policy is for governments to spend more than they tax. If the government's budget is in DEFICIT then the domestic economy must be receiving the money the government is losing (assuming no outflow of international funds). Private sector investment may be low but net injections will rise if public sector investment compensates to build more roads and hospitals, employ more people and pay them wages. An economy in recession can thus be stimulated if the government makes the injections which the private sector is unwilling to provide. Notice in this example that savings outweigh private investment so therefore the government can finance a budget deficit by borrowing from the financial markets which are flush with funds that no one else wishes to employ. As the economy recovers due to the fiscal stimulus, incomes will grow and along with them tax revenues will rise to pay off the (low-cost) loans the government originally borrowed.

The converse of all this also applies. If investment is greater than savings, injections exceed leakages and inflation threatens, then governments can aim to increase taxes and make a budget surplus to take the heat out of the economy and ensure that aggregate demand attains equilibrium at full employment level and not higher.

But just as he challenged the orthodoxy of classical economics which preceded him, so other economists have since had to overcome the intellectual stranglehold that the Keynesian paradigm exerted in the post–war years.

The most famous economist since Keynes, Milton Friedman, is one who has been at the forefront of re-establishing neoclassical economics and in challenging both the Keynesian notions that market economies are not self-stabilising and that they therefore need government macroeconomic regulation.

Friedman, and other neoclassical economists, do not dispute there is a role for government intervention in MICROECONOMICS (for example, to break up monopolies and promote competition amongst suppliers, as discussed in the last chapter). But they say there is more likelihood that government spending at macroeconomic level will be actually destabilising and lead to more problems of unemployment and inflation, rather than the opposite.

This neoclassical position, at its extreme, asserts that Keynesian theory gives governments the excuse to increase spending beyond budgets and, once you let this particular genie out of the bottle you will never get it back. Government spending increases year on year as public officials find more and more reasons to overshoot budgets; budgets are thus revised and yet again they are overspent. The end result is an increasingly bureaucratic public sector that grows with a mind of its own and crowds out the private sector – which loses revenues, dynamism and the potential for supporting the national economy in the long term.

Inflation, Friedman argued, was and is the result of central authorities allowing excessive monetary growth. Cut back the money supplies and you cure the problem. The opposite extreme experienced by the US in the Great Depression of the 1930s was caused by a sudden and severe collapse in money supplies due to a chain reaction of commercial bank failures. Remedy? Friedman was the supreme MONETARIST economist: governments should set a steady course with money supplies growing at a rate just equal to the rate of growth of all goods and services in the economy and then they should leave the market well enough alone. Markets may not be perfect but they are better than the alternative – ham-fisted attempts by governments to "stabilise" the macroeconomy.

THE CONTROVERSIAL CORRELATION

The Keynesian notion that a country's aggregate demand determines the level of economic activity was supported by the empirical findings of Professor A. W. Phillips in 1958 which seemed to show beyond contention that, for almost a century, the UK's rate of wage inflation had varied inversely with unemployment in a remarkably stable, almost predictable way. As unemployment went down, inflation went up, and vice versa.

This finding, it was subsequently argued, thus supported the Keynesian theoretical model that said you either get unemployment if aggregate demand is too low or inflation if aggregate demand is too high. It also supported political advisors who suggested you could get less unemployment, and thus more votes, by increasing government spending.

The Phillips correlation dominated policy thinking of the time. It was an incontrovertible piece of analysis that seemed to prove you had to live with either one extreme or the other or find some not-entirely-happy medium. The compromise that most developed countries chose to live with in the immediate post-war years was a degree of creeping inflation. It was thought to be the necessary price for reducing unemployment.

Friedman's voice (also that of another US economist Edmund Phelps) arguing to the contrary was not heeded outside the field of theoretical economics. Notwithstanding the irrefutable evidence of an inflation/unemployment trade-off stretching way back into the nineteenth century, these two economists separately argued that if governments began spending money to try and reduce unemployment, in effect opting for a bit more inflation, then the supposedly reliable correlation would break down.

Friedman, in a famous address to the American Economics Association in 1967, said that the Phillips curve illustrated in Box 5.3, Figure 5.7 offered a reasonable prediction of policy alternatives in a world where zero inflation was the norm; that is, where years in which there was inflation were counterbalanced by years of *de*flation. But as soon as people *expected* governments to fuel inflation over a continuing period then they would build that into their wage demands. And as soon as that happened, if governments still persisted in their spending plans to reduce unemployment, there was the potential for inflation to *accelerate*.

BOX 5.3 THE TRADE-OFF THAT SHIFTED

The PHILLIPS CURVE *PP* (Figure 5.7) illustrates data for UK wage inflation against unemployment over the entire period 1862–1958. It shows a remarkably stable trade-off. Friedman predicted, however, that if governments deliberately attempted to peg unemployment to some level *B* below what he called the natural level *A* then this original

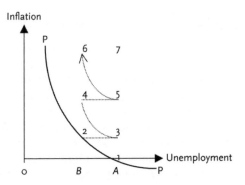

Figure 5.7 The Phillips curve and movements off. Assume government
spending reduces unemployment below *A* (1) but leads to an
increase in inflation (2). Next round wage claims would build
in this increase – which would then lead to a fall in demand
for labour (3). If government increases spending yet again,
inflation now rises to (4). This leads to even greater wage
demands – returning unemployment to (5). If the cycle keeps
repeating, the end result will be that inflation/unemployment
locii explode off the curve: 6, 7, and so on.

trade-off would inevitably break down as the Phillips curve
shifted up and out.

In the 1970s it was more than economists who took note of
what Friedman said. Most of the Western world, in reaction to the
OPEC oil shocks of 1973 and 1979 (see Box 5.4), experienced
accelerating inflation almost precisely as predicted. A shift in inflationary
expectations provoked a wage–price spiral and many democratic governments – unwilling to take the political risk of allowing unemployment to rise – opted to spend money instead with the exact
consequences of accelerating inflation as illustrated in Figure 5.7.

The world seemed to have adjusted to living with inflation – only
to find that once started, it was a notoriously difficult process to hold
in check. Stagflation resulted: inflation with stagnating growth. For
economists and advisors of the Keynesian school, the events of the
late 1970s condemned them to the margins of policy-making
whereas Friedmanite analysis and recommendations now captured
the centre-ground. The macroeconomic paradigm shifted once more.

BOX 5.4 OPEC AND THE OIL PRICE SHOCKS

The Organization of Petroleum Exporting Countries was formed in 1960 in an accord between original members Iran, Iraq, Kuwait, Saudi Arabia and Venezuela. But it was not until the USA in particular, in 1973, began to import increasing amounts of oil as its own supplies fell short of demand that OPEC could act as a successful cartel. The spark that lit the oil crisis was the 1973 October War between Arabs and Israelis when OPEC shut off oil supplies in retaliation to Western support of Israel. The price of world oil soared 400 per cent between October 1973 and January 1974.

For oil consumer countries in the rich and poor world alike, the 1970s was a time of painful adjustment to high oil prices and the inflation this fuelled. Just as they thought they were coming out of it, in 1979 oil prices surged again. This time it was the Iranian revolution when the pro-Western Shah of Iran was deposed by Muslim fundamentalists who again shut down sales of Iranian oil. By the 1980s, however, governments in the West had changed and economic policies had changed with them (see the following section on supply-side economics).

THE SUPPLY-SIDE CONSENSUS

Economics is not an exact science. Things never turn out quite the way theory predicts since – unlike the "hard" sciences such as physics – there are so many variables beyond the economists' control. But for evidence to confirm theoretical predictions as comprehensively as was demonstrated in the inflationary 1970s was really remarkable. Friedman, famous already, became even more renowned and his influence now extended to policies advocated by decision-takers all round the world, just as had been the case with Keynes, earlier.

Any attempt by governments to spend their way out of recessions was now condemned. By extension, almost any initiative for governments to intervene in the economy was heavily criticised. Right-wing, free-market conservatism – with the ascent to power

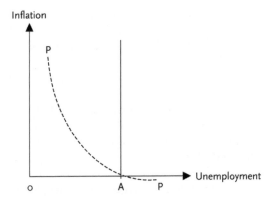

Figure 5.8 The expectations-augmented Phillips curve. A "natural" level of
unemployment which cannot be reduced implies that the original
Phillips curve *PP* becomes superceded by the new version: an
EXPECTATIONS-AUGMENTED PHILLIPS CURVE, which is
a vertical line at point *A*.

of Margaret Thatcher in the UK and Ronald Reagan in the USA –
now dominated the political agenda.

In the short term, it was alleged that a country's productive resources
were more or less fixed and their allocation between competing uses
was best decided by unrestricted market forces. Trying to reduce
unemployment below its "natural" level by increasing aggregate
demand could not increase national income/output/aggregate supplies one iota – it could only stimulate increasing inflation as already
described (Figure 5.8).

What are the policy recommendations that flow from this?
Ignore inflationary meddling with aggregate demand – focus instead
on the microeconomic features of the SUPPLY-SIDE of the economy.

Only policies that are aimed at making resources more flexible and
responsive to market forces could hope to reduce unemployment
and improve a nation's fortunes.

LIBERALISATION, deregulation, PRIVATISATION, removing
the allegedly dead hand of government, were all the new buzz words
of the 1980s supply-side revolution. Markets had to be set free so that
they would restore flexibility and dynamism to Western economies.

The tenets of this latest orthodoxy in macroeconomics were now
as follows:

- Central authorities varying money supplies cause most of the instability in an economy. Money growth should be fixed at a rate commensurate with that of long-run trend growth of the economy and then left alone.
- There is no long-run trade-off between inflation and unemployment.
- The economy is inherently stable such that if disturbed by misplaced government meddling then it will return eventually to the long-run equilibrium at the NATURAL RATE OF UNEMPLOYMENT.
- The natural rate of unemployment is increased by the provision of welfare payments which allegedly give people an incentive not to work, and by minimum wage laws and protective labour legislation that inhibit hiring and firing workers.
- Future expectations, the actions of unions and the flexibility of prices and wages all impact on inflation and misguided government intervention can exaggerate these influences.

Such an economic philosophy dictates a detailed restructuring of the relationship between the government and the economy as a whole:

FISCAL DISCIPLINE

First, supply-side economics requires governments to balance their budgets, live within their means and thereby stop inflationary spending. Loss-making banks and industry should not be bailed out in the mistaken pursuit of trying to protect jobs. Similarly, it also means reducing welfare payments and handouts to workers. This saves government money, lets failing industry fail and prompts workers to move to new, growing firms. On the side of taxation, high MARGINAL INCOME TAX RATES should be cut and the tax base broadened. Such discipline also addresses the problem of incentives. (Why should industry strive to be efficient if government bails out failure? And why should the individual work if earned income is highly taxed and unemployment brings you benefits?)

PRIVATISATION

State-owned or NATIONALISED INDUSTRIES should be sold off to whichever private investors might be interested (e.g. telephones and telecommunications) and closed down where industries have no buyers (e.g. coal). One-off sales of public industry will net large revenues for the government which can be used to pay off the NATIONAL DEBT and balance budgets over the longer term and simultaneously they remove altogether the permanent drain on the public purse of otherwise loss-making dinosaurs.

DEREGULATE AND FREE-UP TRADE

Competition should be promoted wherever possible. Barriers to entry and exit in private industry should be removed. In the public sector, quasi-markets can be introduced in health, education services and in public broadcasting to simulate competition between suppliers. In labour markets, improve labour mobility by breaking up restrictive trade unions that act as monopoly suppliers of labour whilst increasing job information and training to allow workers to move. In finance, remove restrictions on the international movement of money, the barriers to foreign banks, and the demarcation of different loan markets between building societies, banks and all other money houses.

PRICE FLEXIBILITY

Release the price mechanism to operate unhindered. The price of domestic money, the price of labour and the price of international currencies should, in particular, all move up and down without fear or restriction. That is, rates of interest, wages and foreign exchange dealings should be determined by free markets and not fixed by some rule, regulation or legislation.

DE-POLITICISE MONEY

Last but certainly not least, remove politics from the determination of the money supply – that is, make the nation's CENTRAL BANK independent of day-to-day control by government. Give the governor of the central bank a target to keep inflation down and under control and leave him/her to get on with it, irrespective of unemployment effects and free from political interference.

The short-term SOCIAL COSTS of implementing these measures have caused much debate. Cutting industrial subsidies and closing down businesses whilst at the same time reducing spending in the public sector must mean increasing unemployment. Such policies combined with reducing and re-targeting unemployment benefits are likely to increase poverty and hardship. "Broadening the tax base" is coded language for increasing taxes on a wider range of goods and services – that is, increasing prices. Reducing marginal income tax rates may leave high-income earners with more money to spend but doesn't help the lower paid.

Widening extremes of poverty and wealth are the inevitable result of such policies – but this is justified, according to this new classical paradigm, if the value of money and the efficiency of markets is to be restored. It is worth the risk if incentives to work, invest and produce are all improved and opportunities to climb out of the lower income levels are similarly increased. The overall impact on the economy, it is alleged, is to make it more dynamic, entrepreneurial and growthfull. National income will thus grow faster and raise everyone's standard of living over time. And the quicker these reforms are implemented the better – it will reduce any social costs involved in adjusting to the new economic realities (see New Classical school below).

This revolution in economic philosophy – turning back from Keynesian thinking in favour of unfettered markets again – drove major changes in the 1980s not only in the developed countries of Europe and North America but also in the developing world. It was a shift in priorities to address inflation, curtail government excesses and to play down attention to unemployment. The Washington-based and highly influential institutions of the International Monetary Fund (IMF) and the World Bank actively promoted these views (see Box 5.5). There continued some disagreement over the short-term costs of implementing the recommended package of market reforms but mainstream macroeconomic analysis was, on the whole, won over by the new consensus.

BOX 5.5 THE WASHINGTON CONSENSUS

The early 1980s, a time of inflation and recession for many in the developed world, saw the emergence of a major debt crisis for poorer countries. The policy package to reduce inflation, listed above, meant cutting back money supplies in the rich countries – which inevitably raised interest rates. (A shift back in world supplies forces up the price of money.) Poorer nations that had borrowed from them now faced huge debt repayment charges that they could not afford.

The IMF and the World Bank were asked for help – which they offered at a price. In return for providing financial assistance, these Washington institutions insisted that market-friendly, supply-side reforms must be put in place in all countries that had become heavily indebted. Some might argue this was holding a gun to the head of the poor. Others would insist it is simply forcing bad debtors to put their financial houses in order. Either way, the new economic orthodoxy was spread from policy advisors and governments in the rich world to the poor. It became known as the WASHINGTON CONSENSUS and it had a bitter taste for the many whose standards of living were worst affected.

Poor country governments were forced to cut back on costly welfare programmes, to reduce TARIFF BARRIERS and other trade restrictions that protected domestic industry, to devalue their currencies and to free up their internal markets to foreign capital. This entails promoting freer international competition in goods and free movement of (rich country) investment funds to buy and sell (poor country) indebted business.

Taxes were raised, incomes and consumption reduced, budgets balanced and funds generated to pay off debts. But as anyone in debt knows, it is not the overall amount of capital you owe that is important, what counts is how much time you have to pay it off. For many in the developing world the complaint was that they were forced to pay too high a price, too quickly.

For mature market economies, I have described the paradigm shift that occurred in the 1970s: government intervention was now held to blame for subsidising declining industry, over-protecting labour and ossifying wages and prices. In such circumstances, one can understand the call for markets to be freed up and cajoled into competitive efficiency – but even for the rich world this analysis is hotly contested and its dangers are emphasised (see the New Keynesian argument below). For poor countries where modern markets are missing, fragmented or under-developed, there is even less justification for promoting such radical, neoclassical policies.

Where labour is unskilled and uneducated, where land is tied into traditional practice, where capital has accumulated in informal and untitled assets, these resources cannot move freely to new and productive employments in response to market signals. If free trade is introduced in countries where industry is struggling to develop, such business is likely to collapse in the face of unrestricted competition from foreign multinationals. Those skills which the local populace have acquired can be tempted away to take up employment overseas (the BRAIN DRAIN), and untapped natural resources such as mineral deposits and native flora and fauna can be exploited too cheaply. With heavy debts, poor countries might even offer cut-price DEBT-EQUITY SWAPS where foreigners are offered large shares in local business in exchange for paying off the loans these businesses have incurred. (A strategy criticised as "selling off the family silver".)

The Washington Consensus is not necessarily a policy package that fits the needs of all countries, therefore. The directors of the World Bank and of the IMF eventually conceded this – though only after years of forcing painful cuts on Latin America and Africa, in particular. In November 1999, in an IMF conference on what were called "second generation reforms" both Michel Camdessus (then managing director of the IMF) and James Wolfensohn (president of the World Bank) signed up to policies focused on helping the poor and improving equity. Camdessus actually agreed that "too much attention is focused on how markets operate rather than on how they develop". They realised (painfully late) that premature implementation of policies that assume the existence of efficient markets actually inhibits their evolution.

RATIONAL EXPECTATIONS

The pro-market, supply-side revolution that had captured policy-making since the 1980s was based on the rational expectations hypothesis. This was the notion that economic agents form expectations of the future based on all available evidence and that they do not make systematic errors in predicting what will happen. This was taking the monetarist economics of Friedman to a logical extreme. In effect the hypothesis predicts that free markets will never stray far from equilibrium and, if there are such cases, they will only be due to misinformation and must only be very short-lived as agents rapidly learn. You can fool the markets once, but not twice.

Predictions from this hypothesis state that, providing governments do not intervene, unemployment will be stable at the "natural" rate where labour markets are in equilibrium. Any attempt to reduce unemployment below this natural, market equilibrium by boosting money supplies will *immediately* cause inflation (the expectations augmented Phillips curve, above) and, conversely, any attempt to reduce inflation needs only a credible government commitment to slash money supplies and this will not affect unemployment.

According to this hypothesis, markets always clear with no excess or shortage; prices and wages are always in equilibrium, and any movement of such prices signals that the fundamentals are moving and thus for the most efficient outcomes, they should not be interfered with by government intervention.

If people are unemployed it is because their skills are not in demand and trying to support their employment or impose minimum wages cannot help them, not in the short nor in the long run. The best future for stagecoach drivers or miners with no coal left to extract, is to find another job, not beg for governments to employ stagecoaches or keep mines open.

By the same logic, there cannot be anything wrong if house prices are rising rapidly since this is not the result of speculation, only a real excess of demand over supply – which must in due course call forth the equivalent supply response that will reduce prices. All speculation, according to this mind-set, is actually a short-run market *corrective*, signalling where resource movements have yet to catch up.

As theory, these ideas were a return to the beautiful, logically consistent world of pre-Keynesian economics. Hence the name:

the NEW CLASSICAL ECONOMICS which, since it was based on micro-foundations of rational behaviour, was both susceptible to sophisticated mathematical modelling and also had the advantage of disarming its critics who could hardly call themselves opposed to rational argument...

By the 1990s, there was no other game in town. New Classical theory and its supply-side economic policies had carried all before it. Around the world, thanks to liberalisation, financial markets in particular had ballooned in trade; incomes were growing with them yet inflation was rapidly falling; both India and China had introduced pro-market reforms that were transforming their economies and the East Europeans and ex-Soviet satellites were all in full retreat from centralised government.

The only academics to disagree with the New Classical consensus in economic theory were the NEW KEYNESIANS. Swimming against this tide (like Friedman before in the 1950s and 1960s) they still rejected any notion of a stable macroeconomic equilibrium at some "natural" level of unemployment. If inflation was to be reduced by a cut-back in aggregate money demand then, far from markets clearing instantly or even in the short term, the market economy might not clear at all. So long as spending in the economy is suppressed, so will be employment and incomes. Also, like lonely voices crying in the wilderness, they repeatedly asked the awkward (though by then, seemingly not very relevant) question: *if markets always clear, what caused the Great Depression?*

THE GREAT RECESSION

It took the 1930s Great Depression to overthrow the paradigm of classical economics and bring in the Keynesian revolution in macroeconomics. It was the stagflation of the 1970s to introduce the next paradigm shift – the rational expectations revolution that denounced Keynesian economics and heralded a return to a new classical theory. Now the global recession that started in 2007 has signalled the next turn in the cycle – for some, at least, back to a new Keynesian revival. What causes a major depression is no longer of interest only to historians and out-of-favour economists.

The speculative bubble in house prices in various countries; the explosive growth and overpricing of mortgage backed securities;

the bursting of these bubbles; the banking collapses; the international credit crunch, the rising unemployment and the prolonged European recession that we analysed in Chapter 1 are impossible to explain away as a random walk in equilibrium prices that the rational expectations hypothesis would have us believe. These are not markets in a moving equilibrium where "nâtural" rates always apply ... unless, of course, you are so blinded by the beauty of economic theorems that you cannot see anything else. Surely a better hypothesis is that free markets unregulated by government are liable to disastrous, exaggerated swings in fortunes and can get stuck in disequilibria – where confidence collapses and banks go bust; where businesses cannot get loans; where people cannot get work.

Recessions are defined in the popular media as when a country experiences two or more quarters with no growth in gross domestic product. When does a recession become a depression? Some wit said that a recession is where your neighbour loses his job; a depression is when you lose yours. In fact there is no hard and fast definition that economists are happy with but at least this jibe has the merit of implying that the impact of a depression is both wider and deeper than a recession. It also has a long-lasting affect on psychology.

How do you get out of a massive slump? Certain politicians and central bankers have ignored NEW CLASSICAL ECONOMICS and increased injections into the circular flow of their nation's economy. Indeed, where increasing the money supply has been less than productive (since corporate financiers have been rebuilding their bank reserves and have been reluctant to loan these monies out) some governments have resorted to expansionary fiscal policies – bailing out businesses, running big budget deficits, borrowing extensively (see Figure 1.8) and spending money they have not yet earned through tax revenues.

The global slowdown that started in 2007 has, in my opinion, been to a varied extent moderated by some very Keynesian spending policies, otherwise we do not know whether we would have hit the depths of the 1930s or gone deeper. That does not mean that the fight to overcome opposite, non-interventionist policies – insisting on cutbacks in government spending, in balancing budgets and enforcing austerity (that is, a low income, low spending equilibrium consistent with high unemployment) – has been won. Republican critics in the USA and politicians of a conservative bent in Europe still wield a lot of influence and have resisted more expansionary public spending and welfare support for the hardest hit. The recession is Europe in particular has been prolonged (see Figure 1.8) and, politically, is far more difficult to rectify, as will be discussed in Chapter 6.

CONCLUSION

Where is the economics profession today in the light of all these developments? Well, macroeconomics is still hotly debated. Theories of inflation and unemployment have had to be rapidly revised and updated and we are still in the process of learning from recent experience.

Free markets *are* capable of remarkable flexibility, growth and of spreading the rewards around to millions of ordinary people. The gains from market reforms have been enjoyed by countless Asians, Americans and Europeans over the last two decades. Countries as far apart as Chile, China, India, New Zealand, the USA and the UK have all experienced consistent falls in inflation and increases in employment and economic growth as supply-side reforms have slowly brought results. Free markets however *do* need regulating! Insisting that market economies never go astray (New Classical School) or will regain balance unaided in the short term (Monetarist) are theoretical positions that are difficult to hold now.

Similarly, insisting that government intervention in the real economy is inevitably harmful in the long run is unlikely to be argued by banks, finance houses, General Motors and a whole host of other businesses that have only been kept alive since 2008 by massive infusions of public money.

So Keynesian economics is back with a vengeance ... but just as it was supremely arrogant and short-sighted of its many critics to bury Keynes when market-based reforms were enervating over-regulated industries and countries in the 1980s and 1990s, so it cannot be said that spendthrift policies, by governments, businesses and individuals are a long-term, sustainable route to achieve economic growth. Debts have to be paid back sometime.

In conclusion, both macroeconomic *and* microeconomic reforms are necessary to secure growth with stability. The level of aggregate demand must be high enough to prevent recession, and government monetary and fiscal policies *can* work to offset booms and slumps, as Keynes advised. Equally, however, if resources are protected in inefficient and unchanging employments then an economy cannot escape long-term sclerosis and decline. Much time, encouragement and painful effort may be needed to facilitate the occupational and geographical mobility of a nation's productive assets.

Has recent experience demonstrated the failure of supply-side economics and the success (again) of the Keynesian revolution? It is a false dichotomy. Keynesianism does not recommend unrestricted interventionism and neither can deregulating and liberalising trade guarantee growth and development. There is a role for both government action and free markets.

SUMMARY

Classical economics asserts that flexible prices will ensure equilibrium in labour, financial and all other markets such that there is attained one unique level of income and employment for an economy as a whole, where the aggregate supply of goods and services just equals the level of aggregate demand.

The experience of the 1930s depression confounded such confidence. Keynes argued that market economies are inherently unstable and may require government demand management policies to maintain general equilibrium.

Phillips' original findings that inflation increased at the expense of unemployment seemed to corroborate Keynes' analytical model, though the 1970s experience of inflation and recession served to overthrow the Keynesian paradigm and promulgate Friedman's monetarist/neoclassical views.

Friedman argued that monetary discipline combined with microeconomic reforms to liberalise markets could contain both inflation and unemployment.

More extreme theorising by the New Classical School promoted supply-side reforms that were taken up enthusiastically by many right-wing governments ... though unshackling particularly financial sectors led market systems from a boom eventually into a bust and a great recession.

A return to government-led spending in nations across the globe has moderated the slump and vindicated Keynesian economics. Despite this, macroeconomic fiscal and monetary policies to adjust aggregate demand, *and* microeconomic policies to free up trade are today both necessary as important instruments of government economic management.

FURTHER READING

Akerlof, G. and Shiller, R. (2009) *Animal Spirits*, Princeton University Press. A lively celebration of Keynes and a novel interpretation of economic theory after the great recession.

Friedman, M. (1968) "The Role of Monetary Policy" *American Economic Review*, Vol. 58, pp. 1–17. A classic monetarist paper, readable and still very relevant, this is Friedman's address to the American Economic Association in 1967 where he first introduced the world to concepts such as the natural rate of unemployment and what was later to be called the expectations–augmented Phillips curve.

Cleaver, T. (2013) *Understanding the World Economy*, Routledge. My own text with, in the first three chapters, further explanation of booms and busts; micro- and macroeconomics; unemployment and inflation.

For masses of fascinating detail and data on different countries in the world, check the websites for the IMF and the World Bank: www.imf.org and www.worldbank.org.

QUESTIONS

1 Explain how a banking collapse will, via a negative multiplier, lead to a severe contraction in the circular flow of incomes. If such a negative chain reaction begins – leading to incomes spiralling down and down – how and where does such a contraction ever end?

2 The Phillips curve trade-off between inflation and unemployment held up as a relatively stable relationship for almost a hundred years until it was formally identified in the 1960s, whereupon it then broke down. Explain why.

3 Some types of unemployment are best solved by applying microeconomic or SUPPLY-SIDE POLICIES; other types of unemployment are more appropriately addressed by applying macroeconomic, demand-management policies. Can you explain? How could you tell the difference between micro and macro causes of unemployment?

4 Joe Stiglitz, a Noble Prize-winning economist, has claimed that the economics profession and its ruling paradigm are partly to blame for the build-up to the great financial crash of 2007/2008. Can you reconstruct his argument?

6

MONEY, BANKS, BUBBLES AND CRISES

Money makes the world go round. In order to trade, dealers must use a recognised and acceptable form of money and this then enables goods and services to be exchanged and incomes to be paid. The need to use money and yet safeguard its use led to the first banks, and the subsequent creative manipulation of other people's money has since given rise to the modern, massive, international financial industry.

In general, the growth of banking and the resulting globalisation of finance has accompanied the increasing wealth of nations, but it has been a roller coaster ride at times. On occasions, too much money has been loaned out – only to be followed by recriminations all round when creditors, in the attempt to get their money back, close down banks and sell off the businesses they supported. Money is essential to conduct trade; it requires the growth of financial specialists, and there arises, therefore, the occasional irresponsible use and abuse of financial power. It is to these issues that the study of economics must now turn.

THE NATURE OF MONEY

Money is a unique commodity that is only as good as other people think it is. The notes and coins that you have in your pocket may look pretty tangible and appear valuable to you but, first, most money in the world does not have any physical form at all (it exists only as a matter of computer record on bank balance sheets), and second the value of any currency is only determined in exchange – and if someone else won't accept it, it's worthless.

A MEDIUM

Money is first and foremost a MEDIUM OF EXCHANGE. It thus facilitates the circular flow of national income and output described in Chapter 5 and, indeed, without money far less trade and income growth would be possible. Money allows each of us to specialise in our chosen profession, exchange our labour for money income and then trade this for any and all commodities that we may choose to buy in the market economy. Without money we are reduced to BARTER – perhaps swapping work for payment in goods and then attempting to pass off whatever we are given for something else we want from another. Successful barter is very rare since it requires a double coincidence of wants (we can strike a deal only if you've got exactly what I want and I've got exactly what you want). The transactions costs involved in everyone trying to trade in this way are so huge that it inhibits any economic growth for society above subsistence level. Everyone would wear out shoe leather trying to go around bargaining for an acceptable deal, trades agreed in one place would vary with others elsewhere and perishable commodities like essential foodstuffs would deteriorate in the process. Agreeing to an acceptable medium of exchange obviates all this.

What is an acceptable medium? It used to be gold. Something that everyone valued intrinsically for itself, which could be verified for its purity, could be measured out in fine, divisible units, easily carried and which did not deteriorate. It thus possessed most of the ideal QUALITIES OF MONEY. Key to its use as money was its acceptability across cultures – all round the world, people valued gold as a precious asset.

Due to its success as a form of exchange, gold in fact became too scarce. With trade made profitable for payment in gold, production increased, trade expanded and merchants plied the world. But with insufficient gold to support the increase in world output the price of gold must rise and the prices of all other goods and services must correspondingly fall (deflation). The use of other precious metals (principally silver) was thus resorted to. This gave rise to the first quarrels over EXCHANGE RATES – the price at which one currency could exchange for another – but markets grew up to deal with this.

Note however an important distinction: the first monies therefore differ from today's by possessing an INTRINSIC VALUE. Gold and silver had a street value for themselves, based on their usefulness in jewellery and craftwork. This carried advantages and disadvantages. It guaranteed the acceptability of precious metals – thus ensuring they could function as a medium of exchange – but it also meant that world money supplies were susceptible to a steady deflationary drain as these metals were pressed into service as raw materials in the industry of fine craftsmanship. (That is, as gold and silver were slowly taken out of the money supply, that which remained in circulation went up in value. All other goods must go down in price, therefore.)

The invention of paper money avoided this problem. The use of coins – standardised units of precious metal – predates the Roman Empire but we have to thank the medieval goldsmiths in London for the invention of a paper promise to gold or silver. A promise to pay the bearer on demand the sum of ten pounds of sterling silver is the origin of the UK ten pound note. The promise is still there on bank notes today – but the paper itself has little intrinsic value and the promise now cannot be claimed. It is not backed by any precious metal. It is thus FIAT MONEY: its value is declared by fiat, by the central authorities.

In fact today, in the twenty-first century, we have a world monetary system that Friedman calls unprecedented in that no major currency has any link to a commodity and nor is there a commitment anywhere to restoring such a link. Throughout history, he argues, the only times that governments departed from basing their currencies on some recognised and accepted commodity (such as the GOLD STANDARD) were either very short lived or disastrous, or both.

The reason for this claim is that if there is no physical limit to the money supply imposed by, say, the amount of gold or silver that can be mined then there is always the temptation to issue more paper promises – banknotes – by whomsoever holds the licence to print money. And there is no quicker way to undermine a market society than to debase its currency, as HYPERINFLATIONs throughout history have proved (see Box 6.1). Once people lose confidence in the money supply then, unless a ready alternative is available, it becomes impossible to trade.

BOX 6.1 THE GERMAN HYPERINFLATION, 1923

The economic consequences of the peace negotiated at the end of the First World War proved to be disastrous for Germany. The victorious nations in the conflict demanded that Germany pay reparations for the costs imposed on, particularly, French soil. But Germany was an impoverished country and could only pay the massive sums demanded of it by printing banknotes. The more it did so, the more the value of these notes fell and the more, inevitably, were demanded. And so Germany printed more and more and more. Eventually, the banknotes became almost worthless – in the domestic economy people were paid in suitcase loads of cash which they desperately tried to exchange for anything of intrinsic value before the notes devalued even further. Hyperinflations – where prices increase by hundreds and thousands of per cent – destroy people's confidence in currency, make market exchanges impossible and thus provoke economic collapse. In Germany's case, the economic and political chaos created in 1923 led to a vacuum that would later be filled by a nationalist strongman who would only lead his country into an even greater trauma.

At the beginning of the twentieth century the world monetary system operated with all main currencies fixed to a given gold price. The First World War impoverished Europe, most countries came off the gold standard and in the case of Germany hyperinflation ensued since it was unable to pay reparations without printing money. After the Second World War, under the Bretton Woods agreement in 1944, all world currencies operated a dollar standard. That is, they fixed their currencies in terms of the US dollar and this in turn was fixed to the price of gold – and this system lasted right up until 1971 when the system broke down. Since then there has been no anchor to world money.

BOX 6.2 THE GOLD STANDARD AND FIXED EXCHANGE RATES

Prior to the First World War, the currencies of all major trading nations were freely convertible into gold at a fixed exchange rate. This implied they were simultaneously all fixed with one another. Any nation in debt to another would pay the difference in gold and the outflow of reserves from one country would enforce a contraction of money supplies, just as a gold inflow would prompt a monetary expansion. Different countries can only fix their currency exchange rates between themselves over time, however, if they all grow in wealth at the same rate. After the Second World War, the rapid economic growth of West Germany and Japan, in particular, meant that by the 1970s the Deutsch-mark and the Yen possessed an intrinsic worth greater than their Bretton Woods value fixed in the 1940s. A realignment of exchange rates was long overdue, brought to a head by OPEC (see next chapter), and since there was no agree-ment on fixed values in the inflationary 1970s, exchange rates were left to float, or vary, according to international demand and supply.

Confidence has wobbled at times, though so far an international financial system based on non-convertible currencies still survives. Indeed, the mythical attachment to a gold anchor is neither necessary nor sufficient to guarantee the success of paper money. There is only one guiding rule. It is financial discipline imposed by central banks and governments over the long term and the subsequent confidence that this instils in the public that ensures that a given banknote is accepted as "good as gold".

A MEASURE

A second important function of money is to act as a measure of value. A common medium of exchange allows you to put a price, or exchange value, on all things in trade and it is by the operation of the price mechanism that signals of shortages and surpluses can thus be conveyed to all consumers and producers in a market society. Note that no given form of money can fulfil this essential signalling function if its own value is subject to variation. Hence the importance of containing inflation.

Measuring value requires some base line to which all prices can be compared and it also requires a scale of units. The base line against which money itself is valued is a SAMPLE BASKET of everyday commodities – a long list of items which the "average household" in a society will buy and which is weighted according to their relative importance. (A 10 per cent rise in the price of bread will imply a more important fall in the value of money than a 100 per cent rise in the price of golf balls, for example.) All governments appoint statisticians to compile records and regularly calculate whether or not, and by how much, inflation has risen and the value of money fallen.

Note that the "official" rate of inflation may not necessarily correspond with an individual family's estimate of the average rise in prices. It depends on how far their particular purchases match up with the sample "family" (and how far you can trust the authorities to publish properly researched data, as opposed to that which is more politically acceptable!).

A STORE

Money should act as a store of value – if it is perishable in any way then it cannot safely be banked. It makes no sense to accumulate money if it costs to do so – people might as well stockpile all sorts of other assets with intrinsic value instead (salt?). Note the accumulation of capital allows the financial services industry to grow and to invest in all sorts of productive enterprise. People all over the world put their savings into pension funds so that they have some income when they retire. This is only possible if people can trust their money to hold its value over time. What distinguishes "hard" currencies from "soft" ones (terms used at times by financial journals to describe various currencies) is that the former are a better store of value – they are less likely to suffer inflation. This function then facilitates a major feature of all modern money: the ability to buy now and pay later.

Take care – not all that is a good store of value is necessarily money. The price of fine wine increases with age and if you have a lockable cellar it costs little to keep it. Similarly you can have a safe-full of stocks and shares that may more than keep their value. Are they money? No. That is because an essential feature of money is that it is a perfectly LIQUID ASSET that is exchangeable at any time, at no cost, for anything you want. Selling off wine or stocks and shares for their full present value (which may have appreciated considerably) means you have to wait for an appropriate time and buyer. Money, on the other hand, is perfectly transferable or convertible at an instant's notice. It wouldn't be money otherwise.

A STANDARD

Money functions as a standard for deferred payment which allows consumers to buy expensive items (houses, cars) over a phased time period, enables producers of such goods to sell more and better regulate their income streams, and provides the opportunity for bankers to create all sorts of innovative forms of debt and paper money. (Even if the particular form of money in question is a poor store of value, so long as its value deteriorates, i.e. inflation rises, at a predictable rate then a compensating rate of interest can be charged and deferred payment still accepted.)

Being able to conduct trade over time is essential for almost any industry; for funding research; for undertaking any investment and thus for the construction of a modern economy. To build for the future means to delay your rewards until later and so society needs a (financial) means to facilitate this.

Note that deferred payment is only possible if the institutions of society – laws of contract and property rights; the efficiency of bureaucracy and legal systems, and social norms of conduct – all support and reinforce the keeping of promises. If A cannot trust B then even the existence of the strongest and most recognisable of mediums of exchange will not help any trade to take place between them and so will fail to fulfil this essential function of money.

THE FORMS OF MONEY

As has been illustrated already, money comes in many different forms such as given weights of precious metals that have since evolved into coins and notes. The former were originally standardised units of precious metals. The latter were originally promises to pay a given weight of such metal. Coins and notes now are tokens with no intrinsic value but, interestingly, they have assumed the mythical property of "real money" like gold since today what mostly changes hands in trade is not cash but computer orders or pieces of paper and plastic (cheques or credit cards) that represent cash. You know that if shopkeepers or traders won't accept *your* promise to pay then they will accept cash (someone else's…). The transaction is the same, the form of money has changed. In fact the form of money changes all the time – according to what society you are dealing in and what it best recognises and accepts. Money, like beauty, is in the eye of the beholder.

COMMERCIAL BANKING

One unit of currency is as good as another. If I borrow 100 units from you and repay it later it makes no difference if some of the notes are a bit dog-eared. Assuming no inflation, the value is unchanged. Unlike if I use your horse to plough my field and it comes back exhausted, in the case of money there is no deterioration in its worth. Why pay interest on a loan, therefore?

Exactly this reasoning used to operate up until the Middle Ages. To charge interest, to early traders and to many even today, is to commit the sin of usury.

This argument, while understandable, is at odds with modern economics. It ignores opportunity cost. Money is LIQUID CAPITAL – it is capable of productive employment just like any other capital good – and if it can be invested in some profitable enterprise then I lose out if I loan that opportunity to you for free.

(Modern Islamic banks are prohibited from lending money at interest so they must instead find other ways to charge for their services. One common solution is to become part owners, not creditors, of an enterprise that they finance and so be entitled to a share in any profits. That is, they thus receive DIVIDENDS on funds invested, not interest on a loan.)

Commercial banking for profit in the Christian world first started in the northern Italian states of Lombardy and Florence, where certain families with wealth at their disposal held court for potential entrepreneurs. People sat at benches (Italian *bancos*) to arrange the loaning of monies and shrewd deals soon led to increases in investment, production, trade and economic growth of all parties. Northern Italy therefore prospered – fuelling the Renaissance, early advances in science and the progress of European civilisation.

What banking then and now demonstrates is that by mobilising idle funds – lending on the savings of some for the use of others – society gains by employing all its resources. As demonstrated in the previous chapter, capital that just accumulates in unproductive bank vaults acts as a leakage from the society's circular flow of incomes and employment. The most important function of any banking system is thus to circulate these funds from savers to investors and thus stimulate increased production and exchange (see Box 6.3). For this reason all banks and money lenders are known in aggregate as FINANCIAL INTERMEDIARIES – mediating between those who have funds surplus to their needs and those who have insufficient.

BOX 6.3 SAVINGS AND BANKING FOR THE POOR

In the developed world, national savings rates may be relatively high and the great bulk of these funds flow into formal financial institutions. In poorer countries, not only will the percentage of national income saved be lower (see Figure 5.4) but also much saving will not find its way into the formal banking sector at all.

Much economic activity in the developing world takes place in the INFORMAL SECTOR – small-scale enterprise, unlicensed, unrecognised and operating for the most part beyond the protection of the law. This sector includes small farmers, artisans, independent traders and a whole host of self-employed who operate in rural and urban settings with whatever funds they can command. There is no formal banking system that can cater for such small-scale operations – the administration and information costs of serving such a clientele are prohibitive, given the small turnovers involved. The aggregate money flows can nonetheless be great in total – representing between a third and a half of national income in some cases. But as a result of such fragmented and missing financial markets in poor countries, much of the funds that circulate in the informal sector never flow through proper banks and are therefore not recycled as seed investment for the small businesses that need it most.

If people in such communities want to raise capital they typically go to informal moneylenders or pawnbrokers. The rates of interest on loans that such agents charge can be punitive – 50 per cent or more – which represents a formidable disincentive to potential investment. How can this problem be avoided? Financing development is so essential, yet how can poor communities ever raise capital and fund economic growth if the little savings they do make are not recycled?

One encouraging development is illustrated by the Grameen Bank, or Village bank, in Bangladesh. This is a MICRO-CREDIT scheme that its founder, Muhammad Yunus, set up in 1983 on the principle that a small amount of money would be loaned out to a nominated individual in a group of rural poor. No formal COLLATERAL is required but all members of the group sign up as witnesses to the deal and have an incentive to ensure the individual sticks to the terms of the agreement and repays on time since others then may become eligible for future loans. This banking strategy turned out to be incredibly successful. Repayment rates of 98 per cent were far better than those achieved in the regular commercial bank sector.

Yunus reported (2003) that more than half a million houses have been built with loans from the Grameen Bank. Five per cent of borrowers come out of poverty each year. Housing conditions, nutrition, health and education have all improved. As a result, this initiative has been promoted by the World Bank and now nearly 100 countries have introduced Grameen-type micro-credit programmes. By building on the one asset that poor people do have – community spirit – there is hope that this ingenious innovation can liberate the lives of millions from poverty.

THE CREATION OF MONEY

Financiers from Italy set up in London (in Lombard Street!) and oversaw the next stage in the development of banking. By issuing paper promises to return your gold to you whenever you so demand, banks change the form of money that is used in everyday transactions. Instead of gold exchanging hands in trade, promissory notes do. The gold never leaves the bank, therefore – it is just transferred from one person's account to another's. (Note, with several competing banks it may be that after thousands of exchanges at the end of a given trading period, the customers of bank A may owe more to the customers of bank B than vice versa. This net sum is thus transferred – there is no need to transfer gold from one bank to another on each and every transaction.)

As the form of money circulating in the economy changes from gold to paper this leaves banks with stockpiles of gold that are, in effect, idle. This is too good an opportunity to miss! Consider that there will always be a certain percentage of customers who will return to their bank, cash in their promissory notes and claim their gold. But so long as confidence in banks is maintained, relatively few will do this. (After all, it is safer to hold your money in the bank than to store it under your mattress at home.)

Suppose on an average day only 5 per cent of paper promises are ever cashed in. This means that 95 per cent of banks' gold holdings are performing no economic purpose. Why not create more paper promises therefore? People are always coming into banks asking for loans. If they can be given bank notes then the money supply can be greatly expanded and more investment, production and trade financed. Providing that banks are responsible and fund genuine enterprise that increases the flow of goods and services in the economy then the growth in money circulating will be matched by an increase in outputs. Inflation will not result.

In the above example, a prudent bank might work on keeping a safe ratio of 10 per cent gold in reserve. If it has 100 units of gold in its vaults this means it can safely create up to 1000 units of banknotes. Money creation is thus ten times the gold supply! You should see that a more nervous, less confident banking system would need to keep a higher RESERVE ASSETS RATIO and thus be able to create less money. A more financially sophisticated, trusting society may have a much smaller reserve and thus be able to create much more money.

The practice of modern FRACTIONAL RESERVE BANKING follows from this observation. The difference today is that, again, the form of money has changed. Now it is cash that banks hold in reserve and it is the issuing of credit, exchanged by electronic orders, cheques, or plastic cards, that forms the bulk of the money supply.

What exchanges as money and thus becomes prudent to practice in banking depends entirely on what society is willing to accept. Over time, as a financial community gains a reputation for responsibility and caution, so the smaller the reserve asset ratio it can retain and thus the higher the MONEY MULTIPLIER it can employ. At the same time, however, banks have learnt the hard way when they have got it wrong – when, for example, they have issued too much credit and kept insufficient capital in reserve. If ever customers sense that a bank has made more promises than it can keep then there follows an inevitable run on the bank – everybody rushing to try and cash in their accounts and, of course, in such circumstances very few can ever be saved.

In the UK at the turn of the millennium, total money circulating in the economy was 27 times official reserves, implying a reserve to assets ratio of 1 to 27 or 3.7 per cent. In the infamous "credit crunch" of 2008, on the other hand, for a short time in September, banks were unwilling to lend anything to anyone: a money multiplier of zero!

CENTRAL BANKS AND THE MONEY SUPPLY

What determines the supply of money in any economy? This is the business of private, profit-making, commercial banks (theoretically controlled by central banks) and what they produce is the money supply that circulates between us.

Commercial bank collapses are still relatively rare these days (though financial panics, as we know, are not). Central banks – such as the US Federal Reserve, the Bank of England, The European Central Bank – have grown up in all modern economies to regulate the practices of private, commercial banks and moneylenders and in some countries they still insist on a statutory minimum reserve assets ratio to try and prevent over-lending. In fact central banks will offer to bail out reputable financial institutions if ever they are caught short of money. This is known as acting as the LENDER OF LAST RESORT.

Central banks control the issue of cash that forms the MONETARY BASE of society (Box 6.4). They also hold accounts of all recognised financial intermediaries so that, for example, if bank A needs to transfer money to bank B (as explained earlier) the easiest form of so doing is to adjust their respective accounts in the country's central bank.

In performing all these functions, the central bank at the heart of a financial system is thus in a position to control, or rather to *attempt* to control, the national money supply. The mechanisms employed all operate on changing the banking system's reserve assets and, thereby, having a multiplied impact on the economy's total money supply. (With a money multiplier of ten times reserves, for example, if the central bank can engineer a reduction in commercial bank reserve holdings of, say, 12 million units then the economy's money supply will fall by 120 million.)

BOX 6.4 MEASURES OF MONEY

In a society where gold has become demonetised, cash now represents the base which supports a country's total money supply. The amount of cash circulating in an economy can be measured by that quantity which is changing hands in everyday trades, plus that which is held in commercial banks' tills, plus that which is held in these banks' balances at the Central Bank. The sum of this form of money is denoted by *Mo*.

As already explained, much money that finances everyday transactions comes in the form of orders to banks that serve to transfer payments from one person's bank account to another. Actually, this means that it is the BANK DEPOSITS (numbers registered on computer records) that rest in people's accounts that really represent money – different types of paper, cheques or plastic only serve to transfer these funds and these tokens will not be accepted if clients doubt that there are insufficient deposits in the bank to back them up. Monies which you deposit in your bank's current account are called SIGHT DEPOSITS (they are withdrawable "on sight"). Adding commercial bank sight deposits to Mo gives a wider definition of money, which is $M1$.

A complication is added in that many non-bank financial intermediaries now hold sight deposits. For example, building societies used only to deal in long-term loans to finance house buying. With financial deregulation – the removal of restrictions on financial market places referred to in the last chapter – there is now no longer strict specialisation and separation of banks from building societies, there is thus little to distinguish one from the other. $M2$ is the measure of cash plus sight deposits of *all* financial intermediaries that serve the public.

$M2$ totals all sight deposits but does not include people's savings accounts, which normally require a period of notification before withdrawals or transfers can be made. Such accounts are called TIME DEPOSITS and, almost by definition, they are not quite so liquid as sight deposits. Nonetheless individuals and companies do use their savings to pay for transactions on occasions and including these time deposits in the measure of money supply gives us $M3$.

Add to this what we can call wholesale deposits – large accounts managed by businesses rather than by members of the public – and this gives us the widest definition of the money supply, $M4$.

In reality, it is almost impossible to distinguish between some very short-time deposits and sight deposits (indeed, people use some savings account cards to back consumer purchases). Nor is it easy to draw the line between *retail* bank deposits and *wholesale* bank deposits. It is moreover impossible to distinguish between what were once traditional commercial banks and now other financial intermediaries which provide a range of services to all sorts of customers. Definitions $M1$, $M2$ and $M3$ become meaningless, therefore. We are left with only two real measures: narrow money Mo (cash) and broad money $M4$ (all liquid, exchangeable assets).

1   Changing Reserve Requirements

The central bank (hereafter known as the Bank) is the fulcrum of a country's banking system and can insist on a minimum reserve assets ratio that all financial intermediaries must observe. Suppose however the Bank wishes to boost consumer spending to stave off recession. If the Bank decreases this ratio then, with their existing reserves, all intermediaries can immediately issue more loans and thereby increase the money supply (see Box 6.5). The money multiplier increases. Conversely, if the Bank increases the ratio, the money multiplier must fall, loans must be called in and the money supply must contract.

BOX 6.5 THE MONEY MULTIPLIER: AN EXAMPLE

Suppose financial intermediaries hold one dollar in reserve for every eight loaned out. That represents a reserve assets ratio of 12.5 per cent. If they now change to a ratio of 10 per cent, one dollar in reserve can support ten dollars in circulation. That is, banks can now loan out an extra two dollars for every one they hold in reserve. More customers can be given more money and encouraged to go spend it.

---

2   Open Market Operations

Rather than enforcing a change in legal requirements, a more indirect (and more popular) measure to employ is what is known as OPEN MARKET OPERATIONS. The Bank in its every day dealings goes into open money markets and lends money to some institutions and borrows from others. The FINANCIAL INSTRUMENTS it uses to do this are variously called bonds, bills, or securities – all specific promises to pay sums of money over different time periods. Now if the Bank *buys* a bond from some private agent it is in effect exchanging cash in return for a legally binding promise of future payment. The agent selling thus receives cash which that institution can now place in its own commercial bank account.

By this measure, commercial bank reserves of cash increase and so they can increase the money supply by a multiplied amount.

Conversely, if over a period of time the Bank sells more private sector bonds and bills than it buys then clearly there will be a drain on the private sector's cash reserve into the central coffers. The money supply must therefore be reduced by a multiple of the loss in reserves.

QUANTITATIVE EASING (QE) is a modern variant of open market operations. It has been used in the UK and the USA since the 2007/2008 financial crisis to try and stimulate an increase in bank lending and the money supply. QE differs from traditional open market operations in that the central bank buys generally long-term government bonds and other financial instruments *directly* from commercial banks, insurance companies, pension funds and the like. It does not go through the money markets and by trading in long-term assets it directly increases intermediaries' cash reserves (and their ability thus to increase loans) while simultaneously bidding up the price of those assets they purchase and holding down long-term interest rates.

3 The Discount Rate

A third measure that might be used to exercise monetary control is for the Bank to change its discount rate, or the interest rate it charges on its own short-term loans.

The discount rate is the cost to the commercial banks of borrowing at last resort from the central bank. If this cost increases then commercial banks will correspondingly charge more in issuing their own loans.

In addition, with no legally enforced reserve ratio to observe nowadays, private bankers have no wish to keep cash reserves above the lowest practicable levels since stockpiling cash earns them no interest – better to loan it out even for short periods if this can earn them something. Reserves can thus be kept at a bare minimum to meet customer demand.

If the Bank looks like raising its discount rate, however, financial intermediaries have an incentive to keep more cash in their vaults – to avoid having to pay higher than market rates for last resort loans. (Note: if everyone scrambles to increase cash reserves, demand shifts to push up the market price anyway!) Either way, as cash reserves rise, the money supply is reduced by a multiplied amount. Fewer loans can be issued.

THE DEMAND FOR MONEY

The money supply, in theory at least, can be adjusted as described above by the institutions of a country's banking system. What determines the demand for money?

It depends on the alternatives. People may hold their wealth in the form of non-interest-earning money or in the form of some income–earning asset (e.g. bonds, shares, fine art or property). For this reason, Keynes called the demand for money – a perfectly liquid asset, as opposed to demand for other, less liquid assets – LIQUIDITY PREFERENCE.

For simplicity, we can assume like Keynes that the best alternative to accumulating wealth in the form of money is holding it in risk-less, interest-earning assets such as government bonds. (Such a legally binding promise from the government to pay a fixed sum of interest over a stated period frequently comes in the form of a fancy, gilt-edged document. It is a no-risk, 100 per cent secure form in which to hold wealth, unlike promises from some other parties. See junk bonds, later.) Thus the opportunity cost of holding money is the interest forgone in not holding bonds. The higher the interest rate, therefore, the greater the cost of holding money and the lower will be the demand for it. Society's demand for money can thus be illustrated by a normal demand curve where the rate of interest is the price of money (Figure 6.1).

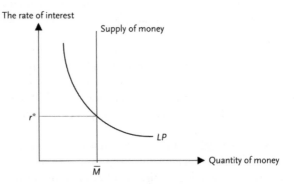

Figure 6.1 Liquidity preference and the market rate of interest. The demand for money is illustrated by the liquidity preference curve *LP*. The supply of money *M* is given by the institutions of the banking system. The equilibrium market rate of interest $r^\star$ is thus determined by the interaction of the supply and demand for liquidity.

There are, of course, benefits in holding money. Keynes identified the transactions motive and the precautionary motive, amongst others:

THE TRANSACTIONS MOTIVE

People demand money for its use in conducting trade or transactions. We all need money to finance our spending over each month though most of us also divert some monthly income into savings or investments such as pension funds. How much money I demand for financing transactions depends on the general level of prices and the frequency at which I am paid. If all prices doubled, for example, I would need to double the size of my money balances. Similarly if I were paid on a weekly basis, rather than a monthly basis, I would need to hold smaller money balances. Lastly, my transactions demand would increase if my real income increased – I would want to spend more money, more often and so would therefore keep larger money balances.

THE PRECAUTIONARY MOTIVE

People tend to keep a small, stable fraction of their income in money form so as to meet unexpected contingencies. We can all expect something unexpected on which we may need to spend some money – an unanticipated celebration or a need to drown our sorrows. The demand for money for this precautionary motive also tends to be affected by the size of real incomes.

What these motives imply is that as real incomes increase so the demand curve for money illustrated above shifts forward (just like any other demand curve, check Chapter 3), thus causing an increase in the market price of money if supplies stay constant. Likewise, a fall in incomes leads to a shift back in demand and falling interest rates.

A rise in real income is not the only reason why societies might hold more money balances over time. Since financial deregulation swept the Western world in the 1980s there has been much greater competition between banks and all other financial intermediaries, both nationally and internationally. One result of this is that many institutions now offer all sorts of temptations to consumers to open bank accounts. Interest is offered on many sight deposits as well as time deposits and overall the real cost of holding money has decreased significantly over the last 20 years. The incentive to hold bonds and other alternatives to money is correspondingly less (Box 6.6).

BOX 6.6 SPECULATIVE DEMAND, BOND PRICES AND THE RATE OF INTEREST

Financial markets allow traders to loan or borrow money over a variety of time periods. For example, you may decide to purchase a bond promising £100 in one year's time – in which case you are in effect loaning out money for a year. What price would you pay for this bond? If you offer £95 then you have accepted a rate of interest of approximately 5 per cent. If the seller will accept nothing less than 98 then the price of bonds has risen and the rate of interest has fallen. (Thus the price of bonds and the rate of interest are conversely related.)

For all financial assets, key influences are the going market rate of interest, the degree of risk involved in the particular asset being traded and the predicted rate of inflation. If the rate on risk-less government bonds (where there is no chance the government will default) is 5 per cent and the rate of inflation is 2 per cent then the REAL RATE OF INTEREST is in effect 3 per cent. (Getting back 5 per cent when inflation has devalued the currency by 2 per cent means you only really earn an extra 3 per cent over the year.) Buying a JUNK BOND from a not so well-known trader, you might thus insist on a real rate of 6 per cent or more, depending on your assessment of the risk involved. That is, a NOMINAL RATE (including inflation) of over 8 per cent.

A one-year security is not necessarily an illiquid asset. You don't have to wait for 12 months to get your money back if you change your mind after you have bought it. You can simply sell it tomorrow for whatever price the market values it for. Dealers buy and sell assets of varying dates of maturity like this all the time since it allows a finance house to possess a portfolio of holdings of differing liquidity. (Generally, the more liquid the loan the lower the risk but the lower the rate of interest it earns.)

What happens if you think that the price of bonds (or any other asset you hold in place of cash) will fall in the future, and market rates of interest rise? If you believe that next Thursday the central bank will put interest rates up you will sell bonds now – and thus demand more money today – rather than wait for prices to fall. Going to the markets to sell bonds/demand money for this reason is to express the SPECULATIVE MOTIVE in demand.

MONETARY POLICY WITH GLOBAL MARKETS

The central bank sells and then buys back, or "repossesses", bonds and gilt-edged securities before their maturity dates in order to supply the markets with assets of varying liquidity. The Bank can thus use these instruments either in open market operations to try and influence money supplies or to dictate a given discount or repossession ("repo") rate. However, central banks in fully deregulated and global money markets have really been found wanting in their attempts to control how financial markets operate. The Credit Crunch and Great Recession can be seen not so much as evidence of central authorities being too lax in controlling credit – thus leading to a boom and bust – but more as an inability both (a) to see what was going on in the boom, and (b) to implement remedies in the bust.

Removing capital restrictions between nations allows for rapid migrations of money in and out, across national borders. This produces both good and bad effects. Many economists support the policy of financial deregulation in money markets since greater competition between banks – as with all industry – increases efficiency and brings prices down for the consumer. Opening frontiers to allow foreign banks to compete is just the extension of this principle.

The City of London is one of the world's major financial centres and the process of deregulation started there back in 1979. The operation of free enterprise in finance, however, once started built up an unstoppable momentum. Breakthroughs in technology helped since it became possible to move money costlessly from one centre to another across the world with just the push of a few buttons. Most money, after all, has no physical form – it is just a record on a computer screen.

Now if banks in one centre can buy and sell money with little government penalty or tax then clearly banks in other centres subject to stricter controls will lose custom and profits. Finance houses in such a situation have usually found ways round central controls since it is in their interest to do so – the end result is that deregulation quickly catches on everywhere.

The problem for central banks is that they must inevitably lose control of their domestic money supplies. Remember that if a commercial bank's reserve assets can be reduced by the central authorities then it must call in its loans, reduce its money supply, by a multiplied amount. But if a bank loses cash reserves to the central bank and then *can compensate for this loss by gaining other liquid assets from alternative sources* (overseas if necessary) it no longer has to worry about supporting its existing pattern of long-term loans. Money supplies need not contract. Moreover *if all sorts of financial intermediaries can now enter the industry* and buy and sell money, the reserves of which institutions does the Bank try to control? Evidence of the authorities' limitations were cruelly exposed in the spiralling growth of innovative types of credit (CDOs) and all sorts of new financial operators (Special Purpose Vehicles or SPVs) that contributed to the speculative boom that preceded the US sub-prime mortgage crisis analysed in Chapter 1.

For these two reasons, in a global financial environment, most countries' central banks cannot fine-tune their domestic money supplies. If a central bank can no longer monopolise the supply of money in its own backyard, however, it can still try to affect the money markets by changing its own discount rate. Cutting prices will usually stimulate demand; raising rates will stifle it.

THE TRANSMISSION MECHANISM

The transmission mechanism describes how a change in the central bank discount rate impacts on an entire economy via a host of different variables.

(This is particularly so if the change is unexpected. Since speculation is rife in financial markets, the decision of a forthcoming meeting of the central bank committee may have already been built into the pricing of marketable assets. Suppose you think the Bank's rate will come down next week and prompt bond prices to rise from 95 to 98 as explained in Box 6.6. If you are selling bonds today, you will hold out for 98 – bringing forward the fall in the market rate of interest. Expectations affect everything in modern economies. If, of course, the Bank is reducing its discount rate to counter a prevailing mood of depression then key to the markets' reactions will be how the Bank's actions are interpreted. Is it too little, too late? A signal of official desperation? Cutting official rates to zero to counter the credit crunch did not – in the short term – have any impact on market rates of interest and the willingness of banks to lend to one another or to viable businesses desperate for credit. If, however, reducing the Bank's rate is, in the longer term, an essential and necessary corrective measure – perhaps combined with other expansionary policies – it will eventually come to be recognised as a stimulus to trade and help to counter the markets' gloom.)

A fall in the discount rate will normally be followed by a fall in most other rates of interest in the market place since, as earlier explained, rates charged on commercial bank loans are usually based on this central bank rate. A general fall in interest rates will likely then induce a boom in asset prices – from speculative paper to property prices. For example, mortgages will be cheaper and thus more demand for houses will push their prices up as was explained in Chapter 3.

Similarly, with credit more easily available – providing manufacturing industry can quickly expand production or where they retain large stockpiles – there will be increased sales of consumer durables. People will buy more cars, computers and household goods.

With regard to external trade, all other things being equal, a fall in market rates will bring a reduction in foreign monies entering the economy to be placed in interest-bearing accounts in domestic banks. Less demand for the currency therefore will cause a fall in the exchange rate. (This may or may not affect the earnings from export sales or spending on imports, depending on how price-elastic the respective demands are. The country's balance of payments may thus be affected – see Chapter 7.)

As all these effects cascade through the economy the level of aggregate demand will rise over time. Particularly influential will be the impact on investment. Cheaper bank borrowing means it is less costly to raise funds to invest but an even greater stimulus occurs if business expectations are shifted. If the change in discount rate secures a more optimistic business outlook then investment will rise and a multiplied increase in national income may result (see Chapter 5): employment will rise and, providing the economy has the capacity to expand, output and incomes will increase and inflation will not result.

EXCHANGE RATES

With global financial markets, note that no one country can implement domestic monetary changes without considering external influences. If a nation places no restriction on money entering or leaving its shores then it must take the consequences. In particular, a country cannot fix its exchange rate with other world currencies, deregulate its financial markets and hope to pursue an independent monetary policy. This is known as the "impossible triangle".

As explained above, reducing domestic interest rates to stimulate domestic demand (assuming no other changes) will result in a DEPRECIATION of the exchange rate. A country can only keep a fixed price of its currency on the FOREIGN EXCHANGE MARKETS if it imposes strict capital controls – that is, prevents dealers from buying and selling the currency in the quantities they desire.

Fixing exchange rates of the domestic coinage to major world currencies such as the US dollar or the euro (see the gold standard, earlier) is something that many countries' governments have desired – now as in the past – as a means of lending stability to their own financial systems.

Especially true with a newly introduced currency that people may not yet have confidence with, if the new paper carries a fixed value in terms of a trusted external currency then dealers are more likely to accept it.

Even with well-recognised currencies, fixed exchange rates generally help trade (see Box 6.7). For example, if you are planning a foreign holiday the last thing you want is continually changing foreign prices – which is exactly what would happen if the exchange rate is floating, not fixed. Whether it is trying to arrange a holiday or to secure a vital business contract, varying prices impose a cost – and thus a disincentive – on trade. Such an argument is particularly relevant if you are in a small country that deals regularly with a big neighbour. With so much business at stake, better to fix the exchange rate so everyone knows the costs involved.

BOX 6.7 DISCIPLINE IN INTERNATIONAL TRADE

A fixed exchange rate imposes discipline on central banks and governments.

Consider the following scenario: if a country is losing out in trade – such that export revenues are insufficient to cover import spending – then there are more domestic importers selling the currency than foreigners wanting to buy it. The price or exchange rate of this currency will be expected to fall in a free market or, in a system of fixed exchange rates, a country's central bank must sell off its gold or foreign currency reserves to cover the difference and thus maintain the fixed rate. No central bank can afford to do this for very long. What a fixed regime ensures therefore is that the central authorities must do something to address the root of the problem: to prevent the country from living beyond its means and buying more in international trade than it is prepared to sell. (This generally means cutting back on domestic demand and attempting to switch resources to promote export production. It generally implies consuming less – a policy that bankers and politicians like to recommend for others...)

The gold standard, when it operated for all trading counties at the beginning of the twentieth century, imposed just this discipline on world economic affairs and some observers with long memories still hark back to these days and the certainties that this system embodied.

THE EURO

Fixing exchange rates between trade partners was an essential phase in the creation of a common currency – the euro – which many wanted to enhance a closer European Union. The eventful track record of establishing this unit of exchange between such very different countries and cultures has excited much controversy, however – from even before euro notes and coins entered circulation on 1 January 2002.

First, joining a common, single currency implies participating countries must sacrifice their own, independent monetary policies to a common, single, supranational authority – in the case of the euro, to the policy decided by the European Central Bank head-quartered in Frankfurt. The Bank's interest rate decided there, and its policy to stimulate or restrict money supplies, is designed to fit the eurozone as a whole but this may not always be entirely com-patible with the specific interests of one or more of the contributory countries to the common currency. (For example, in the European Exchange Rate Mechanism – the fixed exchange rate forerunner to the euro – Britain, under speculative attack in 1992, opted to leave the system rather than hoist up interest rates in order to remain pegged to a common currency. That experience – opting to retain their own monetary policy and the better growth record it enjoyed as a result – contributed to the UK's subsequent decision to remain out of the establishment of the euro. See Box 6.8.)

In addition to countries of the union losing their sovereignty over monetary policy, each independent government's fiscal policy is constrained also. If one government's budget goes into significant deficit and it borrows from international money markets to cover the difference, other member governments of the union will not sit idly by if the reputation of their common currency begins to be questioned. The EU thus insists that a member country's annual fiscal deficit must not exceed 3 per cent of its GDP and its accumulated government debt to GDP ratio should not exceed 60 per cent. However, the first of these criteria is contrary to the Keynesian recommendation that governments should run deficits to inject money into the circular flow if a country experiences a severe recession (see previous chapter). The second criteria ignores the reality that seven of the eurozone countries possessed debt ratios well over the required minimum in the run-up to its establishment *(Debt-to-GDP ratios in 1999 were: for Austria, 65.3 per cent; Belgium, 111.7 per cent; Cyprus, 155.8 per cent; Finland, 66.4 per cent; France, 62.2 per cent; Greece, 100.9 per cent and Italy, 123.8 per cent)* and – see

Chapter 1 – the position of a number has worsened in the sovereign debt crisis since. Trying to enforce adherence to these criteria has meant that a number of governments have been persuaded to implement austerity programmes: cutting back spending and borrowing and, in so doing, only prolonging the Great Recession for their people.

The problem for countries determined to stick with a common currency (same as it is for those in a fixed exchange rate system) is that DEVALUATION and maintaining an independent economic policy is not an option. True, devaluation is a medicine that can be over-used and abused and governments thus may never acquire fiscal discipline – forever increasing spending, borrowing, inflating, devaluing and debasing their currencies. But if a country is suffering from a fundamental disequilibrium in its economic affairs and severe unemployment for many (see Figure 1.2) then a one-off realignment of its currency is better than years and years of continuing recession. The evidence from, first, the interwar years of the Great Depression and, second, the UK's experience outside the euro shows that independent monetary policies have their advantages when global economic circumstances turn nasty (see Box 6.8).

BOX 6.8 SPOT THE COUNTRIES NOT TIED TO A FIXED EXCHANGE RATE OR COMMON CURRENCY

Figure 6.2 compares the size of the respective countries' economies over the 1930s, related to base year in 1913. In the first group of countries (Belgium to the USA) all stayed fixed to the gold standard and their economies either stagnated or declined between 1929 and 1938.

The second group of countries (Norway to Sweden) came off the gold standard in 1931 and maintained floating currencies and independent economic policies. All experienced positive economic growth between 1929 and 1938.

In Figure 6.3, the growth rates of the four biggest economies of the EU are compared between 1994 and the start of the financial crisis and Great Recession in 2007. Of

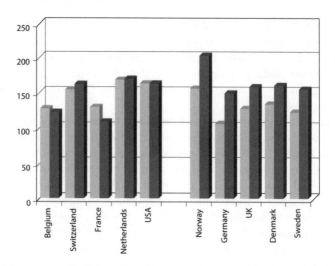

Figure 6.2 Interwar growth: 1929 compared to 1938 (1913 = 100). (Source: Angus Maddison, *Economic Growth in the West*, Allen & Unwin, 1964.)

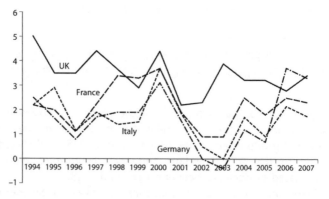

Figure 6.3 Comparative percentage growth rates, 1994–2007. (Source: World Bank.)

these four, only the UK remained out of the fixed Exchange Rate Mechanism and then the common euro. The growth rate of the UK lies consistently above the average of the other three.

INTERNATIONAL CRISES

Trying to maintain fixed exchange rates at times when inter-connected global markets question the value of the currency concerned has been a contributing factor in many modern financial crashes. The East Asian currency crisis in 1997, Russia 1998 and Argentina 2001 all illustrate this characteristic – where incurring excessive debts causes foreign creditors to lose their nerve and start selling the currency in question. Official government statements that all international debts will be honoured are rarely believed in these circumstances. Once-fixed exchange rates can be forced apart. Local banks, businesses and people then find they have to pay enormously increased amounts of their devalued domestic currency to pay off debts incurred in dollars, euros or pounds.

Note, however, that financial crises are not *caused* by fixed exchange rates, nor even by liberalised money markets. Rather, they are all related to unsustainable financial practises: excessive borrowing, speculative innovation and the overconfident belief that "things are different this time" and "we know better now" than in the past. The global financial crash of 2008, for example, was not linked to any particular fixed exchange rate … but it did exhibit these other classic features of financial crises and getting out of the Great Recession has been tougher for those tied to the euro.

Overconfidence can occur for different reasons. A developing country which perhaps has a change of government and pegs its currency to the mighty dollar, removes restrictions on the international movement of money and pursues prudent financial polices familiar to Western bankers may become very attractive to overseas investors. Especially if it is resource rich, needful of capital and with fledgling industry and commerce welcoming to interested outsiders.

Alternatively, a wealthy developed nation with a history of financial strength may get carried away with its technological wizardry, its ability to turn dreams into gold and its resourcefulness at outmanoeuvring official regulators.

Local bankers quick on their feet can now call on far greater supplies of finance if financial markets are open, the markets are booming and foreign creditors are confident about profitable opportunities. And it is easy to make money when everyone else is getting in on the act – entrepreneurs find that in setting up a new company in boom times, everybody wants a share and prices on the bonds and securities they issue keep rising. Does it matter that projected future profits are based on scarce or over-optimistic data? If confidence holds, not really. Those people rushing in to get rich quick will not worry if the paper they hold is overpriced – so long as they are confident that they can sell it later for even higher prices. The market succumbs to feverish buying ... until sometime, somehow, somebody blows the whistle.

All crashes occur when assets become overvalued in a speculative bubble. The readjustment that is inevitable and which everyone knows is coming sooner or later, typically occurs in one traumatic collapse rather than in a gentle and less painful slowdown over time. Why? Because no one wants to hold on to their stocks if prices are falling. Once started, fear of loss terrifies everyone into panic selling.

Blaming the herd instinct, collective myopia and capitalist greed getting the better of wisdom is necessary to describe the problem but not sufficient to fully explain it. The reality is that the prices of speculative assets repeatedly diverge from their underlying values; as we have seen, financial intermediaries can *provoke* rather than contain binge buying; unrestricted international money flows add to the pressure and, when sentiments change, sudden price readjustment can be catastrophic. Immature financial sectors in developing countries can perhaps be forgiven, but when international markets succumb to panic it is not just a few local businesses that go under. Seemingly secure paper proves to be worthless, banks collapse, multinational corporations fail and no exchange rate can hold out against vast and rapid speculative money flows across borders as everyone rushes to sell one currency and buy another. Whole countries can suffer.

The history of any one financial crisis will always illustrate special factors that lead people to think that this time, this place, things will be different. In the case of Japan and other East Asian economies like Thailand, South Korea, and Indonesia they had been amongst the fastest growing economies in the world for the last half of the twentieth century and international banks everywhere were happy to lend them money. The fact that this was fuelling rapid property price rises was nothing special – owning real estate in such a dynamic quarter of the globe seemed a good investment. But if the backing or collateral on too many bad loans is unproductive property and banks all try at the same time to cash in that property to get their money back, then these prices collapse. Confidence is shaken. Many local intermediaries thought at first to be rock solid can be exposed as issuing too many risky loans to undeserving cronies. Then there is panic and wild selling. Debts cannot be paid, businesses and banks go bust. Does this sound familiar? The fact that much the same scenario was played out *al fortissimo* only ten years later in the US sub-prime mortgage crash shows just how little financial markets learn (see Box 6.9).

The descent into the Great Recession was rapid – as explained in Chapter 1 – and the route out is proving to be difficult, showing some serious weaknesses in the structure of financial markets; the limited ability of central authorities to regulate and safeguard them, and – for the eurozone – the incompatibility of establishing a common currency without a common polity.

It has already been mentioned that in liberalised markets, central banks have lost control of domestic money supplies. The explosive growth of credit, created by "grey" institutions and forms of money outside the view and reach of the authorities, led to the subsequent global boom and bust … but exactly the opposite problem – how to stimulate lending in a recession when incomes have fallen, unemployment has risen and trust and trade has evaporated – also illustrates the impotence of the supposed guardians of our financial systems.

Reducing central bank interest rates to zero in the USA and Europe did not at first stimulate any borrowing and investment since expectations were so pessimistic. Further, quantitative easing and making available money almost free to the financial intermediaries does not guarantee they will lend it on to others. It is the equivalent of stating: "here – take these assets on which you can create a multiplied expansion of the money supply!" But the private banking sector has been incredibly reluctant, particularly in Europe, to release credit to others. Bailing out the debts of some of the basket-case banks and even nationalising them could not stimulate an increase in lending. Why? How could the collapse in aggregate demand ever be reversed?

The fact is that with so many unperforming assets on their books – which previously had been regarded as secure – banks reserve assets had shrunk well below the safety line. They had to rebuild their reserve base to secure levels before they would risk any further creation of credit. Badly shaken by the credit crunch and blamed by all and sundry on every side, banks have been (belatedly!) extremely cautious before they would issue any loans. But that was the inevitable consequence of the free market paradigm. If governments and central banks deregulate and liberalise markets then they have taken the policy stance to leave independent operators to make their own decisions. As a result we are all vulnerable to the "animal spirits" that pervade financial markets.

BOX 6.9 THE EFFICIENT MARKET HYPOTHESIS, BEHAVIOURAL ECONOMICS AND BURST BUBBLES

Market forms of economic organisation are alleged to be more efficient than alternatives that rely upon traditional or government decision-making (see Chapter 2). Market prices evolve to an equilibrium between consumer demand and producer supply and, according to the prices that are so determined, resources are allocated between alternative employments.

Any change in demand or supply will impact on prices and thus signal a redeployment of resources so as to efficiently meet the altered circumstances. So long as prices reflect all available market information, it is argued that there cannot be a more efficient way to allocate society's resources.

The EFFICIENT MARKET HYPOTHESIS (EMH) is specifically related to *the prices of financial assets*. It states that prices reflect all relevant, generally available information. The implication is that you cannot beat the market: if information existed that any one financial asset was under- (or over-) priced then the market would immediately adjust. If a speculative bubble was to form, for example, wise investors would soon spot this and cash in, bringing the price down to its proper level. All profitable opportunities are quickly exploited. An analogy is that you can never find free cash lying around on the floor since if any ever existed, it would already be picked up.

The paradigm of the EMH, the importance of rational expectations as a basis for economic theory and the notion that "you cannot beat the market" carried all before it in the world of academic economics since the 1970s. Financial collapses in poorer countries that have occurred on a regular basis through the 1980s and 1990s can be explained away by reference to undeveloped and inefficient markets. This was not supposed to be possible in the wealthier, developed world. Until 2007, that is. If financial assets cannot depart far from their fundamental values then what explains the housing boom and bust and worldwide credit crunch analysed in Chapter 1? A new/old paradigm is called for.

According to new research on BEHAVIOURAL ECONOMICS, people are not always motivated by pure economic interests and do not base their decision-making on rational expectations of the future. Their decisions are influenced by people around them; by feelings of confidence or pessimism. The result is that information is often coloured and imperfectly available. Keynes in an earlier age spoke about "animal spirits".

What happens if confidence inspires bullish spending behaviour? Prices rise. This only reinforces confidence and sparks more spending. The feedback cycle here is a classic cause of speculative bubbles.

Note that if most investors are convinced of the EMH and that markets are never wrong then no one will ever go to the trouble of looking for more penetrating information. Even if some did, if certain wise investors could spot a bubble building, what happens if they are too few to have enough collective clout to cash in and burst the bubble? In such a case, the rational individual *will go along with it* – buying an overpriced asset because he/she (correctly) knows that its price will rise further.

This notion introduces the possibility of asymmetric information and at least two classes of investor: "wise" traders – those that are influenced by all available real information; and "noise" traders – those who cannot discriminate between this and all other noise in the market place. The latter account for asset prices deviating from their equilibrium values; the former are able to dilute this effect but not eliminate it.

Now introduce the notion of "knowns" and "unknowns". If wise investors know of the possibility of exogenous shocks in the near future they can make a stab at calculating probabilities: turning an uncertainty into a calculable risk. This is a known unknown. But by definition, even the wisest investor cannot estimate the probability of an incalculable event such as the US central authorities deciding not to bail out a huge, Wall Street investment bank. This is an unknown unknown. What we can say, however, is that the likelihood of such unknowns occurring *increases the longer the time frame concerned*.

There are two points to be made here: without objective evidence on which to base rational expectations of the longer term then 1. even the wisest investor can be influenced by market sentiment – by general confidence or pessimism; and 2. it becomes rational to concentrate on shorter time horizons.

IMPLICATIONS

Short-term speculative bubbles will occur even in the most efficient markets.

The longer term is uncertain and stock prices may be better explained by movements in mass psychology ("animal spirits") rather than by a rational calculation of probabilities.

UK economist Robert Skidelsky argues the Keynesian view that in a world full of uncertainty, people fall back onto traditional conventions to reassure them. Hence the semi-religious belief in the efficiency of the price mechanism and the herd-like behaviour of financiers. He quotes Keynes: "A sound banker is one who, when ruined, is ruined in a conventional and orthodox way" (*The Times*, December 2009).

We see evidence for this behaviour both in the speculative euphoria leading up to 2007 and in the credit crunch of 2008 when no bank wished to lend. What is the government's response when its monetary policies – trying to regulate the money supply or the central bank interest rate – are rendered powerless by (on the one hand) hyperactive or (on the other) paralysed financial markets? Keynes recommended governments to use counter-cyclical *fiscal* policies: increasing taxes if people are spending too much; increasing public spending if the private sector will not. The eurozone countries, of course, are highly restricted in their use of fiscal policies to address their individual concerns and, despite the economic carnage caused by the 2008 financial crisis and Great Recession, there remain many conservative financiers and politicians on both sides of the Atlantic who still refuse to consider this advice.

SUMMARY

A banking system functions to cycle funds from savers to investors and thus facilitates growth in trade and the circular flow of money, incomes and employment.

Financial intermediaries create credit: commercial banks have every incentive to use idle reserves to back increasing numbers of loans to potential investors.

Providing banks are prudent, the increased money supply generated will be matched by increasing production of goods and services and so inflation will not occur and confidence will hold.

Increased globalisation of financial markets has meant that for most countries controlling the domestic supply of money becomes impossible and most central authorities now opt to control its price by trying to adjust rates of interest.

The demand for money in financial markets comes from the desire to fund transactions, and for precautionary motives, which are directly related to rising incomes. There is also much speculative demand, which is affected by expectations of changing interest rates.

Where monetary flows across frontiers are unrestricted – which they have increasingly become – then exchange rates cannot remain fixed for long. Greater growth and profitability of the international financial industry has resulted – but when memories are overtaken by greed and overconfidence then booms turn to bust and the "science" of economics is betrayed by the all too human behaviour of it participants. Government rescue is then called for.

The euro was created to tie the fortunes of participating European nations together and to enforce a common financial discipline on their monetary affairs. It has certainly done this, but at the social cost of depressing overall growth rates and enforcing austerity and unemployment on a disproportionate number of its citizens.

FURTHER READING

Mishkin, F. S. (2006) *The Next Great Globalisation*, is optimistic about the benefits of free markets and financial liberalisation for developing countries. For an absorbing demonstration that societies never learn, try Reinhart, C. M. and Rogoff, K. S. (2009) *This Time is Different: Eight Centuries of Financial Folly*. Both books are published by Princeton University Press.

For an accessible and more detailed account of the economics of banking, currency union and financial crises, see my own text: *Understanding the World Economy* (2013) published by Routledge.

QUESTIONS

1 The demand for money in the Great Recession fell as quickly as supply as some businesses went broke and, for most others, expectations were pessimistic. Central banks drove their base rates down close to zero to try and induce more business lending, spending and investment. But recovery, especially in Europe, has been sluggish whilst *market* interest rates still differ greatly between some countries. Explain and illustrate each of these developments.

2 Should controls be imposed on international money flows and should the globalisation of finance be restricted?

3 It can be argued that the euro – a common currency between 18 EU countries and possibly more in the future – is unworkable without a common polity. Do you agree?

4. Neoclassical economists and politicians insist that financial discipline and austerity restores confidence and this will in the end promote a return to economic growth for countries caught in the Great Recession. Keynesians argue that this logic is entirely back-to-front: that only policies to stimulate economic growth will restore confidence and this in turn will eventually repair the balance sheets of banks, households and governments. Can you construct both arguments? Which do you believe is most convincing?

7

NATIONAL INCOME, WORLD TRADE AND MULTINATIONAL ENTERPRISE

What did you have for breakfast? Here is a traditional English way to start the day: Florida fruit juice; cereals made from processed US corn; local milk; Demerara sugar; bread made from a mix of local and Canadian wheat; Scottish marmalade made from Seville oranges; New Zealand butter; an English egg with Danish bacon; sea salt and Cayenne pepper and a choice of Colombian coffee or Indian tea.

We daily consume a variety of products that come to us from all over the world – so common an occurrence that we take it for granted. But it is a remarkable feature of modern life nonetheless and it has implications for all parties involved. There may be some people so nationalistic that they wish to purchase only their country's own produce but, first, such people could hardly get out of bed in the morning (bed sheets woven from Indian cotton, mattress of Malaysian foam rubber, and a Japanese alarm clock…) and second, they would be so much poorer if they did indeed achieve this. A country's income and welfare is enhanced by trade, not reduced.

This last point warrants closer examination. The impact of trade on national income; the balance of international payments; the issues of free trade versus protection and the implications for rich and poor countries, domestic and multinational business are therefore the subjects for study in the forthcoming pages.

THE CIRCULAR FLOW OF INCOMES

We analysed the circular flow model in Chapter 5 and noted how domestic incomes fuel consumption, subject to some leakage out of the system by savings and some injection into aggregate spending by investment. We should further note that some fraction of domestic consumption goes on imports – which represent a leakage (they are earnings for foreign suppliers) – and there are additional injections into the circular flow of incomes from domestically produced exports sold overseas.

Equilibrium in the circular flow requires that injections equal leakages. As before, if the sum total of injections are greater (or less) than leakages then national income will grow (decline). In cases of disequilibrium, remember, Keynesian theory recommends that governments adjust their own spending and taxation (fiscal policies) to ensure that aggregate demand equals aggregate incomes, leakages equal injections, at a level of national income consistent with full employment.

We need to add these qualifications to the diagram of the circular flow model in Figure 7.1:

Figure 7.1 The circular flow model with trade and government.

What does this diagram illustrate? That for equilibrium, all income must equal all spending and leakages must equal injections (see Box 7.1).

Note that equilibrium income requires only the equation of these *combined* injections and leakages. It does not necessarily mean imports must equal exports – an imbalance in international payments could be countered by an opposite imbalance in savings and investment or in government finances. An economy in equilibrium at full employment could therefore persist, for example, with a deficit on international trade and a compensating government budget surplus.

BOX 7.1 NATIONAL INCOME ANALYSIS – A FORMAL TREATMENT:

All money incomes (Y) are subject to government taxation (T). The disposable income that remains after tax is spent on consumer goods and services (C), though a fraction of disposable incomes is saved (S). On the other hand, if we consider total expenditure (E), we must note that a part of consumer spending (C) is leaked out of the economy on imports (M), plus we must add spending on investment (capital) goods (I), government spending (G) and foreign spending on domestic goods exported (X).

For equilibrium, national income must equal aggregate expenditure. Thus we get the equation:

$$Y = C + S + T = E = C - M + I + G + X$$

and, by cancelling out C and moving M across, we get:

$$S + T + M = I + G + X$$

or leakages must equal injections.

IMPORT AND EXPORT FUNCTIONS

Leakages from the economy as a result of foreign trade include spending on imports, speculative purchases of foreign assets and also long-term direct investment by domestic firms in overseas markets. Note that consumption of imported goods and services (M) is determined by the level of domestic incomes. Short- and long-run capital

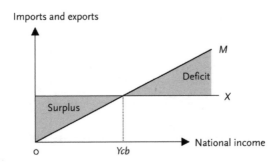

Figure 7.2 Import and export functions.

outflows are affected by expectations of interest rate and exchange rate changes. Assuming the latter two influences are exogenously given, import spending M will tend to rise as domestic incomes rise.

Export earnings (X), speculative inflows of capital and inward foreign direct investment are all injections and are unaffected by domestic incomes. As the opposite of the above, they are more determined by foreign incomes and expectations.

Imports and exports can thus be illustrated as functions of domestic income as illustrated in Figure 7.2. Imports rise with income; exports are exogenously given. The current BALANCE OF PAYMENTS in international trade is in equilibrium at Ycb. For income levels lower than this, exports exceed imports and there is a payments surplus. For income levels above Ycb there is a payments deficit.

A similar analysis can be followed with respect to government spending and taxation. A moment's thought should show you that government direct and indirect tax revenues (based on incomes and consumption) will rise as national income rises. Public sector spending (on education, health, social services, defence, etc.) is determined by other, exogenous factors, however (that is, government policy is liable to change according to political factors outside the realm of economics).

As functions of national income, therefore, savings and investment (see Figure 5.4), imports and exports, taxation and government spending all follow the same outlines. We can sum them altogether as aggregate injections (J) and leakages (L) functions in the diagram in Figure 7.3:

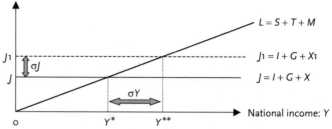

Figure 7.3 Aggregate injections and leakages functions.

Savings, taxation and imports all rise as a function of income, whereas investment, government spending and exports are exogenously determined. Where all leakages equal all injections we know that national income is at equilibrium $Y^{\star}$ with no tendency to grow or decline. An exogenous increase in injections, however (say foreign incomes rise, leading to more export revenues, X to $X1$), will increase injections from J to $J1$. At the level of income $Y^{\star}$ injections are now greater than leakages from the circular flow and so domestic incomes must rise. A new equilibrium will be reached $Y^{\star\star}$ when income has risen sufficiently for the leakages to rise to the new level of injections. (Note, as mentioned above, $Y^{\star}$ or $Y^{\star\star}$ need not be compatible with Ycb in Figure 7.2. The economy can come to rest where there is either an international payments deficit or surplus.)

THE FOREIGN TRADE MULTIPLIER

If exports increase and injections into the circular flow of domestic incomes rise, as just explained, then although the increased export revenues may be limited they may nonetheless induce a much greater increase in national income. That is because the initial injection will be spent on local goods and services which passes over an increase in incomes to others, who in turn increase their spending representing an increase in someone else's incomes and so on. The mechanism by which a rise in foreign trade leads to multiplied income growth at home is exactly the same as the investment multiplier referred to in Chapter 5.

The amount by which incomes are ultimately increased by an exogenous rise in (export) injections is illustrated in Figure 7.3. Distance

σY is much greater than the distance σJ. Clearly, the shallower the slope of the leakages function L, the greater the rise in income any shift up in injections will cause. This illustrates that the smaller the fraction of leakages as incomes rise, the more export earnings are passed on domestically to others in the economy and the less leaves the system. The greater the rise in national income must result. Thus the foreign trade multiplier is measured by the ratio $\sigma Y/\sigma J$ that is, the change in income divided by the change in injections from export earnings.

There are important conclusions here to this analytical model. Export earnings generate multiplied income growth. Extending this principle further we can see that if country A trades with country B, and B with C and C with A then, first, all can stimulate economic growth with each other. *International trade is not a zero sum game where if one country gets richer another must get poorer.* Second, the more that trade extends, the higher the proportion of GROSS DOMESTIC PRODUCT that is exported or imported, then the greater will be the foreign trade multiplier. For good or ill, we tie our fortunes into those of others the more we trade with them (Box 7.2).

BOX 7.2 THE IMPORTANCE OF TRADE

In Figure 7.4 we can see the importance of international trade to certain countries' economies. Large nations such

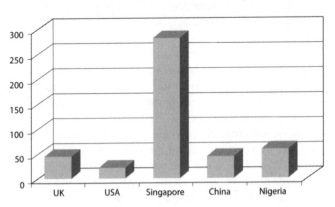

Figure 7.4 Merchandise trade as percentage of GDP (2012) (the sum of imports plus exports as a share of GDP, expressed in current US$). (Source: World Bank.)

as the USA may offer huge markets to smaller countries like Singapore but nonetheless trade only impacts on a relatively low fraction of US incomes. Singapore's economy, on the other hand, revolves around exports, imports and re-exports (which explains why the total rises well above 100 per cent!). Any slight improvement or deterioration in the fortunes of others has immediate implications for a small trading nation like this. Low-income countries like Nigeria which may export relatively few products can similarly be very dependent on trade.

Finally, not only will macroeconomic levels of income be affected by trade as just demonstrated, but microeconomic reallocations of resources – changes in the patterns of national output and employment – will result in all trading countries. These points will be returned to later in this chapter after concluding the analysis on the balance of payments.

THE BALANCE OF PAYMENTS

Money crosses a country's frontiers as a result of international buying and selling of merchandise (the visible balance of trade); purchase and sale of services (the invisible balance) and movements on capital account – short-term, speculative (or "hot money") flows or longer-term, cross-border investment in plant, machinery, etc.

Any imports of merchandise, for example purchasing foreign wine, result in an outflow of money; exports to overseas buyers of, say, locally produced spirits will conversely bring in earnings. "Invisible" imports are represented by, for example, purchase of foreign holidays, which causes an outflow of money from a nation's trade account. Invisible exports could be profits repatriated from domestic businesses operating overseas.

The day-to-day money flows on visible and invisible trade are summed up in the "balance of payments on current account", sometimes referred to as the current balance. Add to this the in or outward movements of capital on the capital account and you arrive at the overall net balance or total currency flow.

Net movements of money between countries can have important implications and it is necessary to examine both causes and effects of such currency flows.

CAUSES

As already mentioned, domestic incomes are an important determinant of import spending. As the former grows, so must the latter – like all consumption spending. The speculative demand for foreign bonds is also in part determined by domestic incomes but is perhaps more affected by changes in interest rate expectations (see last chapter). Short-term capital flows in particular are highly internationally mobile – almost perfectly price-elastic. That is, a slight increase in rates of interest on bonds and securities in country A above those prevailing in country B will result in cashing in bonds in B and transferring the money to A. As regards *long-term* overseas investment, the rate of interest in the money markets is relevant though we noted in Chapter 5 that a more important determinant is the expected future profitability of such investment.

Assuming expectations are exogenously given, we can graph total currency flows of the balance of payments on axes contrasting national income with rates of interest:

The BoP line in Figure 7.5 shows all the levels of income and rates of interest at which a nation's balance of payments is in equilibrium. Consider point *Ycb*. Derived from Figure 7.2, this shows the unique level of domestic income where the current account is in balance. (Recall that any income levels higher than this would see imports rise and the current balance go into deficit; any lower income would produce a current surplus.) Overall balance in the BoP

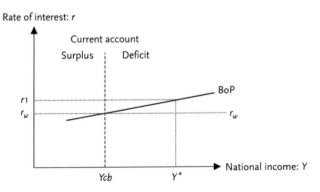

Figure 7.5 The balance of payments curve.

requires that the capital account is in balance at this point also – which it would be if the domestic interest rate was equal to the prevailing market interest rate *rw* obtained elsewhere in the world (Box 7.3).

BOX 7.3 WORLD INTEREST RATES

World money markets offer a variety of different places you can invest your funds – some a lot more risky than others. This is much the same in principle to investing money in your own country – some projects you might consider putting money into are less secure than others. The international scene multiplies potential money-earning outlets enormously and CROSS ELASTICITY OF DEMAND between bonds in one financial centre and another is extremely high. As an example, in September 2013, Ben Benanke, then the chairman of the Federal Reserve Bank in the USA had only to *hint* that he was thinking of reducing US quantitative easing – implying a possible slight rise in the Fed's interest rate – and massive international flows of hot money took place immediately: into the US and out of all other financial centres, forcing up interest rates all round the world to try and offset this movement.

A country's BoP line rises at a relatively shallow line from this point *rw* – signifying it is highly interest-elastic. At income level $Y^\star$ the current balance is in deficit (imports of goods and services exceed exports) but if domestic rates of interest are increased just a little above world rates (*r1* exceeds *rw* by a narrow margin) then foreign capital will flood into the country sufficiently for the capital account surplus to equal the current account deficit. The balance of payments is maintained.

Balance of payments is thus illustrated for all domestic income levels and interest rates, though note the more unresponsive, or price-inelastic, world currency flows are, the steeper will be this BoP line.

There is a problem here, however. If a country needs to raise its interest rate to balance international currency flows it cannot at the same time use monetary policies to stimulate domestic spending and investment. As implied in the last chapter, you cannot use interest rates to regulate the domestic money supply, open your borders to unrestricted financial markets *and* use interest rates to protect the balance of payments. If a country chooses to opt for these first two variables in the "impossible triangle" it must adopt measures other than monetary ones to adjust its trading relations.

Astute readers might also have noticed another problem. If interest rates are increased to secure a capital inflow needed to balance a current account deficit, then it must repay this capital sometime. In the future, the nation concerned must somehow achieve the reverse of the above: a current account surplus that therefore allows a capital outflow. Countries cannot increase their indebtedness forever.

The only *long-term*, sustainable position for a country in international trade, therefore, is to secure a level of income $Y^\star$ that represents full employment at home with balance in the current account *and* balance on the capital account. This would mean a position on Figure 7.5 where Ycb is consistent with $Y^\star$ and local rates of interest equalled the world rate, rw.

How is this possible? The country must adjust its import spending and export sales such that the current account obtains balance at a higher income level than illustrated in Figure 7.5. This can be done in one of two ways (see Figure 7.6): either by direct controls

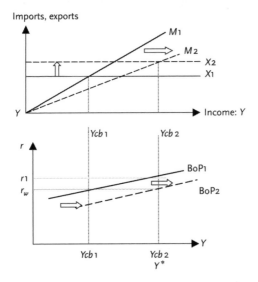

Figure 7.6 A shift in trade relations.

or by devaluing the exchange rate. (Note, if $Ycb1$ cannot be increased to $Ycb2$ by either of these ways then the only other course of action is to reduce or deflate equilibrium income $Y^\star$ until it reaches $Ycb1$ … and forcing austerity on people is not a pleasant option.)

Like in Figure 7.2, the upper diagram in Figure 7.6 shows imports rising with income, exports exogenously given. If imports were somehow decreased and exports increased by the government then the two functions X_1 and M_1 would shift as illustrated to give a new current account balance at income level $Ycb2$.

On the lower diagram, the shift forward in the income level where the current account balances from $Ycb1$ to $Ycb2$ means the BoP line shifts similarly. Remember that the BoP line shows all points where the current account and the capital account are both balanced. The latter is only true where domestic rates of interest equal rw, the former where national income equals $Ycb2$. Line BoP2 now shows these properties. Both capital and current accounts are thus balanced where $Ycb2$ equals Y^*, which is consistent with full employment.

DIRECT CONTROLS

One way of reducing imports and increasing exports is for governments to resort to controls on trade. By imposing TARIFFS or QUOTAS on imports, and by giving tax concessions or direct payments to encourage domestic industry to export, a country can improve its balance of payments. Many different countries have used such policies at various times in the past but, particularly in the case of a large economy, they are not at all popular with trade partners. Direct controls are contrary to the spirit of trade liberalisation and are likely to provoke retaliation. What then occurs is that trade barriers go up in one country after another and all suffer in the end (Box 7.4).

BOX 7.4 US CONTROLS ON IMPORTED STEEL

In March 2002, the Bush administration imposed tariffs on imports of steel to the USA. The move was an attempt to protect jobs in America's declining steel industry in states such as Ohio, West Virginia and Pennsylvania. Coming from the world's largest economy and a valued market for steel-making countries in Asia and Europe, this protectionist action was a powerful blow against the interests of global trade as a whole. If other countries followed the US lead in trying to restrict imports then all international trade would suffer and growth in world incomes would slowly grind to a halt.

An angry European Union was not slow to respond. It threatened to place tariffs on Florida orange juice and a host of other American goods if the steel duty was not removed. A fearful World Trade Organization ruled the US action as illegal.

On 4 December 2003, President Bush declared that the "temporary measure" to help the US steel industry had run its course and he re-stated his belief that America was "better off in a world that trades freely and a world that trades fairly" and he withdrew the steel tariff. Everyone (except US steel producers) breathed a sigh of relief.

Source: *The Economist*, 6 December 2003.

DEVALUATION

All of the discussion so far has assumed that exchange rates are fixed, that trade deficits or surpluses result in continuing outflows or inflows of money into an economy. This is a fair assumption since for the most part countries resist short-term fluctuations of exchange rates. They are very destabilising. Imagine a country trying to sell its produce abroad when the price of its currency, and therefore its exports, is continually changing. It would have great difficulty.

Short-term imbalances in money flows can be financed by a country running down or building up its reserves of foreign currency. For example, a trade deficit means more people are buying imports and thus selling local currency to buy foreign exchange. Excess sales of the domestic currency will *not* result in a fall in its price, however, if the country's central bank can provide the foreign reserves to match supply with demand. Thus the exchange rate can stay fixed.

But long-term deficits cannot be sustained in this way – reserves will soon become exhausted. Sooner or later the local currency must lower, or devalue, its exchange rate.

When this happens, exports have a lower price when quoted in foreign currencies; imports become more expensive. (As all tourists know, when the local currency is weak, foreign holidays become more expensive.) Demand for imports falls as their price rises; conversely export demand tends to rise.

THE J-CURVE EFFECT

These changes tend to correct money flow imbalances and thus restore equilibrium to the balance of payments – though not straight away. Because import orders may be fixed and contracts signed, demand for them will not change as their foreign currency price rises. The immediate effect is an even larger outflow of funds. Demand, however, does become more price-elastic over time. Consumers will place orders with domestic alternatives if foreign sources are now more expensive.

The same tendency can be observed with exports. They will not increase at once. First, it takes time before foreign customers become aware of price falls and respond by increasing demand and there is also a time lag for domestic suppliers to react, to adjust production schedules and to increase output. That is, both demand and supply may be price-inelastic at first.

Total currency flow thus takes the following J-CURVE shape over time: in Figure 7.7, starting from a deficit position at time 0, the balance of payments becomes even more negative as an immediate consequence of devaluation, but steadily improves thereafter.

How long things take before the balance of payments becomes positive is crucially dependent on the supply elasticity of exports. If suppliers can increase production quickly consequent upon an increase in overseas demand then earnings will improve, but if there

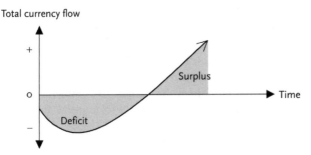

Figure 7.7 The effect of devaluation on the balance of payments over time.

is any reluctance on the part of resources (labour and capital) to move into export production and to increase productivity then the J-curve may be very flat and may not move into surplus for a long time, if ever. In such a circumstance the country will inevitably suffer deflation – a loss of income and the reduction of living standards – as the most painful way to reduce import spending and thus eventually to balance its trade relations.

COMPARATIVE ADVANTAGE AND THE GAINS FROM TRADE

Throughout history, countries all round the world have resorted to various measures to try and improve their balance of payments. The 1930s in particular were years when direct controls and competitive devaluations were attempted by some nations to maximise injections and minimise leakages at the expense of others. They were known as MERCANTILIST or "beggar my neighbour" policies and, as a result, only served to export recession and impoverish trade for all.

If a country tries to protect its own industries from losing out to imports and subsidises exports to try and steal overseas markets from others then it cannot succeed in the long run. It commits the fallacy of composition. What seems a good policy for one country to practise cannot work if all do the same. If nobody wants to buy goods from anyone else then clearly no one can sell any goods. (Even if one nation could successfully and selfishly exploit a partner for some time – if country A's income grows by reducing country B's – then this cannot continue for long before the export market is exhausted.)

As a *general* rule, the World Trade Organization argues that free trade is the best policy. It tries to promote the idea of all countries growing together. Despite the popular protests against globalisation, the WTO insists that *all* nations, whether rich or poor, benefit from a world regime of unrestricted international trade. Rather than protest about bringing down the barriers to commerce, it is alleged that this is the one measure most likely to improve the fortunes of the poorest nations on the planet.

The argument that supports this claim is the principle of COMPARATIVE ADVANTAGE, which has been lauded as the most important, non-obvious principle of economics. Evidently it is a general law that is not well understood by the general public. Certainly it is difficult to implement since domestic voters (especially in rich countries) who consider themselves vulnerable to trade can create a lot of political obstacles. This is one of the most important issues in basic economics and it is vitally important that we analyse it fully here. To emphasise: the argument is that free trade would lead to huge welfare gains (especially for poorer nations) if it were widely implemented.

Some simple examples are necessary to explain the argument. First, take the obvious case where two counties are efficient in producing different goods (say, one in computers and one in cars). It makes sense that each specialises in what they are good at and trade for the other. Both nations clearly benefit.

Now consider the non-obvious case where one country appears to be more efficient in all its industries compared to its less-developed neighbour. What do these two nations have to gain from trade? A common argument heard in the poor world is that they have everything to lose by being exploited by bigger, richer trading partners. On the other hand, a familiar cry that goes up in developed nations on these occasions is that free trade means exporting jobs to low wage countries.

Clearly in this scenario both rich and poor cannot claim they are each losing out to the other. We have to look closer to examine the economic consequences of trade between unequal partners.

Consider the university professor of automotive engineering who happens to be a good car mechanic. Is it worth fixing her own car when it breaks down or should she take it to the local garage?

The engineering professor may be the world's leading expert on the internal combustion engine but while she is producing, say, a revolutionary new design that is lighter in weight, uses less fuel and comes at 10 per cent less cost, she cannot at the same time get under her own car and fix the fault. What should she do?

This is an example of comparative advantage. The local garage mechanics may not be able to redesign the future of the motor industry but they can certainly help fix problematic cars. They may not be as efficient as the engineer in diagnosing and correcting the particular fault in question but, by leaving them to get on with it, the professor can specialise in what she does best. It is simply not worth her while trying to do everything she evidently can do.

Meanwhile the local mechanics have work they can get on with that otherwise they would have been denied and, even more important, by starting with relatively low skill jobs they may eventually develop more exacting careers.

This analogy should help explain the economic strategies open to developed and underdeveloped industrial nations. For example, the USA may be absolutely more efficient than Mexico in both industrial engineering and in car assembly plants. Nonetheless it pays the US to specialise in that pursuit in which it has the greatest comparative advantage, engineering, and leave the car assembly plant to locate south of the Rio Grande.

Mexico meanwhile can start work on producing cars. In this example it has no ABSOLUTE ADVANTAGE but retains a comparative advantage in car assembly (that is, compared to engineering design). It may employ more labour than would be the case in a similar factory north of the border, productivity might be lower and those employed may not develop many sophisticated skills at first, but economic development has to start somewhere and, in this example, car assembly is the place. (INFANT INDUSTRIES like this are in fact a typical way to start the process of growth and development.)

How does a country know in which industries it possesses comparative advantage? Two Swedish economists, Eli Heckscher and Bertil Ohlin, argued that a nation will have an advantage in industries which use intensively those factors of production that the country has in abundance. Thus the USA can specialise in high tech goods that require abundant supplies of highly skilled labour; Mexico can specialise in industrial goods that employ large numbers of lower skilled personnel.

One dynamic implication of the Heckscher–Ohlin theory is that, over time as specialisation occurs, the rewards will rise to the factor in production increasingly employed in trade. This has income DISTRIBUTION EFFECTS for the countries concerned. In the hypothetical example used above, it means that lower skilled workers in Mexico should gain more earnings over time; similarly, returns to technical qualifications in the USA should improve. Note that these distribution effects can have important social and political consequences for the countries concerned and any tensions that arise must be carefully managed. There is no better example of this than the case of Argentina (see Box 7.5).

BOX 7.5 TRADE, SPECIALISATION AND INCOME GROWTH – THE SOCIAL AND POLITICAL CONSEQUENCES

One hundred years ago, Argentina was a fast-developing country with a high per capita income equal to or better than many European states. It stood comparison with Canada and Australia as a huge, resource-rich land of recent settlement that became a world leader in the production of a staple product – beef – for overseas markets.

Staple theory explains the way in which specialisation in the export of a key primary product can create a network of linkages in the developing country – the spread of transport and commercial INFRASTRUCTURE and the development of port facilities that typifies what occurred in and around Buenos Aires and the Argentine Pampas. Note, however, that modern export-led development is not just determined by advantageous overseas demand conditions – it is crucially dependent on supply-side factors. The fact that Argentina became a world leader in the export of beef, rather than wheat which it could also produce, was because the enterprise, investment and expertise that it developed in cattle ranching was far more innovative and dynamic than any other farming or industrial practice at the time. It thus spawned complementary investment in the latest techniques of stock breeding, refrigerated transport and modern banking and financial facilities and attracted great inflows of European capital and immigration in the three decades running up to the First World War.

Argentina was the leading Latin American economy for most of the twentieth century in terms of its national income and national income per capita but the Great Depression of the 1930s resulted in a sudden collapse in overseas markets. The political consequences were immense. The land-owning, liberal aristocracy that favoured export-led policies now lost out to urban-based, nationalist, populist opinion that demanded policies favouring industrial development.

Argentina entered the post-Second World War period with a well-established, domestically owned industrial sector, a well-integrated economy with efficient export orientated agriculture, little persistent unemployment, wide access to education and, relative to the region, less inequality. It came closer to the standard neoclassical ideal, with all factors of production scarce and valuable in market terms, than almost any other less developed country. It was *not* a less developed country.

Juan Domingo Peron was elected Argentine president in 1946, principally by urban voters. He immediately set about implementing an economic strategy that was industrialist, protectionist, based on government direction and subsidy and designed to transfer resources from agriculture and the land-owning elite towards industrial working classes. The policy stance was extreme: reducing farm export incomes by a half of their real value by insisting all sales went through government marketing boards at fixed low prices. (See monopsony, Chapter 2.) Meanwhile urban real wages increased by around 62 per cent between 1946 and 1949.

As a strategy to redistribute incomes, these policies were outstandingly successful but their extremism built into Argentine society major long-term problems: bitter division of industry against agriculture; government as patron and provider rather than market policeman; and increasing fiscal deficits and external trade imbalances. The country was set on a post-war path of sluggish inefficiency and contradictory objectives.

An economy that was based on export agriculture but which protects industry, depresses agricultural incomes and inflates urban ones is bound on the one hand to reduce export revenues while on the other promote increased expenditure on foreign consumer goods. Further, when the main exports are meat and wheat then increased urban incomes and consumption tend to divert these potential exports into the domestic market.

The post-war Peron government thus ran into inevitable balance of payments difficulties and stop-go growth. The only way to stop trade deficits was to stop growth in spending. As soon as spending resumed the deficits came back. Efforts to restore incentives to primary exporters by devaluing the currency only promoted demonstrations from well-organised urban workers and industrialists. Trying to buy off both sides then resulted in fiscal deficits and inflation. A spiral of inflation, devaluations, increased wage demands, increased public spending, inflation, etc. was thus institutionalised: the economic consequences of domestic social conflict. The military forced Peron into exile in 1955 but the basic fault-lines in Argentine society, polity and economy remained and, to this day, they still hamstring attempts to secure economic growth and development.

The Argentine experience shows that international trade can bring immense rewards – and the market may distribute these in ways that are not always popular. Government management of the gains from trade can then be fraught with difficulty (though see Box 7.7 on Korea).

ARGUMENTS FOR TRADE PROTECTION

In all countries there are likely to be winners and losers as trade expands. The most common argument against free trade is that it creates unemployment in those domestic industries that cannot compete against cheap imports. While this is undoubtedly true, it is nonetheless argued that there are sufficient welfare gains to be made by unrestricted trading to compensate the losers and still leave a net gain for the country as a whole. The principle is as true for individuals as it is true for communities: by specialising in certain employments you can earn more than if you try to produce everything yourself.

POLITICAL ARGUMENTS

While the economic equation is clearly weighted in favour of trade, however, the political argument may not be. Try convincing the farmers in industrial countries that they have no comparative advantage. Inefficient (in world terms) farmers in Europe have been blocking reforms to the COMMON AGRICULTURAL POLICY (the CAP) for years – much to the chagrin and cost of both poor country producers and rich country consumers. While it is true that, in theory, a country can compensate losers in a free trade regime, this does not mean that all people who stand to lose out will trust their governments to actually do that. Hence the political pressure for protection (Box 7.6).

BOX 7.6 PROTECTING THE FARMERS

Agriculture is subsidised in many rich-world countries for a variety of reasons. Farming is liable to large swings in output as unpredictable weather, disease and other misfortunes have their impact. Agricultural prices are thus very variable in free market conditions – hence the demand for government intervention to stabilise prices and farm incomes. In many countries, also, the agricultural lobby is a powerful political force – partly as a result of strong emotional attachment to the countryside and the historic (now redundant?) strategic need to guarantee domestic food supplies.

Government subsidies to farmers in the developed world, however, act against the interests of poorer countries who have little else to export. Far from free trade, we have a global system that fixes the rules to keep rich farmers' incomes up and poor countries' incomes down. In the last round of world trade discussions (The Uruguay Round, 1986–93) between rich and poor nations, agriculture was deliberately kept off the agenda. The World Trade Organization has insisted that in the Doha round of negotiations (which were supposed to end in 2005!) agriculture is kept very firmly in centre focus. Unfortunately, the European Union have made no sizeable concession to modify its system of farm subsidies in the CAP and the USA has not moved either. It seems that free trade in agricultural products – which would be the single most important measure to improve developing country incomes – is still a long way off.

INFANT INDUSTRIES

The fastest growing economies in the world, in East Asia, have not pursued blanket free trade policies as a means of raising their incomes. They have, in fact, been careful to protect their infant industries as a means of developing their potential.

Consider the case of car production. Korea had no comparative advantage in this industry at first. Enormous US, European and Japanese car giants could exploit economies of scale to keep costs of production down and – with product names and logos well-recognised all round the world – there were considerable barriers to entry into this global market place. Nonetheless, the South Korean government realised that comparative advantage is a dynamic, not a static concept. What seems impossible today might not be so tomorrow. Policies were therefore implemented to raise levels of general education and to support management training. Similarly the growing capital markets (domestic banks and money traders) were instructed to give low cost access to finance to certain chosen sectors, and the government gave tax breaks, subsidised investment and, directly and indirectly, encouraged the growth of fledgling export industries that would otherwise have been unable to compete in world markets. The strategy worked. Korea now has a highly skilled and hard-working urban, industrial workforce *and* a capital market structure that gives its motor industry a competitive advantage.

Infant industries need protection from world competition until they have grown up enough to cope with it. Free trade may be the best policy in the long run but in the short term there are sound economic arguments to grant protection as a means to that end. (Note, however, that all involved must accept that government protection is short term only. Dependent infants have no incentive to grow up otherwise.)

"EXTERNAL" EFFECTS

The Korean example above introduces the concept of EXTERNALITIES. Markets will fail to allocate resources efficiently if their prices do not reflect all the external costs and benefits involved in both production and consumption. If many of the rewards for a certain enterprise are all external (for example, workers receive excellent training in accountancy then leave to set up their own businesses) then it profits the entrepreneur little to start up. Government must take a lead in these circumstances (Box 7.7).

BOX 7.7 KOREAN STEEL AND ADMINISTRATIVE GUIDANCE

The case of POSCO, Korea's state-owned integrated steel industry, is an excellent example of how governments can overcome MARKET FAILURE. In the early 1970s the Korean government applied for a concessionary loan (that is, at a lower than market rate of interest) from the World Bank to build a steel mill. The application was rejected on the grounds that Korea possessed no comparative advantage in steel. The World Bank, using standard market valuation, was correct in its decision. There are enormous economies of scale in building such capital equipment (see Chapter 4) which implies a long gestation period before output is large enough to be efficient. And where was the market for all the steel that was proposed? World markets were glutted and domestic steel demands in this developing country were not great. Thus returns on any investment in Korean steel seemed to be way below market rates for the foreseeable future.

> The government went ahead with the investment anyway and found its own finance. Additionally, the government provided essential infrastructure such as water supplies, port facilities, power stations, road and rail communications. Manufacturing in chosen sectors – like the motor industry – was also subsidised so that steel production when it eventually came on-stream had a ready-made market. Current market signals were, in effect, ignored and producers were responding to government commands – a system in East Asia known as ADMINISTRATIVE GUIDANCE. Some years later, POSCO eventually won the World Bank accolade of being "the world's most efficient producer of steel", out-competing many other producers around the globe. Moreover, its success stimulated a host of domestic supply industries to set up which could now sell a range of products to the steel mills: the fraction of local content in POSCO's output increased from 44 per cent to 75 per cent between 1977 and 1984.
>
> Source: Rodrik, D. (1995) "Getting Interventions Right: How South Korea and Taiwan Grew Rich" *Economic Policy* 20.

Where there exist significant externalities, direct government allocation can thus lead to greater efficiency than free markets are able to secure on their own. Countries learn by doing. Management skills improve in coping with developing industries. Technology (like skills) can be expensive to develop but quick to disperse. Linkages between industries can be exploited – both forward and backward. A cement plant provides construction materials for office blocks (a forward linkage), whilst pulp and paper industries set up to produce sacks for cement (a backward linkage). No one industry would contemplate starting on their own but if all set up more or less together the costs for all would be reduced. Co-ordinating such decisions and implementing them requires the hand of government.

There are negative externalities that markets omit also. Free trade and specialisation can promote the exploitation of exhaustible natural resources. For example, Borneo in East Malaysia has a wealth of tropical rainforest which supports irreplaceable ecologies – yet the profits received by private logging companies for selling hardwoods to customers overseas do nothing to compensate for the loss of precious eco-diversity. Similarly, tourism is frequently cited as an industry that many poor countries can develop but this too can bring problems. Cultural pollution occurs – a superficial materialism that begins to erode a rich cultural and spiritual heritage.

As a general aim, therefore, free trade has much to commend it but arguments above show that it must be carefully managed. There are a variety of private *and* social costs and benefits involved in opening up sectors of an economy to trade. National income and welfare may be enhanced by trade in the long run but development takes time and governments may need to give guidance, support and, indeed, protection to certain natural and cultural assets whose values are not recognised in the short term. Getting the policy mix right in all circumstances in not easy.

MULTINATIONAL COMPANIES

The dilemma of how best to secure free trade but not to lose out in the process is central to the relationship between MULTINATIONAL CORPORATIONS (MNCs) and host governments in the developing world.

Two-thirds of international trade nowadays is handled by businesses that own assets in more than one country. For example, much internal firm trade now crosses borders: a firm producing raw materials in one country sells supplies to a manufacturing affiliate in another and the finished product may be marketed by a sales office of the same corporate family located in yet another part of the world.

There is no doubt that one of the major economic trends of the last 50 years or so has been the phenomenal growth and global reach of MNCs. Business empires have built up all over the world such that companies like the Swiss-based *Nestle SA* own assets worth US$ 234 billion (2013), 93 per cent of which are held overseas, and turn over annual sales of US$ 100.6 billion, which are more highly valued than the Gross Domestic Products of many poor nations: e.g. Ghana, US$ 40.7bn; Guatemala US$ 50.2bn; Morocco, US$ 96.0bn (Forbes and World Bank data, 2012/2013).

The concentration of economic power in the hands of profit-seeking global enterprises has become a source of much controversy.

The huge flows of foreign direct investment (FDI) into and out of different countries is potentially very unsettling for any national economy. What represents a good business decision for any one MNC may not be good business for the country that hosts its operations. At the same time, nations can benefit greatly from the resources and technology that foreign firms can bring into (particularly) developing countries. There are therefore arguments both for and against opening borders to international business and governments, academics, journalists and many members of the public have all expressed concerns over the issue (see Box 7.8).

CAUSES FOR GROWTH

Economists must seek to understand why there has been such great growth in multinational enterprise. What drives this particularly successful economic animal? For example, given that there are inevitable costs in any one business attempting to set up producer affiliates abroad, why do it? Why not stay at home and export, or sell the license to produce to a local, overseas enterprise?

One reason is to by-pass any host country restrictions on trade. Japanese car producers were originally barred from access to European markets by tight quotas on all imports. They thus invested in building large-scale, host country car plants behind the trade walls the European Community had erected. Exports may not always be possible, therefore, so in such circumstances MNCs are inclined to invest in overseas production instead.

One reason for not taking out licensing agreements is to retain tight control over all stages in the production and marketing process. If a particular business thinks it has a winning formula for its product in world markets it may not wish to let any other business get within arm's length of it. Research and development costs in some industries are immense yet imitation may be quite cheap and easy to achieve. If the parent company is not able to secure a high price from a potential licensee then the MNC will wish to enter the foreign market itself rather than pass over the rights too cheaply to an outsider. This is particularly relevant in developing countries that offer little patent protection in law. (See the argument in earlier chapters about the importance of property rights – no protection means no deal.)

BOX 7.8 MULTINATIONALS AT BAY?

Some high-profile MNCs make easy targets for anti-globalisation critics. There are many arguments to be found in books, articles and websites protesting about the injustices perpetrated by global capitalism. It is the responsibility of all students to examine the economic issues for and against these criticisms. Here are two well-known examples:

In the Indonesian financial crisis of 1998, rioters in Jakarta demonstrated outside a local McDonald's hamburger bar, protesting about alleged US cultural imperialism. The owner of the FRANCHISE rushed out to try and placate the crowds. Contrary to the shouts and criticisms being aired, he reassured those outside that he was an honest local citizen, he and his assistants were all devout Muslims and the shop was always closed in the holy month of Ramadan.

Wal-Mart, the US retailer, as well as many other inter-nationally known European and North American chain-store companies, purchases apparel (clothing) from Bangladesh, a country with one of the world's lowest industrial wages and, in some cases, positively dangerous working condi-tions. In April 2013 over one thousand workers were killed when an eight-storey garment factory in Dhaka collapsed on top of them. It provoked a storm of protests by workers in the world's second biggest garment industry. The workers brandished placards demanding that Western MNCs pres-sure the Bangladesh government to improve wages and working conditions. As a result Wal-Mart hired independent inspectors to check the safety conditions in the 200 factories it buys from (reported by Associated Press, November 2013).

In the first case, McDonald's hamburgers are undeniably an American concept. Your friendly neighbourhood store is, however, locally staffed and managed. The parent com-pany sells franchises to local owners who receive manage-ment training, start-up capital and all the production technology to ensure that the final product sold to customers is recognisably the same as any other Big Mac sold anywhere else in the world. The franchise owner is free to keep any profits after all costs are paid, including a fraction to the MNC.

From the point of view of development economics, this is excellent business for the host country – capital, management training, TECHNOLOGY TRANSFER, increased employment are all benefits gained. Linkages established with local supply chains are similarly beneficial. So what is the problem here? There are issues of cultural imperialism involved but they can be overstated. Are Indonesian customers selling their culture short by buying American style products, rather than traditional meals? Are they really innocent victims of sophisticated US marketing techniques? (Could not the same be said of US customers visiting Mexican or Indian restaurants ... ?)

In the second case, Western chain-stores like Wal-Mart and Primark are retailing and marketing businesses, not manufacturing companies. They will send their designs to any factory anywhere that can deliver on contract at least cost. Developing-country firms that sign up to this are given access to modern designs and knowledge of customer tastes in rich overseas markets. They learn essential international business practice where delivery to contract – honouring a deal – is the key to economic development and growth. The producing factories are all locally owned, managed and staffed and rates of pay are determined by local markets under the jurisdiction of national governments. Poor countries have lots of unskilled labour but scarce capital and enterprise. Pay scales will inevitably reflect local demand and supply. If wages were higher (in fact, those MNCs that do operate in low-income countries usually pay above local rates for labour since they have more to lose from poor publicity) more people would flood into the cities than could be employed. (Hence the rise of shanty towns that disfigure many urban areas in developing countries.)

Bangladesh is a country that was born out of poverty, chaos and conflict when in 1971 it fought a liberation war against (the former East) Pakistan administration. Its economy was ruined in the struggles and did not begin to revive until the establishment of the first garment factory devoted to exports in 1980. In the 30 years that followed more than four thousand ready-made garment factories have bloomed. The industry is now the country's biggest foreign exchange earner, it employs over four million women, mostly from low income families, and it is the multinational retail stores – who wish to protect their international image – which have been pressing Bangladesh factory owners and politicians into raising local wages and working conditions.

Behind these political influences on the spread of multinational enterprise there are some basic economic laws. These businesses are all subject to significant economies of scale, not just in production but, particularly, in co-ordination, administration and technological research. MNCs are also an efficient form of economic organisation in situations where sources of supply are spread around the world in diverse locations and, similarly, potential markets are huge, global and not subject to major national differences in tastes and preferences.

An industry that demonstrates all these conditions *par excellence* is oil (see Box 7.9). It is also true of industries such as chemicals, pharmaceuticals and electronics. (The motor industry has more problems since it has to accommodate differences in preferences but does so successfully by restricting choice to a limited range of models. Giant food and beverage conglomerates have even greater diversity to cope with: they seem to have grown in spite of wide differences in consumer tastes. How? By maintaining a large portfolio of varied products – Nestlé's instant coffee, chocolate bars and breakfast cereals are the same in South Africa as they are in Singapore.)

International business looks around the world to answer a number of different questions: where is the least-cost location for gaining raw material supplies? Where is production best based? Is closeness to sources or to markets more important? Driven by the pursuit of profits and the need to seek a competitive edge, once a given market or source of supply has matured, the MNC must move on.

Host governments in developing countries have different objectives to MNCs wishing to locate within their realm. Whether or not they welcome incoming foreign direct investment, and on what terms, depends entirely on the nature of the agreement signed between the two parties. There is no *a priori* reason why the economic activities of MNCs should on balance be beneficial or harmful to the interests of host countries. As implied above, opening frontiers to Foreign Direct Investment (FDI) can bring both advantages and disadvantages.

BOX 7.9 THE INTERNATIONAL OIL INDUSTRY

Oil is a homogenous product. My car cannot tell the difference between one brand of petrol and another. The fact that different oil company products are therefore perfect substitutes for each other means this industry is characterised by intense rivalry and thus sometimes collusion (see Chapter 4). The growth of the major oil oligopolists has come as a result of fierce competition – one company on occasions buying up another – and strategies employed by the more successful to build huge vertically integrated enterprises that safeguard production from finding the basic raw material in one part of the world right through to marketing the finished product on the other side of the globe.

For much of the twentieth century, the international oil industry was dominated by a handful of oil "majors" (famous names such as Esso/Exxon, Shell, BP, Mobil, etc.) which controlled all stages in production and distribution. Since most oil was bought and sold between affiliates in the same company, only relatively little was ever freely traded internationally. The oil majors were thus able to dictate world oil prices and declare profits in whichever country they wanted, according to where tax laws were least.

Rich world customers of petroleum products could be charged high prices; poor world producer countries could get relatively little for their supplies of crude. The oilmen in the middle made fortunes. All this changed, however, in the 1970s. This was when, with consumption outgrowing production, the USA became a net importer of oil and then the OPEC governments nationalised the assets of the oil majors that had previously controlled the output of crude oil. For the first time ever, a group of underdeveloped nations could now exercise real economic power. A series of oil strikes imposed by the OPEC nations forced up the international price of oil and caused a major redistribution of world incomes – away from consumer countries and into the pockets of OPEC, *not* the oil companies (see Chapter 5).

Since those days, host countries have become much more adept in bargaining for a good deal with incoming oil companies and, with the hold of the majors weakened, the structure of the industry is now more open, less collusive and more liable to change. As a result, countries with significant oil reserves can now play the field and hold out for better prices from MNCs. Note, however, oil is a commodity that is much in demand and few other natural resources confer such bargaining power on developing countries fortunate enough to possess scarce supplies. The road to riches pursued by OPEC governments is unlikely to be followed by others.

THE BENEFITS OF MULTINATIONAL ENTERPRISE

FDI can bring in much needed capital to developing countries. One of the more significant obstacles to economic development in poor countries is that their level of savings is low. They are caught in the trap of low incomes, a low propensity to save and thus an inability to invest. Additionally, given underdeveloped banking systems, what savings are made are not necessarily efficiently recycled into the most productive investment outlets. Low investment means low, or no, growth.

MNCs can help raise the level of investment in developing countries by calling on resources denied to host countries. FDI also tends to be the sort that is long term – the construction of plant and

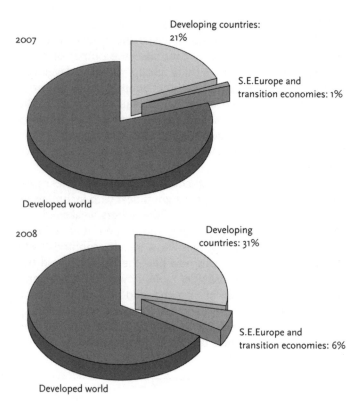

Figure 7.8 The increasing share of world foreign direct investment going to developing and transition economies, 2007–2008. (Source: derived from James X. Zhan, *World Investment Report* [2009], UNCTAD.)

machinery that will *not* be subject to destabilising, short-term speculative movement: in one day, out the next.

One of the benefits of increasing globalisation, therefore, is that billions of dollars of investment have flowed into developing countries recently (see Figure 7.8) which would otherwise not have occurred. Whereas the recent international recession has led to a decrease in worldwide FDI from US$ 2 trillion to 1.7 trillion between 2007 and 2008, this international allocation has changed direction: it fell 29 per cent between countries in the developed world but increased by 17 per cent to developing and 26 per cent to transition economies. And in 2012 – for the first time ever, according to the World Investment Report of 2013 – developing economies absorbed more FDI than developed countries. Like any investment anywhere, these funds will be placed in profit seeking outlets (perhaps manufacturing products for the domestic market) intended to reward the businesses concerned. This does not mean, however, that the interests of the host country are not also served.

First, of course, new investment means the creation of new jobs. Many MNCs locate production facilities in poor countries to take advantage of lower production costs – especially lower wage costs. This is not prejudicial to local labour. As mentioned earlier, MNCs, if anything, are guilty of providing better than local rates and conditions – a practice that they should contain. Better to employ thousands at relatively low (by Western standards) wages than give out only a few jobs at much higher rates and leave the rest in poverty.

If, indeed, a MNC affiliate is set up to serve the local market then the welfare of domestic consumers is increased. (People only buy goods if the value of the product consumed is greater than the value of the money – and thus all other alternatives – exchanged for them.) If the investment is instead designed to export local produce then local infrastructure will be set up to facilitate this trade (see Box 7.5 on Argentine beef exports) and other domestic enterprise in the host country can benefit by gaining knowledge of how to access foreign markets. Recent evidence from Latin America and Asia shows that multinational firms can and do act as export catalysts for local businesses interested in following their lead.

Another spin-off from inward investment for the host country is the possibility of increasing not only the quantity of capital but also its quality, or productivity. Technology transfer takes many forms. MNCs can bring in not only the latest glitzy machines, they can also provide excellent management development opportunities plus workforce training in high tech skills. If the skills gap between local and foreign personnel is great then the MNC will bring in its own people, and technology transfer will be relatively little, but nonetheless the opportunity is there for increased skill transfer if the host country can upgrade its own education systems and provide the local labour force with the start-up human capital required. There have certainly been complaints that some developing countries have not gained as much as they originally hoped for from incoming technology. Other nations however, like Singapore, have grown up on the back of FDI that has undoubtedly added value to the local skills base.

The role of government is important in determining the distribution of eventual rewards from MNC operations. The example of the oil industry (see Box 7.9) is a classic case where MNCs can offer countries with crude oil reserves the sophisticated technological expertise to develop their untapped natural resources. One party has supplies of capital and the latest technology; the other has the undeveloped raw material. Clearly both parties stand to benefit: it is all down to striking a mutually acceptable agreement. Note that the deal will be better for the host country the more competitive, less collusive, is the multinational industry with which it has to negotiate and the more honest, incorruptible and commercially astute is its government.

Lastly, free trade – wherever it obtains – brings with it the drive for efficiency. So long as local businesses are not sheltered from competition behind tariff walls they must be efficient in order to survive. Giving access to the local market to MNCs means that domestic monopolies cannot evolve and nor can they grow up dangerously close to government. Efficiency is thus promoted not only in industry but also in public service: government officials are open to bribery and corruption if local business believes that the path to profits is best pursued by RENT-SEEKING – securing subsidies, tax protection or exclusive government contracts rather than striving to be competitive.

THE DISADVANTAGES

A popular argument against multinationals setting up offices in host nations is that they act to siphon off profits back to their parent. Over time, MNCs therefore act as a conduit for capital to move *out* of developing countries, not into them.

Evidence for this particular argument needs to be convincing nowadays. If the market is developing then MNC profits are frequently ploughed back into further investment in the host country. In those countries where local stock markets are up and running, the MNC will raise share capital and thus distribute profits to local owners. In total, MNCs generate a lot of trade, in goods, services and some of it in financial instruments, and it would be premature to conclude that the net balance for host countries must always be negative. Nonetheless, the historical experience of oil companies and other extractive industries has been one where great profits have been made and contracts signed with developing country governments have left the hosts with only a small slice of the overall cake. There should be little surprise then if newcomers are now greeted overseas with more cynical, distrustful attitudes (see Box 7.10).

BOX 7.10 EXTRACTING THE WEALTH OF NATIONS ON THE OLD GOLD COAST

Africa is a resource-rich continent and Western developed nations have been scrambling to extract its wealth for centuries. The first European settlements in the old Gold Coast of West Africa were built by the Portuguese in 1482 and they were followed by many others up until the establishment of the British colony in 1821.

Through the nineteenth century the British built railways and a transport infrastructure to export gold, metal ores, diamonds, ivory, pepper, timber, grain and cocoa, amongst others.

After independence in 1957, Ghana finds itself still today with an economic structure that favours the export of primary produce as the main revenue earner of the country. Only today, the main conduits for the exploitation of its mineral wealth are not colonial administrators but multinational corporations like Newmont of the USA – the world's second biggest gold miner.

The *Financial Times* reported (23 March 2010) that gold revenues totalling US$ 2.1 billion were earned by mining companies in Ghana in 2009 ... but only US$ 146 million (7 per cent) of that revenue was returned to the state in royalties and other payments.

At the same time, spills of cyanide – used in the process of separating gold from the ore in which it occurs – poisoned local fish and devastated the fortunes of local villagers who are dependent on their catch.

Ghana is left to reflect on the mixed benefits of exploiting its natural endowments. Foreign capital is needed to develop the country's main source of income but how hard a bargain do host governments drive with incoming multinational corporations? Impose too many restrictions, push for too high a tax take, and MNCs will not come.

Variable commodity prices, and a volatile political climate, have for many years made it very risky for businesses to invest in developing country mining industries. At the turn of the millennium, commodity prices in real terms were at their lowest level for 50 years. Gold in particular slumped in price from the heady years of the Oil Crisis – over US$ 800 per oz. in 1980 – to a low of US$ 270 per oz. in 2001.

Given this background, with World Bank encouragement, host nations have tended to offer better and better terms to get foreigners to stump up capital and invest. But maybe they were too generous. Recent booming demand from China, added to doubts over the safety of international banks, has now pushed gold prices higher and higher. In the eyes of many, foreigners again seem to be getting most of the wealth out of Africa, leaving only pollution, a sense of injustice and increasing social unrest.

Employment effects of MNCs may not always be beneficial. The incoming, modern-equipped factory may out-compete domestic rivals and lead to the closing down of many jobs. This is all the more likely if the technology employed by the MNC is capital intensive. Relatively few employment opportunities in high tech skills for foreigners will therefore be created whereas thousands of unskilled domestic workers may be forced out of their jobs in local firms that now go bust.

By the same token, technology transfer may be minimal. MNCs may jealously guard access to research and development benefits – perhaps keeping the important value-added functions of design and technology in the parent country and releasing only assembly operations to locations abroad where they are disparagingly known as "screwdriver plants". The first MAQUILADORES in Mexico were originally of this type – US-owned factories built just south of the border in tax-free zones set up to serve the markets further north.

Spin-off benefits to local industry, which might be expected to win contracts to supply the MNC with a variety of inputs were also disappointingly low where the said assembly plant just put together mostly imported components.

Lastly, multinational corporations bring a way of life to developing countries that threatens local cultures. Western capitalist culture promotes materialism and rewards individualism, not the communalism of the extended family or village. It brings an obsession with the pursuit of profit and economic growth and it inevitably results in widening income differentials as some seize opportunities to enrich themselves while others do not; where some skills and attributes are valued by the market and others are not. MNCs are enormously powerful engines of modernism. If this is progress, not all communities are prepared for it.

CONCLUSION

We live in an international marketplace. In fact it has always been so: national sovereignty is a thing of the past, and the long distant past at that. The chance to make fortunes in trade has driven the expansion of empires from before Roman times, through the race to establish European colonies, to the emphasis on globalisation today. World economic fortunes are inextricably intertwined.

There yet remain some corners of the world where the global reach of trade has not made significant inroads – such places may retain prized traditional cultures but they also support very low material standards of living. Given the choice, people in such communities usually want the increasing incomes that access to world markets gives them.

Multinational corporations have played an increasingly dominant role in world trade since the early twentieth century and we have seen that their operations can bring advantages and disadvantages to countries that host their operations. National governments, however, are responsible for setting the rules for commerce within their borders and MNCs can only do business within the terms of contracts agreed. It is for host nations therefore to monitor the balance of interests served. Economics argues that the more competition that obtains, the more efficiency and less corruption is likely to result. Note that efficient markets require the free exchange of information – open access to the media can thus help safeguard against closet deals being signed that enrich only a minority. Lastly, growing multinationalism in business is, in the end, the best defence against certain countries being exploited for the alleged benefit of others. ECONOMIC IMPERIALISM, as it is called, was the result of companies of one distinct nationality trying to maximise their returns at the expense of a foreign nation. But the more a MNC raises long–term capital from stock holders in host countries and the more it employs local managers in senior positions – that is, the more truly multinational it becomes – then no country becomes "foreign" and thus the more likely the ethos *within* the firm will seek to promote equitable outcomes for all parties.

SUMMARY

Imports act as a leakage, and exports an injection, into the circular flow of national income in any country.

For long-term equilibrium, a country must attempt to secure a balance of all its international payments consistent with the full employment level of national income.

As a general rule, the more that international trade is free from controls and restrictions, the more all participating countries can benefit.

Free trade, for poor countries in particular, may be a long-term goal that requires short-term management. It is important that they are not shut out of rich country markets, nor are they stifled by the economic power of huge multinational corporations.

Where economies of scale exist and where markets, resources and risks are all geographically dispersed, multi-national corporations have evolved as remarkably effective mediums in the organisation of world trade.

The experience of past abuses, the global spread of information, increasing competition and the growing inter-nationalism of multinational labour and capital can moderate the exploitative tendencies of modern business. Growth in world trade and incomes, and the increasing dispersal of both, is thereby possible for the future.

FURTHER READING

For up-to-the-minute news and information on specific countries, for regular surveys on trade, development, finance and the environment, and for a consistent argument in favour of free trade, *The Economist* magazine is without equal.

For a more advanced textbook on international trade theory and policy there is none better than Krugman, P. and Obstfeld, M. (2011) *International Economics*, Pearson.

For a contrary, more sceptical view on the forces of globalisation, but also including a wide range of offerings from an interesting selection of economists, visit the trilingual Chilean website: www. rrojasdatabank.org.

QUESTIONS

1 If a country's current balance of payments moves steadily into deficit as the level of national income and employment grows, what must be done in this country to promote a sustainable balance consistent with higher levels of income and how can this end be achieved?

2 A number of trading countries have demonstrated that comparative advantage is a dynamic concept: industries in which it is profitable to specialise change over time. What economic policies can promote such dynamic comparative advantage? What qualities must an industry, and the country in which it is located, possess to facilitate this dynamic growth?

3 Under what circumstances can protectionist policies be beneficial to a country's long-term economic prospects and under what circumstances will they be prejudicial?

4 What has driven the increasing growth and global reach of multinational corporations (MNCs)? Consider the case for more multinational investment and trade organised and controlled by MNCs; and the case for less. Might international regulation improve their net impact on world trade?

8

CAN WE REDUCE POVERTY AND PROTECT THE ENVIRONMENT?

This final chapter brings together a number of the concepts, themes and theories introduced and analysed in the preceding pages. We are thus finally able to examine the important question that we asked earlier: how to improve living standards for all *without* sacrificing the needs of future generations.

Economics is concerned with scarcity and the need for choice. Clearly, if Earth's resources were limitless then there would be no need to economise on anything – but instead humankind's ideals must always be constrained by the finite means at our disposal. Since we cannot always have everything, we are faced with trade-offs. What goals do we seek to prioritise and which do we therefore have to sacrifice?

Society can employ one of three decision-making systems to address these issues. Central authority can issue commands as to what, how and for whom things should be produced. (What legitimises this authority is a question of political economy. It could be democracy or dictatorship.) Free trade between independent buyers and sellers may instead arrange all economic affairs, with market prices signalling which, and how efficiently, social needs should be met. Finally, there are some communities that leave economic orga-nisation to tradition – following the pattern of past decision-making to embrace the demands of the present.

Economic logic dictates, and history demonstrates, that communities are not always left alone to decide their future. The more effective the decision-making system adopted by society, the more it will secure economic growth and the more its influence will spread. Market-based societies have thus evolved to become dominant. Command and traditional elements have their role within them but, with the eclipse of the centrally planned economies, systems which are predominantly market organised are now unrivalled in the world.

What goods and services a market society produces depends on the pattern of consumer spending. How production is organised is determined by the nature of market competition. Whose needs the market serves depends on the power of individual spending – which in the long run is decided by each person's productivity and thus ability to earn income.

This neat circular ideal illustrates the importance of CONSUMER SOVEREIGNTY. The market serves the individual; the individual serves the market. It is a form of economic democracy where, as Friedman has argued, everyone is free to choose. In all and every trade that is undertaken, buyers and sellers agree a price that is freely arrived at and therefore mutually beneficial. There would be no deal if the welfare of *both* parties to an agreement were not enhanced.

The problem with this economic democracy, of course, is that first, not everyone has an equal vote and second, we are not all perfectly informed of the consequences of our choices. Markets are not perfect. The productivity of some people may not be recognised nor rewarded sufficiently and they will therefore exhibit very little economic power. And those commodities and production processes that *do* receive substantial votes of consumer confidence may in fact prove to be very harmful to the environment and thus our overall welfare.

Why some countries have grown rich while others have not is a question that has troubled economists since Adam Smith wrote *An Inquiry into the Nature and Causes of the Wealth of Nations* in 1776. Examining the costs and benefits involved in the economics of the environment is, in contrast, of relatively recent concern. Both issues are interlinked but we can begin by looking at recent developments in growth theory.

GROWTH THEORY

In a recent article (*What do we know about economic growth? Or, why don't we know very much?* by Kenny and Williams, in *World Development*, 2001) two economists list what mainstream economics has come up with to explain economic development worldwide. In chronological order, from the 1940s up to the 1990s, the key factors explaining growth have been: "physical capital, human capital, policy reform, institutional reform and social development". They add that "a cynic might note that this list moves from the relatively simple to over-come toward the impossible to change (even more so if we take the story into the later 1990s and add geographic factors)." There is much theorising and debate summarised in this pithy comment. Some of the key points are drawn out below.

PHYSICAL CAPITAL

Investment in capital goods has always been emphasised as essential for economic growth. If a wheat farmer wants to increase produc-tion next year he must save some seed from this year's crop, plant it – along with quantities of fertiliser, water and other inputs – and wait for the following year to harvest the result. The more seed is saved and not consumed but invested, the more future outputs can increase. Seed capital is thus vital for growth.

The economic history of the Soviet Union shows the importance of investment in physical capital. This nation grew to become a world power after the debacle of the First World War due mainly to the Stalinist system of ruthless central planning that devoted increasing resources to building up capital goods in oil, iron and steel, transport and communications, machine tools, defence, etc. (Rates of investment in the Soviet Union in the inter-war years were the highest in the world.) Individual civil rights were trampled upon but enormous economic and military might was thus constructed. Recognising this, mainstream economics in the post-Second World War era made capital accumulation central to its growth models also. NEOCLASSICAL GROWTH THEORY, however, emphasises the free market (not central command) as the key allocating mechan-ism. The decision whether to consume or invest resources is thus dependent on market price signals, not on orders from government.

Neoclassical theory assumes PERFECT COMPETITION, mobile resources, fixed technology and prices determined in free markets. An important constraint on economic growth in this simple model is the fact that investment in capital is subject to the law of diminishing returns (see Chapter 4). For example, in the example given above, a farmer cannot keep ploughing-in more and more seed on his land every year and expect that outputs will grow in constant proportion. Future outputs are instead likely to grow in smaller and smaller increments (unless, of course, the farmer adopts some new revolutionary technology – which for the time being we assume he does not).

What determines the level of investment as opposed to consumption in any given year? It all depends on market rates of return. A business may decide to invest past profits in new capital goods if the expected return from taking such a decision is greater than any alternative. Alternatives in a market society include distributing these profits to shareholders for their own consumption, or the return that might be expected by placing these profits in a bank. Note that if the rate of return anticipated on a new investment project is likely to be *above* the going rate of interest in the financial markets, the entrepreneur is likely to back his investment.

The market rate of interest is a measure of how the economy as a whole values future versus present funds. Suppose you loaned out £100 for one year to a friend. What interest would you charge? If you say you wanted £105 back in a year's time you have just expressed a RATE OF TIME PREFERENCE. That is, you have placed a price – of 5 per cent per year – on time. If now you as a shareholder can consume £100 today or can invest and receive, say, *£110* in a year's time then you will opt for the latter. The rate of return on the proposed investment is greater than the interest needed to persuade you to wait. You will thus prefer more money in the future to the lesser amount now.

Putting all these elements together in 1956, Nobel Prize winner Robert Solow derived a theory of economic growth. Investment in capital will take place so long as the rate of return on each project envisaged is above the market rate of interest/rate of time preference. Given an unchanging population growth rate, if capital stock grows faster than the labour force then eventually the rate of return on capital will fall as a result of diminishing returns. (As more and more capital is employed for each person, the optimum ratio of

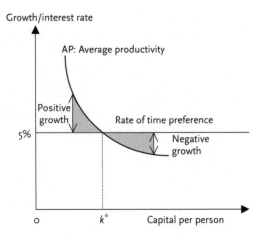

Figure 8.1 Neoclassical growth theory.

labour to capital is passed. Average productivity will fall.) The rate of economic growth must slow down and eventually stop. There must evolve a steady state where investment, and thus the stock of capital, grows just fast enough to equal that needed to equip the labour force. Faster than that means increasing capital stock, diminishing returns and thus a fall in investment. Slower than that and there will be higher than equilibrium returns so investment will increase – see Figure 8.1.

In Figure 8.1, the AP curve illustrates the diminishing returns to capital, that is, the higher the level of capital per worker the lower is its average productivity.

The market determines a rate of time preference equal to 5 per cent p.a. and thus the equilibrium quantity of capital per person equal to $k^\star$.

If the capital stock is as yet insufficient to equip all the labour force such that capital per person is less than $k^\star$ then productivity of capital will be above 5 per cent and investment will increase. There will be positive growth in the economy. Conversely, if the capital stock increases above $k^\star$ then productivity will fall, investment will fall and the capital stock will eventually decrease as the economy shrinks (negative growth). Eventually, the economy evolves a steady state where the rate of growth of capital just equals the rate of growth of the labour force such that capital per worker is constant at $k^\star$.

The conclusion to neoclassical growth theory is therefore pessimistic but consistent with the law of diminishing returns: if capital and labour both grow at constant and equal rates, capital per person must be constant and, since physical capital is the cause of growth in the economy, income per head must remain constant. That is, living standards can improve in the short run only up until capital per person has reached equilibrium value (k^*). Thereafter, living standards are condemned to stay the same. No further growth is possible *unless* exogenous technological progress occurs.

TECHNOLOGICAL PROGRESS

What happens in the neoclassical model when technology does change? A sudden revolutionary change can shift up the productivity of capital. The AP curve in Figure 8.1 will thus shift to AP1 (see Figure 8.2). Note that the downward sloping curve still remains – diminishing returns to capital accumulation still operates – but now the equilibrium capital per person will be arrived at point k^{**}. Standards of living have risen. A technological breakthrough in this model causes a short-term boost in growth rates, only for the eventual result to be zero growth again (albeit at a higher income level).

Thus with a one-off technical change, income per head will rise to a new level and then remain constant again.

The only way that per capita incomes can continue growing, according to this theory, is for technical change to keep happening;

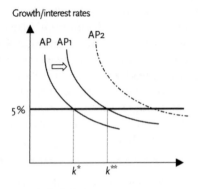

Figure 8.2 Exogenous technical change.

for the stalemate of diminishing returns – where average product equals the rate of time preference – to keep being postponed. Thus *AP* shifts out from *AP* to *AP1* to *AP2* to *AP3*, etc., and equilibrium capital per person keeps moving from $k^\star$ to $k^{\star\star}$ to $k^{\star\star\star}$, etc.

Neoclassical theory predicts, therefore, that the only explanation for long-run growth is technological progress (Box 8.1).

BOX 8.1 TECHNOLOGICAL PROGRESS AND THE SOVIET UNION

The late history of the Soviet Union seems to corroborate the neoclassical claim that technical change is essential. In the last decades of its life as a command economy, the USSR was faced with declining economic growth. The nation had the highest investment rates and the highest labour participation rates in the world. More and more marginal lands were also devoted to production of agriculture or industry but growth rates still declined and, fatally, rates of productivity were stagnant. No matter what innovations were tried, output per person and output per capital both failed to rise. The command economy had increased the *quantity* of inputs in production up to the limits of full employment but the country could not increase the quality or productivity of those inputs. It was thus condemned to suffer diminishing returns. Advanced technology was employed in Soviet military applications where its use could be strictly controlled but the command system prevented its free deployment elsewhere. As a result, the standard of living of the average Soviet citizen stagnated. There were queues for even the most basic of essentials such as bread and meat. In the end it was the dissatisfaction of ordinary people with their economic circumstances that brought about the overthrow of central planning in the enormous command empire that stretched from Berlin to Vladivostok.

The problem with the neoclassical growth theory, of course, is that it has no explanation for technical progress. Where does it come from?

In the earlier theories it is simply assumed to drop like manna from heaven, yet this theory concludes that technology is the only means to break the hold of diminishing returns. Subsequent empirical studies showed that for countries such as the United States and other developed nations it was not so much physical capital but increases in its quality, TOTAL FACTOR PRODUCTIVITY, that accounted for a significant fraction of their modern economic growth. How and why? More theorising was clearly called for.

ENDOGENOUS GROWTH THEORY

Solow's neoclassical model led eventually to a growth theory that was built upon, or endogenised, the process of technical change. If growth spawns advances in technology and, in turn, such advances are not subject to the principle of diminishing returns, then the spread of technology will engender increased growth and this will cause further technical change, ad infinitum. What might explain such a chain reaction? In the 1980s, Paul Romer introduced just such an ENDOGENOUS GROWTH MODEL by emphasising the roles of ideas and of human capital.

Unlike most other economic goods, a profitable idea is non-rivalrous. My use of this idea does not deny yours. For example, in the agricultural revolution that first led to economic growth in the UK in the eighteenth century, ideas like sowing seeds in straight lines and rotating crops in fields represented a great breakthrough in technology. So too was the invention of calculus; steam power, flow-line production; healthy diets; DNA; the internet. Profitable ideas like these may have taken years to evolve but they can be copied quickly and without denying access to the original inno-vator. One person or a thousand people can thus pursue a new technology with no diminution in the productivity of the idea. That is, ideas are *not* subject to diminishing returns.

Profitable ideas do not come like manna from heaven nor even from a broad cross section of the population. They are themselves the product of much education, training and active experimentation – the accumulation of human capital. Primary and secondary education, universities, research laboratories, media of mass communication all need to be set up. As Thomas Edison said: genius is 1 per cent inspiration and 99 per cent perspiration. True, there is an irreducibly

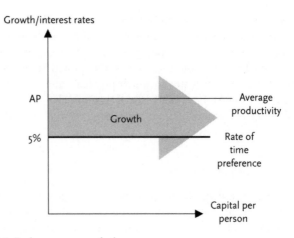

Figure 8.3 Endogenous growth theory.

random element involved but there is nonetheless a lot that can be done by investing in research and development if you want to generate improved technological progress.

Romer's growth theory makes the same starting assumptions as the neoclassical model – competitive markets, flexible prices, mobile resources – but not with respect to the returns to capital. As explained, the productivity of ideas applied to industry – technology – will *not* lead to diminishing returns but instead to constant returns to capital invested. Thus in Figure 8.3 average productivity does not fall as capital per person increases. And so long as returns are higher than the rate of time preference, then business will continue to invest and growth will continue to raise incomes, engender more ideas, more technology, more growth and on and on…

SOCIAL CAPITAL

Endogenous growth theory gives a role to governments as well as to markets. Although much investment in research and development can be undertaken by private business concerns, it can only be based on the social capital that the public sector already provides and it could not occur without it. Free markets fail to supply what we know as PUBLIC GOODS AND SERVICES since there is no profit to be had from so doing. Millions of people receive state primary and secondary education because an educated populous confers external benefit to society. For the same reason, the state builds transport and communication networks of open access that facilitate the mobility of resources. No independent business will educate all children and provide roads for the entire nation since a private enterprise cannot recoup this investment. But without basic education and transport and communication services, how can the private sector ever recruit the resources necessary to invest in technological development? The state must provide the foundation upon which the market can build (Box 8.2).

BOX 8.2 PRIVATE AND SOCIAL RETURNS TO EDUCATION

Pure public goods like national defence confer social benefits that are non-excludable. They cannot be packaged, restricted in supply and sold only to paying customers for a profit (if I am protected by my country's armed services then so too is my neighbour). MERIT GOODS, such as education and health services, *are* excludable (and thus can be provided to some by private enterprise) but the social benefit in opening access to all is judged to be so great as to warrant their public provision.

Formal education is an excludable merit good (schools can decide which students to exclude or not) though it nonetheless confers many external benefits on society. You and I benefit if we both live in a community where everyone else is educated.

Primary and secondary education provided only by a market system is likely to be highly inefficient and inequitable. Just a minority would be able to afford private schooling and who knows what talent would thus go undiscovered, uneducated? How many potentially brilliant scientists, engineers, artists and musicians escape the net in poor countries whose genius, if cultivated, might otherwise transform these nations?

State provision of schooling is thus necessary, though expensive. To produce one Einstein you have to educate

> millions at primary level before a process of selection, much later, can identify the research abilities that can be employed at postgraduate level.
>
> Note that market allocation of educational services becomes less inefficient the more able it is to spot talent. The most prestigious universities can pay for themselves in the private sector since in their late teens and early 20s students can better calculate whether or not they have a reasonable chance of gaining the skills and career contacts from these institutions that will enable them to earn high financial rewards. That is, at this age, the private consumer can make a good guess that the rate of return on his/her educational investment will, or will not, be measurably above the rate of time preference.

Without the support of the state, therefore, technical progress will be limited and insufficient to generate growth. But having opened this Pandora's box, Romer's growth model cannot give precise instructions as to what exactly must be done next. All sorts of variables can impact on technological progress – for example, should government allocate funds to basic research or should this be left to the financial markets? Should infant technological industries be subsidised, and if so, for how long? Public officials might find an excuse for all manner of government interventions. Where do you draw the line?

Growth theories can go only so far. Reviewing the empirical evidence helps to fill in the gaps in our knowledge and this has led to an active debate over which precise policy recommendations are important to stimulate growth.

POLICY REFORMS

Throughout this text, a number of instances have been quoted of government successes and failures in framing economic policies. Governments can protect infant industry or promote inefficiency; can promote competition or promote corruption; can stimulate a declining economy or stimulate inflation. Get the policies right and sustainable growth is possible; get it all wrong and wild swings in economic fortune result.

Chapter 5 describes the supply–side paradigm shift that captured mainstream economic thought and policy-making in the 1970s and 1980s. The early post-war, interventionist stance was rejected in favour of a liberalising, privatising, free trade economic philosophy, actively promulgated not only by academic economists but also by institutions such as the IMF and World Bank – which had the power to tie financial strings to such policy recommendations (Box 8.3).

BOX 8.3 CASHEW NUTS IN MOZAMBIQUE: AN EXAMPLE OF WORLD BANK INFLUENCE

Cashew production in Mozambique has been an important income earner for the country since Portuguese colonisation. With independence in 1975 however, following the strategy of many other developing countries, the incoming government banned the export of raw cashew nuts as a measure to stimulate the domestic packaging and processing industry.

Mainstream neoclassical economics disapproves of such practice. A ban or export tax on raw materials depresses their internal price and effectively subsidises the domestic processors. Cashew farming is discouraged and labour and capital are drawn into urban industry which is protected and inefficient in world terms. Urban employment and incomes are propped up whilst poor farm incomes are depressed. That is what theory dictates.

The World Bank became involved and insisted that (in a country torn apart by civil war) if the Mozambique government wanted to qualify for much needed World Bank and IMF financial support then it had to liberalise the cashew nut export trade and reverse the trends outlined above. In spite of fierce opposition from the government and domestic industry, the World Bank got its way. The ban on exports was removed in 1991/1992 and related tax restrictions were reduced from 60 per cent down to 14 per cent in 1998/1999.

As a result, farm prices rose, raw cashew exports increased and resources were pulled out of the domestic processing industry. The benefits for the farmers were, however, very small whilst the costs imposed on the infant packaging industry – which went into steep decline – were substantial. Recent analysis (published by the US National Bureau of Economic Research, see source below) shows that, so far as Mozambique's overall development was concerned, the World Bank got it wrong.

Estimates have revealed that the extra income benefits farmers stood to gain from liberalisation were probably "no greater than ... US$5.30 per year for the average cashew-growing household" and 50 per cent to 60 per cent of this gain was anyway siphoned off by urban traders and middlemen. The actual benefits were thus described as "puny" compared to the enforced unemployment of 11,000 processing-industry workers in 2001. Neoclassical theory dictates that resources made redundant in "inefficient" industries that are forced out of business by free trade should thus relocate in sectors in which the country does possess a comparative advantage. But poor countries have inefficient markets constrained by lack of transport, information, and credit needed to aid the mobility of labour and capital. Mozambique's urban workers stayed unemployed.

Worse, the export trade in raw cashew turned out to be less competitive, less beneficial than that for processed cashew. (India is the dominant buyer – a monopsony – of raw cashew and is thus able to keep its price, and Mozambique earnings, down...) Had the government's strategy of supporting an infant industry been left to follow its course, therefore, the nation's overall earnings would certainly have been greater, and dynamic gains would have been realised in domestic processing technology and also in government economic management.

The real world is always more complicated than theory presumes. The World Bank's world view had been captured by the "Washington Consensus" – the policy paradigm of supply-side economics – and this clouded its vision of what specific measures were appropriate in a particular instance.

Source: McMillan, M., Rodrik, D. and Welch, K. "When Economic Reform Goes Wrong: Cashews in Mozambique" *NBER Working Paper 9117, August 2002.*

There is no doubt that some developing countries' policies have been inflationary, destabilising and financially unsustainable. Others have been protectionist, isolationist and anti-growth. Essential reforms in some cases were necessary. But to insist on cutbacks in all public spending, to tar all government intervention with the same brush, is to fall foul of the fallacy that one extreme is better than the other. Since the late 1980s, however, we have seen the steady rise of a consistent challenge to the free market, neoclassical paradigm.

NEW INSTITUTIONAL ECONOMICS

It has been argued so far that economic growth cannot occur unless investment takes place to create the capital goods necessary to produce increased future outputs. Technological progress must also occur to ensure that productive resources are liberated from the constraints of diminishing returns.

Market economies use price signals to decide the pattern of resources to be invested in capital but will need the hand of government to provide support for technology.

In addition, sound macroeconomic policies that prevent inflation and its distorting effect on the price mechanism, and policies to guarantee free trade that give opportunities for all to participate in wealth creation are equally held to be necessary conditions to secure economic growth.

All these conditions taken together are still not, however, sufficient to explain why some countries grow rich and others do not. There is a growing consensus, particularly from economic historians who have taken a longer view of the process of development, that the missing factor, the key explanatory variable that links all these issues together is the presence or absence of stable social, political and economic *institutions*.

In this argument, capital and technology are the product of economic institutions that embody confidence in the future. Sound government policies are similarly the product of sound, stable political institutions. Secure property rights, legal systems, political stability, LAND REFORMS and efficient capital markets, are amongst those institutional features that facilitate economic growth and development.

A country blessed with enormous natural resources (the Soviet Union, Argentina) will make a mess of them if they have bad institutions. Conversely, a nation with very few resources and/or starting from a very disadvantageous situation (Singapore, Taiwan) can nonetheless achieve rapid advance if it has good institutions. A country with bad institutions will institute bad policies and be unable to reverse them; whereas a country with good institutions may make policy mistakes but will be able to recover and redesign them.

These are the views of an increasing number of different economists and historians who have studied the factors affecting the economic development of a wide range of countries, past and present. They include the very first, famous economist as well as some recent Nobel Prize winners:

Adam Smith, the professor of moral philosophy of Glasgow University in 1776 was well aware of the ethical foundations of a market society. It was he who first emphasised that economic growth takes place with increasing specialisation consequent upon the expansion of markets. Trade can occur all over the world – providing one party to a contract trusts the other to keep their end of the bargain. This emphasis has returned to modern economics in a concern about transactions costs.

It is fascinating to see how different societies do business. One of the problems of Western tourists visiting developing countries, for example in the Middle East or Latin America, is that many fail to understand the culture of trade in these countries. In an Arab *Souk* or bazaar, for example, there is much haggling – face-to-face trading on a repetitive basis – over small transactions. A lot of effort is thus devoted to clientisation.

What you are in effect doing in these circumstances is establishing a personal relationship and reputation. In such societies, reputation is everything. Other examples are traditional caravan trade in the Middle East, or in Native American culture, or in Mafia trade – if you have the blessing of the local chief or sultan you go with his protection and you can establish an efficient trade. Similarly, the Latin American traditional method of doing business is to go through the extended family – you rarely deal with someone you do not know; you always go via family or personal recommendation of someone whose reputation is recognised by both parties.

What all these trades have in common is that they take place in an environment where there is no over-arching rule of law – where a dealer who is wronged has no recourse to some authority that can compensate him or her in full. Without such authority, the trader has to bargain to establish his or her own rights. The essential economic point to be made here is that the transaction costs involved in doing business this way are excessive. Since trust in trade is established on a personal basis, then market trade cannot develop very far. The cost of doing transactions on this basis soon becomes prohibitive.

The contrast when people who are used to such personalised dealings relocate in a wealthy market economy can be fascinating – some are amazed at how trusting people can be in Western society. To open a bank account, to buy a car or to make a deal and exchange money over a telephone is so easy.

Highly specialised market societies can only operate if transactions costs are minimised. We thus have elaborate systems of monitoring and enforcing contracts that are embodied in law as property rights. It is only because we possess such systems that transactions costs can be reduced and thus we can do business.

Property rights allow individuals in highly complex trading situations across space and through time to have the confidence to deal with others of whom they have no personal knowledge and with whom they have no reciprocal and ongoing exchange relationship. Even if you only deal with such people once, you should be able to rely on them just as much as if you were in daily contact and whether they need your business or not.

Such trading is only possible if:

- formal institutions exist to specify property rights and to enforce contracts,
- and NORMS OF CONDUCT exist to maintain the same confidence where – even where authority exists – there are deficiencies in measuring and enforcing compliance.

The importance of formal institutions (government) and informal institutions (norms of behaviour) tend to be ignored by academics of neoclassical persuasion who in the words of economic historian Douglass North: "persist in modelling government as nothing more than a gigantic form of theft and income redistribution".

Yet the key to growth and development is the same today as in Adam Smith's time – the increasing specialisation and development of markets – which is absolutely dependent on a complex web of institutions which run from measurable property rights to well-run legal systems to incorruptible bureaucracies. There are vast differences in the relative certainty of contract enforcement over time (empires have grown and fallen according to the strength of their customs and laws) and in space – between the developed and developing world.

It is argued that, *without exception*, countries grow slowest where property rights are weak or absent, the rule of law is unreliable and where governments are corrupt. In such cases the custom of trust and respect between citizens breaks down, the costs of transacting business soon becomes excessive and no great growth in trade beyond personal contact is possible. In contrast, countries grow fastest where these institutions are all in place and it becomes the norm to abide by them (Box 8.4).

BOX 8.4 INSTITUTIONAL REFORM

Land in poor, agricultural economies is the main source of wealth. Such societies tend to be feudal in organisation: where ownership is concentrated in the hands of a few and peasant labour is paid a low wage to till the fields and deliver the product to the landlord. Quite apart from any injustice in such arrangements, so long as labourers cannot earn the full reward for their efforts, there is no incentive for those who do most of the work to strive to be economically efficient. Both land and labour productivity tends to be very low.

The Chinese communist revolution in 1949 was driven by a sense of injustice to dispossess landlords and redistribute lands in huge communes to be owned by "the People's Republic". In this way previously poor peasants were to be given altogether greater access to wealth-creating land.

Agricultural production stagnated, however, despite all sorts of efforts to inspire revolutionary zeal such as in the inappropriately named "Great Leap Forward". It was not until well after the death of the communist leader Mao Tse Tung that China was able to experiment with market incentives in the communes. In the 1980s, with the introduction of the Household Responsibility System, individual households could lease their own land and were able to keep or sell off any produce they made in excess of official targets. As a result, farm production took off and China has never looked back.

The moral of the tale is that where property rights are confined to a few, or held in some collective ownership, then the majority are denied access and incentive to utilise productive resources efficiently. Give people entitlement to the fruits of their own labour, however, and economic growth will result.

By this argument (i) land reform in agricultural societies, (ii) privatisation and wide share ownership in industrial societies and (iii) high levels of general education in knowledge societies are all essential institutional reforms that promote growth and development.

GEOGRAPHY?

One of the oldest and, curiously, most recent explanations for the difference between rich and poor nations is alleged to be geography. According to the traditional argument, tropical climates provoke debilitating diseases, inhibit agricultural productivity and militate against hard work. Geographical reasons for poverty have been made for centuries and on occasions they have been used to justify unsavoury colonial, if not downright racist, attitudes. However distasteful they may be, social scientists must nonetheless examine this old claim.

Recent research has in fact added a new twist to the story. There is no denying that colonies of European settlement in temperate latitudes have generally been more successful in achieving economic growth than those established in the tropics. This is true, however, not for the reasons given immediately above but because different geography and climate has led to the establishment of different institutions and it is these institutions which determine the pace of development.

Surveys have been undertaken of former colonies in different parts of the world in order to control for a variety of factors. It is found that where the death rate of settlers was high – typically due to diseases in the tropics – the Europeans stayed away and set up institutions that were designed to be extractive, using local or imported slave labour. Whether it be mining precious resources (silver in Bolivia, diamonds in South Africa) or farming in planta-tions (sugar in the West Indies, rubber in Malaysia), the laws and institutions introduced were essentially hierarchical – conveying economic and political power to a tiny elite and denying any substantial rights to those below them in society. Where geography and climate was agreeable to Europeans, however, settler mortality was low and so colonists moved in, set up property rights and democratic systems that devolved power, promoted trade and generated growth. (The original inhabitants of these temperate lands, it must be emphasised, generally lost out in the face of this immi-gration. They had little say in what was to be established in their homelands [see Box 8.5].)

BOX 8.5 WHICH IS THE WILD WEST?

Dances With Wolves (Orion Pictures, 1990), directed by and starring Kevin Costner, is one of a long line of Hollywood Westerns that depict the culture clash between native Americans and European settlers. It only differs from its many predecessors in that it is overtly supportive of the former in the dramatisation of the conflict between a traditional society of nomadic hunter-gatherers and the land-grabbing, modern market economy that overruns it.

The North American native experience was also shared by the fate of aboriginal inhabitants of Argentina, South Africa and Australia. Those not killed off by non-native diseases against which they had little defence were dis-possessed of their communal lands by immigrant settlers who recognised only private property rights – established by their own laws and modern firearms. Removed from the economic basis of their less sophisticated tribal socie-ties, native populations could not compete against the well-organised, economically and militarily powerful new-comers who transferred the land they acquired into alternative employments. US corn, Argentine beef, South African gold and diamonds and Australian wool have since been marketed around the world and enriched the lives of millions of producers and consumers alike ... though try convincing the few descendents of those who lost out in the process that the ends justified the means.

An interesting illustration of this argument is the geographical differences in institutions between the northern and southern states of the USA. Types of farming, patterns of ownership, employment and incomes in the more temperate climates contrast markedly from those in the southern, plantation states where the nature of society still bears the scars of its origins in slavery.

Geography in its own right, it should therefore be emphasised, is not a good explanatory variable. Nor is colonialism, *per se*. Tropical countries with good institutions can enjoy economic success (like Singapore) – it is just that they have been the exception. The fact is that even after the imperialists have gone, there are too few tropical nations that have succeeded in throwing off their inheritance. Too many countries with hierarchical social structures have still not been able to change them, and remain saddled today with feudalistic institutions that inhibit their advance. Those colonies established with good, pro-growth institutions – typically but not always in temperate zones – have meanwhile reaped the economic benefits that have come with them.

CAN THE PLANET AFFORD IT?

The population of China numbers 1.4 billion (2014) and for the last 30 years or so it has enjoyed increasing economic growth that has lifted the great majority of its people out of poverty. The widespread introduction of market institutions and incentives has transformed the former highly inefficient, centrally planned, command economy into the latest, and biggest "Asian tiger".

Although slower to introduce institutional reforms, India has also shaken off some of its more restrictive economic shackles and, with a population of 1.3 billion, it too has now found its way on a steady path of economic growth that is beginning to bring improved living standards to all.

The average annual growth rate for these two giant countries (which together account for 40 per cent of the world's population) over the period 2009 to 2012 was, in the case of China, 9.2 per cent and, in the case of India, 7.1 per cent. This compares to a world average of around 2.3 per cent per year (an average, of course, pushed up by these two outliers).

These statistics represent a steady improvement in the fortunes of billions of lives and must accordingly be celebrated. The question to ask, however, is – can this trend be sustained?

The environmental pressure group WWF calculates how much of the Earth's resources are consumed to provide for its population. The ECOLOGICAL FOOTPRINT measures the total area of productive land or sea necessary to produce the food, materials, energy and living space currently used to provide for one person in each different country. The results are given in Figure 8.4: the vertical axis registering the hectares of land required per capita and the horizontal axis measuring the relative population sizes for the respective continents.

As can be seen, the average North American citizen consumes nearly ten times the resources of the average African or Asian individual. Note, however, the numbers of those who consume least greatly exceed those who consume most. What happens therefore, if current Chinese and Indian growth rates are maintained and

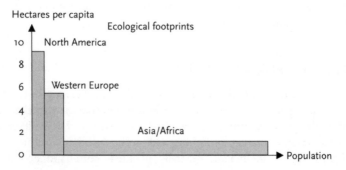

Figure 8.4 Hectares of land needed per capita to support consumption in different continents, against population, 2000. (Sources: WWF, World Bank.)

every Asian gets eventually to drive around in cars the size and gas-guzzling capacity of the average North American? The column for Asia/Africa in Figure 8.4 will grow in size to the height of the others. If this were to happen then the planet will be devoid of resources and polluted with waste!

Quite clearly, this brief example shows that future populations cannot enjoy the wasteful lifestyles practised at present by the world's richest. The heavy ecological footprints left on the Earth today by Americans and Europeans would devastate the natural environment and exhaust the planet if repeated by future billions in the rest of the world.

There seems to be even more injustice for the developing world implied in this prediction. Just as soon as these countries seem to be on the way to implementing the institutions and policies to produce growth, so the finite resources of the Earth will hold them back – thanks to the profligate behaviour of those who got there first. Is this really true? Would the replication of current North American consumption patterns in developing countries impoverish the planet?

Fortunately for us all, that is unlikely to happen. The major reason for this – despite some of the scariest scenarios painted by a few environmentalists – is the operation of the free market. To explain how markets can assist in protecting scarce resources we can take one important example as an illustration: the supply of oil reserves.

In 1972, in a famous publication by a number of authors referred to as the Club of Rome, *The Limits to Growth* (by D. H. Meadows et al.) set out a pessimistic scenario where the world was destined to run out of oil and other essential, exhaustible resources by the year 2000. World economic growth was thus destined to come to a full stop.

Evidently this has not happened. People can still fill up their cars at the local petrol station with no restriction. Growth rates of the wealthier consumer nations are still positive and the newly indus-trialising countries are growing even faster. What went wrong with the calculations?

Based on US patterns of oil consumption in 1972, if all other nations as they grew richer emulated such practice then there is no doubt that there would be much less oil left in the ground today. Maybe world growth would have stopped. Similarly, if all Asia tomorrow drives the US cars of today, then world economic growth might indeed come to an end. But of course the problem of basing predictions on current practice is that this assumes future behaviour will not change ... and it always does. That is the fascination of economics – it is a *social* science and people, unlike phenomena in the "hard sciences", are capable of choice and change.

Free markets, in particular, provide powerful incentives for people to alter their consumption and production habits. Consider the implications of continuing high demand for oil.

If the rate of world consumption continues to grow steadily, or even accelerate, such that existing oil resources become depleted then, in the open market, prices would rise – slowly at first but at an increasing rate also, as supplies reduce. The effect of this price rise is twofold: it immediately puts a brake on demand and it simultaneously increases the profitability of oil and alternative energy production.

Demand is affected in two ways. Some people may reduce their consumption directly where possible (they may take fewer car journeys). They will also seek out alternatives. Since oil is a basic energy source, immediate change is unlikely but *so long as the price rise is sustained* then consumers (in private homes and in industry) will find ways to economise and will seek out alternatives in the longer term – other forms of transport, other forms of heating, and so on (see Box 8.6).

BOX 8.6 THE MOTOR CAR

The major consumer of oil is transport. But consider what has happened over the last 30 years or so to the technology involved in producing the internal combustion engine. Because oil is expensive, car engines today are far more efficient in their consumption of fuel (and far less polluting) than they were in 1972. The cars that Asia buys tomorrow will certainly not be anything like those Americans use today. Americans will not buy today's cars tomorrow either. In fact, if the price of oil does rise much further then alternative fuel technologies (batteries; biofuels; LPG, and fuel cells) will receive yet another impetus. The big car multinationals have already produced the prototype motors – they are currently racing to try and get prices down and engine performances up. Their future profits depend upon it.

Imagine now if there *is* a breakthrough in alternative fuel technology. What would happen to oil prices? As alternatives come on-stream the price of oil would first stabilise and then, depending on how quickly renewable supplies would displace fossil fuels, the price would then fall. This process has not happened yet – alternative technologies are still too costly to develop, though progress is being made and so the cost of green technology has been falling. In the meantime OPEC countries are urgently attempting to develop other industries. Their worried actions are the clearest possible indication that oil resources in future will not be exhausted and put a limit to world growth.

Supply also responds to price changes. More exploration and development will take place since anticipated future profits are a spur to action. Oil reserves in diverse locations previously thought uneconomic to exploit now become profitable to do so. For example, US and Canadian oil and gas shales (rock formations that contain diffuse organic matter within them) are technologically difficult to exploit but as oil prices have risen continuously then this enormous resource has been pressed into service. Hydraulic fracking has caused a boom in US gas production and employment, brought gas prices down, led to a plateauing of oil prices and is en-route to making the USA energy self-sufficient again.

The price mechanism is thus a sophisticated device that works to economise on scarce resources. What *are* prices? Nothing more nor less than an instant indication of relative scarcity. The fact that the real price of oil today (corrected for a fall in the value of money) is lower than it was in the late 1970s is an indication that oil is now less scarce than it was. It changes in the daily or spot market in response to fluctuations in current demand and supply – and it will continue to rise and fall in the future in response to the variety of factors that impact on this (currently) important resource.

MARKET FAILURE

If all Earth's resources were marketed in the way described then we would have a fully automatic environmental protection system already in place. We could all rest assured that there is no environmental crisis. It has been argued consistently throughout this book, however, that free markets frequently fail. The hand of government is needed to adjust the price mechanism since markets do not factor into their signals all the many important influences that profoundly concern people and the environment.

We have seen throughout this text a number of instances where markets fail to organise a society's resources efficiently:

- Where there are substantial externalities – where any individual consumption or production decision impacts significantly on third parties (see Chapter 2 and further below).
- Where there is a lack of information for consumers to exercise efficient choices.
- Where there is a need for pure public goods yet there is no incentive for their private production (see earlier in this chapter).
- Where economies of scale lead to monopoly or oligopoly and the erosion of the public's interest (see Chapter 4).
- Where the sum of society's choices add up to a level of aggregate demand inconsistent with the level of aggregate supply (see Chapter 5).

The first two points are particularly relevant to environmental economics:

EXTERNALITIES

Certain basic resources we depend upon – like the air we breathe – are free goods. They are not marketed, are commercially costless to utilise and carry no price. Economics predicts therefore that consumption will rise up to the point where the marginal utility equals price. That is, we will consume as much air as we want with no limit up to the point where the usefulness of an extra breath is zero. (That happens when we die!)

Since there is no economic restriction on the consumption of the atmosphere, so air and road traffic will burn its oxygen and spill out poisonous emissions with no market penalty. Farmers, logging companies and crazy arsonists will burn off natural vegetation as they so wish. Levels of carbon dioxide in the atmosphere will continue to rise. If the market cannot reign in such practice, government must – or we will be condemned to live (and die) with the consequences of global warning, acid rain, climate change and all the other effects of atmospheric pollution.

Such external costs to society are not included in market prices. Neither producers of cars, or food, nor consumers of these goods, pay directly for the costs imposed on society of excessive oxygen consumption. Hence the argument for governments to impose a carbon tax to restore a "market" incentive to economise on this otherwise free good.

It is a good idea in theory. The problem is trying to calculate the appropriate level of tax. Exactly how much oxygen is consumed by farmers, car drivers, everyone else who burns anything? And even if you could calculate the damage done by each individual consumer or producer, how then do you charge them? Governments must struggle with this conundrum.

If we could get the answer right it would internalise in the price of each good or service all the external costs (and benefits). Markets can thus operate efficient price signals. Unfortunately, the task is immense: externalities are everywhere. How do you account for all the possible environmental impacts that may exist with every production and consumption decision?

IMPERFECT INFORMATION

This last point pervades all environmental concerns. Exactly how much damage are we doing to the environment in the course of our everyday choices? Discharging aerosol cans and disposing of old refrigerators we now learn releases CFC gases that harm the ozone layer. Had we known earlier we might not have done this. No doubt all sorts of other practices carry environmental consequences too. First we need to know of the damage we are doing to the planet and second we must also be able to place a monetary value on this data for comparative purposes.

We can only adjust our collective behaviour on the basis of reliable information. This requires that those who speak out against the wasteful excesses of economic growth do so with responsibility. The essence of economics is opportunity cost: making intelligent trade-offs where every option carries a price. For example, those protesting about the construction of the Three Dams hydro-electric power project in China ought to contrast the (undoubtedly serious) environmental costs involved against the proposed benefits of increased energy supplies to a poor population and the removal of the threat of floods that have drowned millions in the past. Have such protestors fully measured and valued the costs and benefits concerned?

The Economist magazine reports that it comes as a shock to discover just how little reliable information there is on the environment. Look at almost any scientific investigation and you get a different picture. One scare story follows another in the popular press but a balanced overview is impossible since, especially for the larger concerns such as global climate change, comprehensive data is not available. Environmental audits at present underway on numerous proposed ventures are undoubtedly steps in the right direction but the road is infinitely long.

COST BENEFIT ANALYSIS is a form of educated guesswork at placing monetary values on impacts that we know of. (It includes, in the Three Dams example above, attempting to measure the value of human life and quantifying the reduced risk of drowning. There are sophisticated procedures to follow; though they are not flawless.) But how do you measure the value of environmental consequences that scientists are at present only barely aware of?

Public officials designated to compile reports on these issues must proceed with caution since in many cases environmental impacts are long term, difficult to foresee but often irreversible past a certain crisis point. Issues are also frequently clouded by political concerns. In the end we have no choice other than to work with uncertainty.

SUSTAINABLE DEVELOPMENT

A key concept for environmentalists is sustainable development; defined as meeting the needs of present populations without compromising the needs of future generations. This is a worthy ideal. It is nonetheless difficult to achieve if we cannot measure environmental costs and benefits accurately – although it is an important principle that can give rise to valuable guidelines for practical policy.

All economic development is based to some extent on the exploitation of natural resources. These include non-renewable environmental assets such as fossil fuels, RENEWABLE RESOURCES such as fish stocks and wildlife, and certain borderline assets that are capable of regeneration though with a certain loss of uniqueness, such as rainforests.

To insist that no exploitation of Earth's rich bounty should take place for fear of dispossessing future generations is nonsensical. Living standards would collapse and there would then be no further generations created to enjoy the future. The question, as always in economics, is what price is acceptable in trading-off present exploitation for the future? Paying too high a price to protect the environment means condemning present populations – and unborn future generations – to low levels of consumption and hardship; too low a price means depriving our children of the environmental opportunities we ourselves inherited. It is a matter of INTERGENERATIONAL EQUITY.

EXHAUSTIBLE RESOURCES

Depletion of some non-renewable assets is inevitable if present living standards are to rise and embrace millions more of the world's poor. As technologies improve, humankind can be more efficient in its use of Middle Eastern oil and South American rainforests, and alternatives can be increasingly generated, but there is no ultimate substitute in the end for using some form of mineral, exhaustible resource to fuel economic progress.

The loss of existing natural resources can be compensated for to some extent by replacing them with man-made ones. Unique native forests in much of the Earth's temperate lands, for example, have been largely been replaced by agricultural landscapes and plantations that are capable of much greater economic outputs and yet are not environmentally impoverished. Similarly, there may well be less coal, oil and iron ore left for the future but maybe we can camouflage the holes we have left in the ground and replace these supplies with more renewable energies and materials.

If, however, we are bound to consume exhaustible resources by some irreducible amount – albeit less in the future than at present – what then is the OPTIMAL DEPLETION RATE of such assets that balances present against future needs?

Consider an exhaustible resource that is a basic raw material used in industry. If current extraction increases faster than demand is growing, prices of this resource will fall. Conversely, if it is left in the ground while current demand is mounting, prices will rise. Should we mine it now or later, and by how much? It depends on how we value the future – a concept we have met earlier – embodied in our rate of time preference.

At equilibrium, the rate of growth of mineral resource prices should just equal the market rate of time preference/rate of interest. If interest rates are lower than the rate of growth of mineral prices, we exploit and sell more resources now – bringing their price down (see Box 8.7). If the prices are growing more slowly than interest rates then exploitation of resources will fall. Prices will begin to rise faster. (As explained earlier, changes in technology will impact on the rate of growth of prices and thus slow down or speed up the rate of resource extraction accordingly.)

BOX 8.7 DEPLETION RATES: AN EXAMPLE

Suppose oil prices were rising at a rate of 12 per cent per year as supplies cannot keep pace with demand. Suppose, however, that the market values the future at 5 per cent. That is, invest 100 now and you will earn 105 next year.

Clearly you have an incentive to buy oil now and sell it in a year's time – you would make 12 per cent rather than 5 per cent that way.

With fast rising oil prices, there would be a surge of interest in developing oil reserves and increasing supplies. This increased rate of exploitation would eventually bring prices down and the rate of growth of oil prices would fall until eventually it equalled 5 per cent. There would be no incentive to increase exploitation and drive down the rate of price increases below this.

RENEWABLE RESOURCES

The rate at which we can safely run down fish and animal stocks, harvest timber and use fresh water reserves depends on their natural regeneration rates. These differ for different species. Rabbits reproduce faster than rhinoceroses and can accordingly be hunted more. Bamboo grows faster than oak. The costs of harvesting are important too. The further and more expensive it is to travel to cut down timber or fish for disappearing stocks will have to be compared against the revenues gained from selling the scarce supplies.

Note that extinction becomes an imminent danger where:

- property rights are ill defined (see Box 8.8),
- the costs of harvesting are low,
- the prices and revenues from selling scarce resources are high,
- stocks have fallen to a CRITICAL MINIMUM SIZE for natural regeneration and,
- people involved place little value on the future loss of the asset concerned.

All these conditions are met, for example, in those African big game parks where poachers are unlikely to be caught and their targets are easy to identify. The same scenario obtains where certain large wildlife species have nowhere to hide and are competing for habitat with poor people (see Box 2.3, p39–40). The safety of your children has a higher priority than the freedom to roam of tigers or wild elephants in these circumstances.

BOX 8.8 THE TRAGEDY OF THE COMMONS

Common property, by definition, belongs to everyone. No one user has a strong incentive to conserve it, therefore. History shows that, as populations rise, village pastureland that is open to all local farmers tends to be exhausted by the first ones to place their livestock upon it. "Use it or lose it" is the maxim.

The same principle applies to native forests, fish and wildlife stocks, underground reservoirs of fresh water and oil – indeed wherever there is a common resource and access is open to all. Stocks of North Atlantic cod, for example, have been reduced almost to the point of no return where there has been open competition between rival nations' fishing fleets – except in the case of Iceland's territorial

> waters. Where Icelandic waters are concerned there has been a conservation policy observed and enforced and cod stocks are healthy as a result. Where there is a lack of international agreement, however, and property rights are absent or weakly enforced, then excessive exploitation will take place. That is the "TRAGEDY OF THE COMMONS".

MARKETS AND GOVERNMENT

Economic development need not be at the expense of the planet if we get our policies right. If market prices do not reflect substantial environmental costs in the sale of certain goods and services then taxes can be imposed to bring their production and consumption in line with sustainable limits. Exploitation of common property can be reduced by allocating property rights where possible and by active policing wherever not. North Atlantic cod and African elephants need not go the way of the Dodo.

Governments can use the ingenuity and efficiency of markets. For example, given agreement on the amount of pollution reduction that must be achieved by a certain date, different countries (or regions within a country) can trade POLLUTION PERMITS between themselves to determine who does what. If zone A finds it more expensive to make cutbacks than zone B then A can pay B to do more than its share of greenery. So long as there is agreement all round and targets are met then everyone gains.

Another innovative means of using markets to protect the environment, particularly of relevance to poor countries that carry excessive debt burdens, is in the use of DEBT FOR NATURE SWAPs (see Box 8.9).

BOX 8.9 DEBT FOR NATURE SWAPS

Madagascar is a poor African country of little over 22 million people with a Gross Domestic Product of US$ 10 billion and an external debt of US$ 2.9 billion, owed in foreign currencies to overseas banks and governments (2013, World Bank data).

The main resource of this country is its unique biodiversity: nearly 98 per cent of Madagascar's land mammals, 92 per cent of its reptiles, and 80 per cent of its plants are found nowhere else on Earth. But with 71 per cent of the population living below the poverty line, the great temptation is for such deprived people to consume the biodiversity just to survive.

Given that the Western market economies do not want this country's unique environmental heritage to be depleted is there a solution they can find? Surely: it is called a debt for nature swap.

There are numerous agencies, both public and private, that are willing to provide funds for the protection of the environment. Take one example: in 1996, WWF, a conservation agency, was keen to act for the Netherlands Development Cooperation in using US$ 1 million of their funds to take over Madagascan debt. That is, they negotiated a payment of US$ 1m to international creditors to cancel US$ 2m of Madagascan debt. They then presented this deal to the Central Bank of Madagascar which agreed

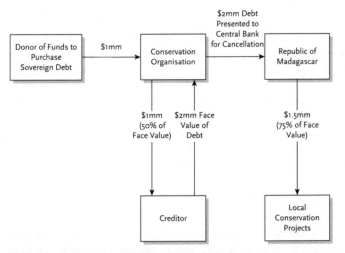

Result: **$1mm Donation generates $1.5mm in Conservation Funding**

Figure 8.5 Debt for nature flowchart. (Source: WWF.)

to pay the equivalent of US$ 1.5m *in local currency* to Madagascan environmental projects. Local forests were protected and villagers trained in conservation in an eight-year WWF project as a result.

This is just one of a number of debt-for-nature swaps that the Madagascan government approved over a period between 1989 to 1996 that involved a cancellation of US$ 12.5 million of external debt.

Humankind's ingenuity is the only resource that is not in short supply and shows no sign of reaching exhaustion. Although there are problems, scientists and economists can come together and calculate the costs and benefits of each and every practice that seems to threaten the environment and make their recommendations accordingly. The political will to apply our energies to safeguard the future is hard to come by but successes like the Montreal Protocol in 1987 – which agreed to phase out the production of CFCs and protect the ozone layer – show that, however difficult, international accord *is* possible.

I finish on a note of caution, however. The poor world cannot wait. Some countries are already growing fast and others are desperate to follow in their footsteps. Having waited so long and watched how others have enjoyed the fruits of the planet without them, poor people naturally have a high preference to get rich quick and may discount the effects on the environment quite highly. Populations in temperate lands who have dammed their rivers, consumed their native forests and burned off their coal reserves in the course of industrialisation may be rudely received if they protest about developing countries doing the same. If people in the developed world want others to ease up on their exploitation of the planet they will have to pay them to do so. That is, after all, what their own markets would suggest. So: what is a fair price?

SUMMARY

The wealth of nations is derived from trade with expanding markets. A country can only benefit from such trade, however, if it first has in place the social, economic and political institutions that reduce transactions costs and give people confidence that agreements will be honoured over time and through space.

People will invest in the future if risks can be reliably calculated and the rewards are judged sufficient. Capital can thus be accumulated and technology can be employed to postpone the onset of diminishing returns.

As economic growth occurs, external environmental costs are likely to be incurred. So long as these costs can be quantified, however, and governments can adjust market prices and practices accordingly then a fine balance between present and future needs can be struck.

Markets can and should be employed to determine the equilibrium price that balances these contrasting, and ever-changing, needs – in this way we *can* reduce poverty and protect the environment.

FURTHER READING

An excellent text on economic growth theory is by Daron Acemoglu (2008) *Introduction to Modern Economic Growth*, Princeton University Press.

There is no general consensus on the nature and content of development economics but a comprehensive book of readings is Meier, G. M. and Rauch, J. E. (2005) *Leading Issues in Economic Development*, Oxford University Press.

Particular insights into new institutional economics can be found in North, D. (June 1994) "Economic Performance Through Time" *American Economic Review*, Vol. 84, pp. 359–68 and de Soto, H. (2003) *The Mystery of Capital*, Basic Books.

Environmental Economics: An Introduction can be appraised in the book by Barry and Martha Field, McGraw-Hill (2012).

QUESTIONS

1 What are (a) the assumptions and (b) the predictions of Solow's neoclassical growth theory, and how do these differ from Romer's endogenous growth model?

2 What role is there for government if it wishes to promote economic growth?

3 Examine the economic costs of exploiting the Earth's fossil fuels (a) too slowly, and (b) too quickly. How quickly should fossil fuels be exploited?

4 What role is there for (a) markets and (b) governments in promoting sustainable economic development?

GLOSSARY

ABSOLUTE ADVANTAGE Where one country is more efficient than another in the production of a common range of goods and services (contrast with *comparative advantage*).

ADMINISTERED PRICES Prices of goods and services fixed by planners according to political or social considerations, and they are not, therefore, automatically responsive to economic shortage or surplus (see *Black Market* and *National Health Service*).

ADMINISTRATIVE GUIDANCE The East Asian model of development where government, via industry and workers' representatives, has led industrial strategy and economic growth.

AGGREGATE DEMAND All spending within the economy that contributes towards national income: *consumption*, *investment*, government spending, exports less imports.

AGGREGATE SUPPLY The total supply of all goods and services in an economy, less exports plus imports (see also *general equilibrium*).

ALLOCATION OF RESOURCES How land, labour, capital and enterprise are distributed between various employments.

BALANCE OF PAYMENTS The record of a country's payments in international trade. The import and export of goods (**Trade**

Balance) and services (***Invisible Balance***) is included in the ***Current Balance***. The international movement of investment, or speculative, funds is listed on the ***Capital Account***. The current and capital accounts taken together sum to indicate the ***total Currency Flow***.

BANK DEPOSITS Money listed in people's bank accounts – most of which exists as a matter of record only and has no physical form but which nonetheless acts as a medium of exchange and is transferable via cheque or plastic card.

BARRIERS TO ENTRY The cost incurred by a firm in entering a new market and competing with existing suppliers.

BARTER The exchange of goods and services in payment for other goods and services.

BEHAVIOURAL ECONOMICS This is a relatively new field of economics that looks at the microeconomic foundations of decision-making. In particular, it embraces psychological and emotional influences and so departs from the neoclassical assumption of rational economic agents.

BLACK MARKET Wherever scarce resources have an exchange value greater than that assigned to them by officialdom then an illegal, or black market will tend to appear.

BRAIN DRAIN The flow of highly skilled personnel out of a country in pursuit of employment elsewhere.

BRAND The unique identity given to a product by its producer.

BUDGET A record of income and expenditure over a given time period. *The* Budget is a reference to the government's annual financial record.

BUDGET CONSTRAINT The limits imposed by a finite income upon a consumer, producer or public administrator.

CAPITAL A man-made means of production.

CAPITAL INTENSIVE PRODUCTION Where more capital than labour is employed in production.

CAPITAL STOCK A stock of assets that is capable of producing a flow of goods or services over time. Note that the stock of *capital* can be *Fixed* or *Variable* as output changes (see also *liquid capital* and *investment*).

CARTEL Firms that act in deliberate *collusion* to avoid competition and thereby rig the market for their mutual benefit at the expense of the consumer (see *oligopoly*).

CENTRAL BANK The hub of a country's financial system which acts as banker to the government and to all recognised *financial intermediaries*; it issues the domestic currency; it conducts the government's monetary policy and it monitors a nation's financial affairs.

CENTRAL PLANNING An economic system where the *allocation of resources* is decided by some central committee of administrators.

CLIENTISATION The process by which buyers and sellers bargain with each other and thereby establish trustworthiness – typically in circumstances where there is no overarching rule of law to protect either party in case of default.

COLLATERAL Some recognised asset offered by the borrower to secure a loan.

COLLATERALISED DEBT OBLIGATION (CDO) These are the infamous securities that fuelled the panic at the heart of the credit crunch. You can raise a loan pledging the collateral of some desirable property. If you pool together lots of properties of varying quality you can use these to back the issue of a single CDO. The highly complex structure of some of these derivatives made it impossible to calculate their riskiness – especially at a time when property prices were volatile.

COLLUSION The action, usually of a *cartel*, of conspiring against consumers to increase prices, revenues and profits. Such action is normally illegal, unlike *tacit collusion* – which refers to an unspoken, unwritten mutual understanding between *oligopolists* not to actively compete.

COMMAND ECONOMY An economy where all decisions about what, how and for whom goods and services are to be produced are communicated to subordinates via command.

COMMON AGRICULTURAL POLICY The European Union's costly system of supporting agriculture.

COMPARATIVE ADVANTAGE Where a country may be inefficient in producing a range of goods and services but has a relative cost advantage in specialising in the production of one, or a few, only (contrast with *absolute advantage*).

CONSUMER EQUILIBRIUM That pattern of purchases which maximises a consumer's utility, given existing prices and incomes.

CONSUMER SOVEREIGNTY How in an ideal market system, by the pattern of their purchases, consumers determine what, how and for whom goods and services are to be produced.

CONSUMPTION The sum of a nation's consumer spending on goods and services.

COST BENEFIT ANALYSIS The comparison of all *costs* and benefits (including *externalities*) which determines whether or not a given course of action should be recommended.

COSTS OF PRODUCTION Costs internal to a firm incurred in the business of production. *Fixed* costs do not change as output changes; unlike *Variable* costs which do change. Fixed plus variable costs equal *Total* costs. Total costs divided by the number of units produced equal *Average* or unit costs. The increase in total costs brought about by the increase in production of one extra unit is defined as *Marginal* cost.

CREDIT CRUNCH The time in 2008/2009 when the world's financial markets were in panic and no one wanted to loan to anyone else since no one knew which institution would go bust next.

CREDIT DEFAULT SWAPS These are insurance-like contracts that promise to cover losses on certain securities in the event of a default. Except unlike insurance, the risks involved are neither finely calculated nor are they subject to regulation. They are just a means of hedging bets between traders who, if they gamble poorly, find out they have purchased a promise to bail out enormous losses. Oh dear...

CRITICAL MINIMUM SIZE The smallest viable population of a threatened species.

CROSS ELASTICITY OF DEMAND The percentage change in the demand of one good or service consequent upon the percentage change in price of another. For substititues as the price of one increases the demand for the other increases – the sign is positive. For complements, the sign is negative.

DEBT-EQUITY SWAPS The sale of shares in domestic industry to (typically foreign) investors in return for their agreement to pay a given proportion of accompanying debt.

DEBT FOR NATURE SWAPS Many underdeveloped countries are blessed with rich environmental resources but have borrowed excessive amounts from the rich world and have difficulty in paying this back. Rather than plundering their natural resources in order to pay their bills, rich countries can agree to cancel some of these debts if precious resources can be preserved. Typically, an international conservation agency is involved to broker the deal.

DEFICIT Expenditure exceeding income (contrast *surplus*).

DEFLATION 1. A sustained period of falling prices and incomes. 2. A process of adjusting records to remove the distorting effects of *inflation* over the period under study.

DEMAND The quantity of a good or service consumers are willing to purchase at a given price.

DEMAND-DEFICIENT UNEMPLOYMENT Resources that are unemployed because of a lack of *aggregate demand*. Sometimes known as Keynesian or cyclical unemployment.

DEMAND MANAGEMENT The attempt by government to adjust a country's level of *aggregate demand* by spending more when such demand is low and less when demand is high.

DEPRECIATION 1. The reduction in the value of a capital asset due to wear and tear in production. 2. The fall in market value of one currency in exchange for others in international trade (see *devaluation*).

DERIVED DEMAND The *demand* for any resource is derived from its ability to produce.

DEVALUATION The downward re-fixing in the official value of a currency, a term very similar to *depreciation*.

DIMINISHING MARGINAL UTILITY The decreasing additional satisfaction one derives from consuming an extra item. "The more you have of something, the less you want more of it."

DIMINISHING RETURNS, THE LAW OF This refers to how, when other resources remain fixed, increasing the employment of just one factor causes output to increase – but in steadily diminishing amounts (contrast with *returns to scale*).

DISCOUNT RATE 1. The base *interest rate* offered by the *central bank*. 2. The rate used to calculate the present value of some future income.

DISTRIBUTION EFFECTS The impact on the division of national income between rich and poor.

DIVIDENDS The return distributed out of *profits* to a company's ordinary shareholders – not to be confused with *interest*, which is paid to creditors whether a business makes a profit or not.

DOMINANT STRATEGY In any game where there are alternative moves to consider, a dominant strategy exists if your best choice is the same, whatever your rival chooses to do.

ECOLOGICAL FOOTPRINT The environmental resources it takes to maintain an individual in his/her current lifestyle.

ECONOMIC IMPERIALISM The economic influence exerted by rich nations, or *multinational corporations*, over poorer countries' consumption and/or production decisions.

ECONOMIES and DISECONOMIES OF SCALE See *returns to scale*.

EFFICIENCY A production technique is **X-Efficient** if it meets the required standards at minimal cost. Such a technical definition of efficiency, however, does not indicate whether or not the resource in question is optimally employed. **Allocative Efficiency** requires not only that each individual resource is giving its best but also no redeployment can lead to any improvement in overall output.

EFFICIENT MARKET HYPOTHESIS Related to financial markets, this is the (now controversial) theory that the prices of *financial instruments* reflect all available information; there is thus no remaining easy money to be made by buying some unnoticed undervalued stock; the market is perfectly efficient, always at equilibrium and asset prices cannot deviate from their fundamental values.

ELASTICITY *Price*-elasticity measures the responsiveness of demand, or supply, to a change in the price of a good. *Income*-elasticity of demand measures the responsiveness of demand to a change in consumer incomes. *Cross-price*-elasticity of supply measures how quickly producers can switch resources to produce an alternative which has now increased in price.

ENDOGENOUS GROWTH THEORY Devised by Paul Romer to explain how economic growth generates technological change which generates further growth, and more change, etc.

EQUILIBRIUM PRICE That price which evolves in a free *market* to equate *demand* with *supply*.

EQUITY 1. An equitable arrangement is that which is considered socially just, or fair. (This may or may not be economically efficient.) 2. Ordinary shares in a *joint stock company*.

EXCHANGE RATE The price of one currency in terms of another.

EXHAUSTIBLE RESOURCES Finite, non-reproducible, environmental assets.

EXOGENOUS CHANGE The variation of some factor assumed constant in the model being considered.

EXPECTATIONS The view that agents possess of future changes in economic variables – such that it influences current behaviour.

EXPECTATIONS-AUGMENTED PHILLIPS CURVE The assertion that no long-run *trade-off* between *inflation* and unemployment exists; that any level of inflation can obtain at the *natural level of unemployment* if money demand so facilitates this.

EXTERNALITIES Costs or benefits experienced by individuals or firms other than those directly engaged in the market production or consumption of a commodity (see *social costs*).

FALLACY OF COMPOSITION The erroneous belief that what holds true for one action also holds true of all actions aggregated together.

FIAT MONEY A form of money of little *intrinsic value* and whose worth is derived solely from the authority of the *central bank.*

FINANCIAL INSTRUMENT A written claim to some asset, such as a promise to pay a certain sum at a future date, which itself can be bought and sold.

FINANCIAL INTERMEDIARIES Profit-making commercial banks, finance houses and money dealers that act in the money markets to match lending and borrowing.

FISCAL POLICY The policy of governments with respect to levying taxes and spending revenues.

FOREIGN EXCHANGE MARKETS Markets where foreign currencies are bought and sold and *exchange rates* determined.

FRACTIONAL RESERVE BANKING The practice of modern banks whereby they create credit by some multiple of their retained reserves (see *money multiplier* and *reserve assets ratio*).

FRANCHISE Where a business supplies much of its own capital and labour and contracts producer and marketing support to supply a branded product, for which it pays a royalty.

FREE GOOD An asset which can be consumed for free. Typically, a market does not exist for its exchange and the determination of a price. As a result, its consumption, use and abuse might proceed unchecked unless some means can be found to prevent over-exploitation.

GAME THEORY This applies wherever strategic decisions between parties are interdependent. "If player A chooses option X, what is my best response?" Game theory is a form of applied mathematics first published by mathematician *John von Neumann* and economist *Oskar Morgenstern* in *The Theory of Games and Economic Behaviour,* 1944.

GENERAL EQUILIBRIUM The simultaneous balance of all markets in an economy and of *aggregate demand* with *aggregate supply.*

GOLD STANDARD Where all currencies are convertible into gold at a fixed price.

GROSS DOMESTIC PRODUCT (GDP) Everything a country produces in a given year. Used as a close approximation of national income, though note that some GDP of country A represents income to citizens of country B, and vice versa.

HAGGLING The process of bargaining to determine an *equilibrium price* that satisfies both buyer and seller.

HUMAN CAPITAL The acquisition of skills that increases the *productivity* of labour.

HYPERINFLATION An extreme form of *inflation* where the percentage rate of increase in prices is measured in hundreds or thousands.

INDIFFERENCE CURVES Lines drawn on a diagram joining points of equal consumer utility derived in the consumption of varying combinations of two goods or services.

INFANT INDUSTRIES A newly established industry, not yet grown to its *optimum size*.

INFLATION The rate of increase in the general level of prices (see also *deflation*).

INFORMAL SECTOR That part of a country's economy that functions without recognition, protection or official approval. An unregulated market of small-scale native enterprise catering for domestic, usually low-income consumers and producers.

INFORMATION COSTS Markets cannot function efficiently without all relevant information concerning the trade in question being made available to the parties involved. The extent of the market through time and space for any given trade is in effect determined by the information costs involved (see also *transaction costs*).

INFRASTRUCTURE The *public* and *merit goods* and services needed to support industry – transport facilities, water, electricity supplies, etc.

INJECTIONS Money injected into an economy's circular flow of income via *investment*, government spending and export spending (see *leakages,* also *multiplier*).

INTEGRATION The combination of businesses. **Horizontal** integration is where a firm grows by joining with others performing the same process in production (such as two bottling plants becoming one) whereas **Vertical** integration is where one firm joins with another performing a different process in the stage of production (such as a bottling plant joining with a transport company). **Lateral** integration is where two firms performing unrelated processes join together (such as a bottling plant with a cement factory).

INTEREST RATE This is the reward for investing capital. It is typically paid at an annual rate for the use of productive services that a stock of capital supplies and it will be higher the riskier the *investment* (see *capital stock,* also *rate of time preference*).

INTERGENERATIONAL EQUITY Equality of treatment between generations. Intergenerational equity is best served if exploitation of a finite resource proceeds at a rate inversely proportional to its rising value (see *optimal depletion rate*).

INTRINSIC VALUE The value of something in terms of the direct utility it provides to the consumer, as opposed to its officially declared value or *administered price*.

INVESTMENT The creation of new productive resources.

J-CURVE The way that *total currency flow* tends to decline and then recover over time, consequent to a *devaluation*.

JOINT STOCK COMPANY A business created by many owners jointly pledging capital – each owner being liable for only the share he/she has contributed.

JUNK BOND A *financial instrument* which carries a higher risk (and a higher return) than those issued by the government or the most recognised and secure commercial banks.

KEYNESIAN ECONOMICS The argument of John Maynard Keynes and followers which claims that *aggregate demand* need not equal *aggregate supply* at a level sufficient to generate full employment and therefore that *general equilibrium* may not be secured by the untrammelled forces of free markets.

LAND REFORM A redistribution of land ownership to benefit the poor and, ideally, to increase agricultural outputs.

LEAKAGES Withdrawals from the circular flow of income of an economy due to *savings*, taxation or import spending (contrast *injections*).

LENDER OF LAST RESORT This is an important function (and source of influence) of the *central bank* – to lend money to recognised *financial intermediaries* if they are caught short of cash.

LIBERALISATION The freeing up of markets by the removal of controls, regulations and other impediments to the flexible movement of prices, and of the entry and exit of economic agents (see also *supply-side policies*).

LIQUID ASSET The ease at which a physical or financial asset can be sold off and converted into money. Cash is 100 per cent liquid. Assets which can only be sold quickly at a greatly reduced price are illiquid.

LIQUID CAPITAL Money which is available for investment purposes.

LIQUIDITY PREFERENCE The *demand* for money, in preference to some income–earning asset.

LONG TERM The time period in which all costs can vary and all relationships originally assumed fixed can change.

LOW-LEVEL EQUILIBRIUM TRAP Where income and expenditure is balanced at very low levels but there is no potential for incomes to grow (typically because people cannot afford to save and invest).

MACROECONOMICS The economic theory of levels of *aggregate demand* and *supply*, *general equilibrium* and disequilibrium (contrast *microeconomics*).

MAQUILADORES Mexican assembly plants set up close to the US border.

MARGINAL PROPENSITY TO CONSUME/SAVE The fraction of the last unit of income earned that is spent/saved. Given an increase in income of £100, what percentage would you spend, and which save?

MARGINAL TAX RATES The rate of tax paid on the last unit of income earned by an individual.

MARKET An arrangement where buyers and sellers can trade and determine *equilibrium prices*.

MARKET FAILURE The inability of a market to equate *demand* with *supply* and avoid waste or hardship (see *information costs* and *transactions costs*).

MEDIUM OF EXCHANGE Any money which acts to facilitate trade.

MERCANTILISM The view that one country's wealth should be secured at the expense of another's, if necessary.

MERIT GOODS Goods and services (such as schools, hospitals) provided on a limited scale by private businesses but which convey substantial *external* benefits such that society may choose to supply them nationally via public enterprise (contrast with *public goods*).

MICRO-CREDIT The provision of small loans to small-scale enterprise.

MICROECONOMICS The economic theory of individual market *demand* and *supply*, and partial equilibrium (contrast *macroeconomics*).

MISMATCH UNEMPLOYMENT Where those people looking for work do not possess the skills and abilities required for the jobs available. Otherwise known as structural unemployment.

MOBILITY Flexible markets which respond to changing *consumer sovereignty* are only possible if resources are **occupationally** and **geographically** mobile.

MONETARIST The assertion that an increase in money supply is the only cause of inflation.

MONETARY BASE The reserves which act as the support for the creation of a country's money supply (see *fractional reserve banking*).

MONEY MULTIPLIER Where an increase in *financial inter-mediaries'* reserves by one unit can be used to support an increase in loans and thus create money by some multiple (see *reserve assets ratio*).

MONOPOLY A single producer that dominates the market so that consumers can only buy from this source or go without, since they have no alternative supplier.

MONOPSONY A single buyer that dominates the market. Suppliers can sell only to this outlet and have no other choice.

MORAL HAZARD If you guarantee to bail out another enterprise when they get into difficulty then that party is likely to take on more risks. For example, if a large bank carries with it the fortunes of millions of innocent depositors then a government cannot easily let it go bust. It is "too big to fail". Distressingly, the knowledge of this fact is then only likely to reinforce irresponsibly risky bank behaviour.

MULTINATIONAL CORPORATIONS Commercial enterprises operating in a number of different countries – the biggest with international share-ownership, employment and management.

MULTIPLIER The ratio by which an initial *injection* is multiplied to equal the overall income flow generated – hence *investment multiplier* and *foreign trade multiplier*. (Not to be confused with the *money multiplier*.)

NASH EQUILIBRIUM This may result if all players in a game have no incentive to change their position; that is, if any unilateral move by anyone leads to them making a loss. This equilibrium was first analysed by John Forbes Nash.

NATIONAL DEBT The outstanding debt that a country's government owes to its citizens.

NATIONAL HEALTH SERVICE (NHS) The UK national supplier of health services.

NATIONALISED INDUSTRIES Former private sector industry that has been taken over by the state and maintained under public ownership for political, social or *market failure* reasons.

NATURAL RATE OF UNEMPLOYMENT The level of unemployment that remains when all labour markets are in equilibrium. Those not employed are those allegedly not wanting work at the going wage rates.

NEOCLASSICAL ECONOMICS Modern mainstream economic theory that is built upon the classical writings of the founders of economics. It emphasises the supremacy of flexible *markets* and *general equilibrium* and recommends limits to government action (see *supply-side policies*).

NEOCLASSICAL GROWTH THEORY Based on neoclassical assumptions of flexible *markets*, this theory predicts that growth based on increasing *capital* accumulation will slow down without exogenous improvements in *total factor productivity*.

NEW CLASSICAL ECONOMICS An extreme form of *neoclassical economics* which asserts that *markets* can clear instantly if people act according to rational *expectations* and are not frustrated by government intervention.

NEW INSTITUTIONAL ECONOMICS A restatement of the importance of institutions, and the limitations of *neoclassical economics*, in explaining market systems and the causes of economic growth and development.

NEW KEYNESIAN ECONOMICS A modern school of thought that asserts that there is no unique *natural level of unemployment*. Following *Keynesian economics*, it is argued that a low level of *aggregate demand* will cause unemployment to rise, with market forces being insufficient to restore *general equilibrium* (see *hysteresis*).

NOMINAL INCOME Income in money terms (which must fall as prices rise). Similarly, the **nominal rate of interest** is that which is quoted before correction for *inflation*.

NON-PRICE COMPETITION A situation, typically in *oligopoly*, where businesses find it too risky to alter the price of their products in competition with rivals and thus prefer to compete in terms of advertising, marketing gimmicks and other less provocative promotions.

NORMATIVE ECONOMICS The offer of value judgements and personal recommendations in the subject matter of economics.

NORMS OF CONDUCT Informal but economically productive customs which regulate and facilitate trade in the absence of central authority.

OLIGOPOLY A *market* dominated by a few large producers, each keenly aware of the actions of the others.

OPEC The Organization of Petroleum Exporting Countries was formed in 1961 to coordinate petroleum policies among oil-producing nations. Its members now consist of Algeria, Angola, Ecuador, Indonesia, Iran, Iraq, Kuwait, Libya, Nigeria, Qatar, Saudi Arabia, the United Arab Emirates, and Venezuela. Saudi Arabia has traditionally dominated the organisation, owing to its enormous oil reserves, and OPEC used to supply far and away the dominant fraction of world oil. That fraction has diminished somewhat as non-OPEC supplies have come on-stream but at 40 per cent of world production it still controls the crucial hold over marginal supplies.

OPEN MARKET OPERATIONS The dealings of the central bank – buying and selling *financial instruments* in the money markets.

OPPORTUNITY COST *All* economic goods or services have an opportunity cost – that is, the decision to pursue one course of action means going without the opportunity to pursue the next best alternative. Note that where there is no opportunity cost involved, there is no need to economise.

OPPORTUNITY SET The choices of goods and services available for a consumer to purchase, given his/her income and ruling prices.

OPTIMAL DEPLETION RATE The rate of exploitation of an asset that minimises its environmental impact and balances present against future needs (see *intergenerational equity*).

OPTIMUM SIZE OF FIRM That level of production where the firm is most efficient: where average costs are minimised. (This may *not* be at the most profitable level of output.)

OVERHEADS The *fixed costs of production*.

PARADIGM A worldview, or set of beliefs that inform general scientific opinion.

PARADOX OF THRIFT The disconcerting finding that if everyone saves in an economy, everyone becomes worse off as national income falls (see *fallacy of composition*).

PATENT An exclusive government license to supply a given product.

PAY-OFF MATRIX A concept in Game Theory which identifies the rewards possible to (typically) two players faced with alternative courses of action – the gains or pay-off for any one being dependent on the actions of the other.

PERFECT COMPETITION A *market* where no one producer is influential enough to determine the price of the product traded – typically because there are no *barriers to entry* to prevent competition.

PHILLIPS CURVE The empirical finding, published in 1958, that unemployment decreased as wage inflation increased (see *trade-off*).

POLLUTION PERMITS A scheme which allows different consumers/firms/countries to trade their respective responsibilities in reaching an overall pollution target.

POSITIVE ECONOMICS Economics that attempts to be objectively scientific in providing testable propositions.

PRICE MECHANISM The way that changing prices automatically organise the *allocation of resources* in a market economy: signalling shortages and surpluses, giving incentive for resources to switch employments and equating demand with supply.

PRIVATISATION The return to private ownership of state-owned or *nationalised industries*.

PRODUCTIVITY The ratio between outputs and inputs.

PROFITS This is the reward for enterprise – the payment to entrepreneurs for organising production and taking the risks involved. **Normal** profit is defined as that minimum level of reward required to keep an entrepreneur in business; any level of profits above that is a form of producer surplus that can be called

abnormal, supernormal or monopoly profit. See also *transfer earnings* and economic *rent*.

PROPERTY RIGHTS For successful exchange to take place in modern market systems, it requires that clear, unequivocal, private property rights exist so that what is mine and what is yours can be established without dispute. This extends not only to material goods but also to unique ideas and intellectual property rights. (A tenet of *new institutional economics*.)

PUBLIC GOODS Goods and services – such as national defence or urban street lighting – that convey sizeable *external* benefits but which cannot be supplied on a restricted basis to paying customers only and thus will not be produced by private enterprise (contrast with *merit goods*). Pure public goods are ***non-rivalrous*** (my consumption of this service does not reduce its availability to others) and ***non-excludable*** (if supplied to me it is simultaneously supplied to others).

QUALITIES OF MONEY Those characteristics a commodity must possess if it is to function as a form of money – prime amongst which is acceptability.

QUANTITATIVE EASING This is where the central bank directly increases the reserves of commercial banks. Similar to *open market operations*, the central bank buys securities directly from commercial banks (not indirectly from other agents) and thus transfers cash into those commercial bank accounts, which can in turn be used to back a multiplied increase in the money supply.

QUASI MARKET A simulated market, usually of a public service, where at least one of the following conditions are absent: private ownership of resources, consumer choice, a market price, producer competition.

QUOTAS A fixed limit on the number of imports.

RATE OF TIME PREFERENCE The price paid on time: how much the market will compensate an owner for postponing his use of risk-less capital (contrast *interest rate*).

REAL INCOME What your money or *nominal* income can buy in real goods and services. Similarly, the ***real rate of interest*** is the return you can expect after inflation is accounted for.

RECESSION A slow down or fall in the rate of growth of an economy. An imprecise and less alarmist term than slump or depression.

RENEWABLE RESOURCES Environmental assets reproducible within an economic time-frame.

RENT 1. Commonly used to refer to the payment for land or property. 2. A surplus payment above that economically necessary.

RENT-SEEKING The action of economic agents to seek government favours, especially lucrative *monopoly* licences, to restrict competition.

RESERVE ASSETS RATIO The ratio of reserves to loans that *financial intermediaries* have created (see *fractional reserve banking, monetary base* and *money multiplier*).

RETURNS TO SCALE How revenues perform in comparison to costs as the size of a business increases. If total revenues increase faster than total costs as all input and outputs expand then this represents **increasing** returns to scale (also known as *economies of scale*). If revenues and costs expand at the same rate, this implies **constant** returns to scale. If total revenue increase more slowly than total cost as production increases then this represents **decreasing** returns to scale (also known as *diseconomies of scale*) (contrast with *diminishing returns*).

REVENUE Earnings from sales. *Total* revenue equals the number of goods sold, times their price. *Average* revenue equals total revenue divided by number of goods sold (it thus equals price). *Marginal* revenue is the addition to total revenue caused by the sale of one extra unit.

SAMPLE BASKET A sample of everyday consumer purchases which is used to calculate the rate of change of prices, that is, *inflation*.

SAVINGS Income that is not spent.

SHIFTS IN DEMAND/SUPPLY The movement of a demand/supply curve caused by a change in some factor other than the price of the good in question.

SHORT TERM The time period in which at least one factor under consideration does not change.

SIGHT DEPOSITS Those *bank deposits* (e.g. current accounts) which can be withdrawn on sight.

SOCIAL COSTS *External costs* imposed on society in the process of producing or consuming goods and services.

SPECULATIVE MOTIVE The demand for money for its use in financial speculation.

SPOT MARKET A market where goods or services are traded for immediate (as opposed to future) delivery.

SUPPLY The quantity of a good or service producers are willing to supply at a given price.

SUPPLY-SIDE POLICIES are those designed to increase efficiency of *aggregate supply*. They include *liberalisation*, deregulation, *privatisation* and reducing government spending and *budget deficits* (see *neoclassical economics*).

SURPLUS Income exceeding expenditure (contrast *deficit*).

SUSTAINABLE DEVELOPMENT Economic development that attempts to conserve the environment such that it provides for both current *and* future needs.

TARIFFS Taxes placed on imports.

TECHNOLOGY TRANSFER The passing of management or technical know-how from pioneering firms/industries/countries to those following.

TIME DEPOSITS Those *bank deposits* (e.g. savings accounts) where notice must be given before they can be withdrawn without penalty.

TOTAL FACTOR PRODUCTIVITY The overall increase in *productivity* of a number of resources which is not directly attributable to any specific one.

TRADE-OFF Where gaining one outcome is only possible by sacrificing an alternative. The loss one incurs in trading off one for the other. Minimising this loss means minimising the *opportunity cost*.

TRADITION Social custom. A form of organisation that relies on precedent, which is resistant to change but which lends stability and certainty to any society.

TRAGEDY OF THE COMMONS The degradation of a communal resource since no one user has a vested and exclusive interest in its protection.

TRANSACTION COSTS The cost of bringing buyers into contact with sellers and facilitating trade. Where these costs are high, markets will be small, underdeveloped, inefficient or unable to function (see *market failure*).

TRANSFER EARNINGS The level of earnings required to keep a resource in its present employment.

TREASURY BILLS The government's treasury borrows money by issuing a Treasury Bill which promises to pay the purchaser a given sum, say 100, in three months' time. If you pay 99 for this now, gain a return of 1 after one quarter and repeat the purchase again and again, you can make a profit of 4 in a year (and so the market rate of interest is determined at 4 per cent on risk-free government bills).

UTILITY Level of satisfaction.

WAGES The reward for labour.

WASHINGTON CONSENSUS A term used to describe the *neo-classical*, pro-market, *supply-side policies* actively promoted by Washington institutions such as the International Monetary Fund and the World Bank, amongst others.

WORLD TRADE ORGANIZATION (WTO) The body responsible for negotiating common rules in international commerce, with the intention of reducing barriers and promoting free trade.

INDEX